It always amazes me that from another man's jou.... connection that will help you continue successfully along your pathway. In Randy Butler's wonderful book, *Heaven's Covenant with Earth*, I made such a connection. I believe you will as well.

H.B. LONDON, JR., Vice President, Church & Clergy
Focus on the Family, Colorado Springs, Colorado

Randy Butler's book, *Heaven's Covenant with Earth*, is a testament to God's tenderness in the wake of unspeakable tragedy. It is a book about healing and hope, renewal and wonder. "A strange thing happens when your child dies," says Butler. "Suddenly doctrine is no longer important." *Heaven's Covenant with Earth* is a compass by which to navigate the deep waters of faith when the coastline of doctrine falls off the horizon. Butler will make you laugh, cry, ponder, and pray. This book will not only change the way you think about God and life; it will change you!

CHARLES J. CONNIRY, JR., PhD, Vice President and Dean
George Fox Evangelical Seminary/George Fox University, Portland, Oregon
Author of *Soaring in the Spirit: Rediscovering Mystery in the Christian Life.*

Through the lens of his own tragedy, Dr. Randy Butler explores a fresh vision of covenant as fundamentally a love relationship with God, rather than a set of belief statements and behavior standards. He writes candidly and honestly, drawing us into his journey and compelling us to re-imagine a faith set free in Christ.

MARYKATE MORSE, PhD, Professor of Leadership and Spiritual Formation
Director of Seminary Hybrid Programs, University Director of Strategic Planning, George Fox Evangelical Seminary, Portland, Oregon

In his book, Dr. Butler challenges prevailing assumptions regarding Christian spirituality by arguing for a recovery of a more complete model by which to relate to God. To address this problem, he proposes to direct Christians to discern the voice of the Holy Spirit, guided by Scripture, which will move them from a judicial and legal relationship with God to a covenant relationship with God. He shows how the transition from the Penal Substitution Model of Christ's work to the Covenant Renewal Model resolves this tension.

DR. JULES GLANZER, President, Tabor College

In *Heaven's Covenant with Earth,* Randy Butler has captured the profound interpersonal implications of the covenant relationship between God and creation. Looking beyond the traditional Western world's framing of the divine-human encounter primarily in legal terminology, he presents the relational and interpersonal foundations of every aspect of pastoral concerns. His inductive use of the biblical covenant concept as the foundational image of the divine-human relationship enables him to reframe salvation, spiritual formation, views of Heaven, stewardship, marriage, parenting, morality and the church in covenant-relational terms that appeal profoundly to the variety of cultural forms represented in global Christianity today. The result is a radical reinterpretation of the Christian life that is based solidly in the covenantal concepts of the Trinity, creation community, and Israel's covenant history. This book is an invaluable contribution to 21st century pastoral theology and intercultural conversation.

R. LARRY SHELTON, ThD
RICHARD B. PARKER, Professor of Theology
George Fox Evangelical Seminary, Portland, Oregon
Author of *Cross and Covenant: Interpreting the Atonement for 21st Century Mission* (Paternoster Press, 2006)

RECLAIMING HEAVEN'S COVENANT

God's Blueprint for Restoring All Relationships

Dr. Randy R. Butler

Proverbs 3:5-6

Randy R. Butler

Reclaiming Heaven's Covenant

Copyright © 2011 by Dr. Randy R. Butler

All rights reserved. This book or any portion thereof may not be reproduced or used in any manner whatsoever without the express written permission of the publisher except for the use of brief quotations in a book review.Scripture quotations taken from the New American Standard Bible®, Copyright © 1960, 1962, 1963, 1968, 1971, 1972, 1973, 1975, 1977, 1995 by The Lockman Foundation. Used by permission. (www.Lockman.org)

Published by
Deep River Books
Sisters, Oregon
http://www.deepriverbooks.com

ISBN 10: 1-935265-84-9
ISBN 13: 978-1-935265-84-9

Library of Congress: 2011927210

Printed in the USA

Cover design by Joe Bailen, Contajus Designs

Dedicated to ...

... my wife Joanie, my daughter Kristi, her husband Charles, and my son Kevin. One day soon we will be together again forever.

... Randy Alcorn, who put me on the road to studying Heaven. I am eternally grateful!

... Larry Shelton, who put me on the covenant path. Thanks a million!

TABLE OF CONTENTS

ACKNOWLEDGEMENTS

I wish to acknowledge those who made me into the person who wrote this book.

... my friend John Brietmeier, who called me shortly after Kevin's home-going and asked me to attend a class with him about Heaven that some guy named Randy Alcorn was teaching.

... our friends Jon and Sheryl Strutz, who stood by our side during the dark days and with whom we now enjoy many bright days.

... other friends who were a huge support and stood by our side during our loss: Dan and Tammy Bowers, Andy and Shirley Sheldon, Jeff and Genell Lewis.

... my friend Bill Post, who has always been an encouragement to me. When I need to laugh, I can count on Bill!

... my prayer partner, Stan Rogers, who I can always count on for spiritual support.

... our church family at Salem Evangelical Church, which has been a wonderful family during the very best of times and never left our side during some very difficult days.

... the staff at George Fox Evangelical Seminary, who ministered to my needs and taught me some priceless truths during my doctoral program. They encouraged me to turn my dissertation into a book. This is that book.

... Dr. Larry Shelton who showed me the path to covenant. His work on this subject and his research are simply brilliant.

... my friend Randy Alcorn, who has done more for me in this life than I can recount. I will always be indebted to him for starting the healing that began in my life in 2003. He has promised me a walk in Heaven with Kevin! I also want to acknowledge Randy's assistant, Kathy Norquist, who so generously and graciously cares for communication between Randy and me.

... Mel Hurley, who took my handwritten notes and turned them into the appendix of this book by taking the 731 scriptures and lovingly typing them out for me in the early days of this process. His work is much appreciated!

I wish to thank the dear people at Deep River Books—specifically Bill and Nancie Carmichael, Lacey Hanes Ogle, and Rhonda Funk—who took a chance on my manuscript. They have become family to me. Without them there would be no book!

I wish to thank my editor Sue Miholer, who took a rough manuscript and made it a readable book and a whole lot more. She was a joy to work with, always affirming and encouraging me.

Lastly—and most importantly—I wish to thank Joanie, Kristi and Charles for loving me just the way I am. I am the richest man in the world because of their love for me and the love from the rest of my family.

FOREWORD

by Randy Alcorn

I met Randy Butler while teaching a seminary course on the theology of Heaven nearly seven years ago. When I asked the students to share why they were in the class, I'll never forget Randy's answer. He said it was because his teenage son Kevin had died three months earlier. Randy took the class on Heaven so he'd understand what Kevin, who he said was "both my son and my best friend," was experiencing. What Randy said that day touched me deeply, and we quickly became friends.

A few months later, he came to my office and handed me a gift. It was a beautiful reddish, polished stone. He said it was jasper, a stone that will be part of the walls of the New Jerusalem (Revelation 21:18). The stone was a reminder of his son Kevin and of the assurance that he and his son will live together again in a glorious city with strong and beautiful walls.

Randy insisted I keep that jasper stone, which I have on my desk to this day. He said, "I want you to know I'm praying for you as you write your book about Heaven. And I want you to have this stone to remind you of Heaven's reality."

I've often looked at that stone and held it in my hand. It's not ghostly; it's solid and substantial—just like the place that awaits us. This is my view of Heaven, and it's Randy Butler's as well. You'll see that conviction surfacing throughout this book, which resonates with an eternal perspective.

I trust Randy Butler. He's devoted to his wife Joan, his daughter Kristi, and his son Kevin who's with Jesus. He is a faithful pastor. Every time I meet people from his church, they speak of his character and his heart for Jesus and the church. He preaches the whole counsel of God, even the unpopular parts, including Hell. He lets God be God and seeks to be faithful to Him. And he has prayed for me regularly, for which I am deeply grateful.

In *Reclaiming Heaven's Covenant*, Randy opens God's Word and lets us in on his life journey. He is honest, wise and true to Scripture. He emphasizes genuine relationship and doesn't reduce the Christian life to principles. Rather, he focuses on knowing God personally and walking with Jesus.

I'm a better person for knowing Randy Butler, and I think you will be too. I thank God for his life of faithfulness, and I congratulate him on this book.

Randy Alcorn
Author of *Heaven* and *If God Is Good*

INTRODUCTION

Heaven's covenant with earth is God intersecting with the human race. Heaven's covenant with earth is a welding together of God and humankind, who were once separated by sin. In welding, the bead is stronger than either of the two pieces of metal being welded together. When Heaven and earth are welded together, God is satisfied, and humankind is made complete. The bead serves as a memorial that something intentional and purposeful has taken place. I call this "Heaven's covenant with earth"!

Indeed, God's weld bead is Jesus Christ. Prior to the earthly life of Jesus Christ, God and humankind were joined together with a contract. From man's viewpoint it was a cold-blooded contract void of life and filled with legalism, which means there are rules to follow. God always wants a relationship, but human beings usually view obedience as duty. God always desires for us to see obedience in light of relationship, but every time humanity has felt God was unnecessary, humanity has bolted, breaking the strand that held together a fragile relationship.

This book is about relationships. Like the Trinity, the three relationships in this book are meant to live in harmony with one another, so much so that they are like the Holy Trinity, three in one. First, there is the relationship between God and me or God and you. This relationship requires the weld bead of Jesus Christ. The second relationship is the one between me and me and you and you. The third relationship is the one between people. This relationship is very broken. I contend we are not getting this one right because we are not getting the other two right. I address all three in this book.

I believe it is possible to restore the broken relationship between God and people. I believe it is possible to renew the relationship within. Likewise, I believe it is possible to rescue broken relationships with one another. How? Covenant!

The Bible is a book of one story, one God, one purpose: covenant! Since Genesis 3, when the human race bolted from God, God has sought to bring us back to Himself through an interpersonal relationship.

In the Old Testament, Ezekiel 36:26–27 gives us God's blueprint to restore *all* relationships! In the New Testament it is manifested in the cross. The cross is not only about atoning for sin, it is also about restoring relationships. I cannot think of one person who would not want restored relationships with God, within, and with one another.

I invite you to join me in this journey on a road called covenant. You have nothing to lose and everything to gain on this road I call covenant. It is an old path filled with beauty. Unfortunately, like many old roads that have been destroyed by bigger and faster roads we call freeways, relationships are hurried, and in the hurrying, we see burnout. We live in an era when relationships are fragile.

The covenant path is not about racing through relationships. We race through relationships like they're just so many dirty disposable diapers, probably because of the smell, certainly because something is wrong inside! The covenant path is about redeeming relationships. It is a path that requires time.

Covenant relationships have no hidden agendas. In fact, like Adam and Eve in the Garden before they sinned, covenant relationships require no outer garments. Covenant relationships are about the clothes we wear on the inside of the relationship. Imagine relationships with no agendas, no pretense. Who is coming to your mind as you imagine such a prized relationship? Covenant relationships take the business deal out of the relationship. Covenant relationships take away all threats, leaving only the joy of being together without any pretense.

This book will show you how the joy of being together in all three arenas previously described can be attained by each one who names the name of Jesus. I am writing this book because I have discovered something I believe to be a universal, timeless revelation from God to us. It is a revelation on relationships.

We each have a story, a journey we call life. My life's journey experienced a catastrophic breakdown in 2003. Some people, perhaps you, have experienced a blowout traveling at a high speed in your car. In 2003 I had a blowout while traveling at about 140 miles per hour. I hit a cement wall, crashing so hard that my life came to an immediate stop, crushing my heart, my soul, my spirit. I thought I was going to die. I wanted to die. I didn't die. In fact, for the first time in my life, I began to live a special relationship I never knew existed.

We each have a story to tell. In this book I tell you my story, my tragedy, and God's triumph in my life. I also give you some helps in finding triumph in your own personal journey of setbacks. It is a true story about my discovery of Heaven's covenant with earth!

Life is what you make it. Once you recognize you have less control than what a society may advocate, the closer you are to moving into covenant relationships. Covenant relationships are not about gaining control. They are about giving it away.

The only thing we really have control over is what we do with God's invitation to come to Him. The rest of life is personal choices that fall under the sovereignty of God. I am a both/and Christian. You will see this throughout this book, which at times will frustrate you to death. I believe in personal choices as well as God's sovereignty. I don't fit into a doctrine. I fit into a covenant relationship with God.

God meant for life on earth to be a very good thing. Why is it, then, that there are more evidences of hell on earth than Heaven on earth? (Please, if you are a theologian, refrain from barking out your pre-rehearsed answer.) The Bible teaches the earth is fallen. I have always felt sorry that the rest of creation has to suffer for humankind's stupidity!

We really messed things up in the Garden of Eden. That covenant relationship in the Garden of Eden is what God desires to have with you and I every single day. The sooner you can make a transition to covenant relationships, the more you will enjoy life on earth. We are all looking for the same thing in this world … PEACE! The only way to have peace is to restore broken relationships. I call these covenant relationships.

Covenant relationships move you and I into harmony with God, both within ourselves and with one another. In fact, if you apply covenant to God and to self, then applying it to others becomes natural. Like plagues of the past that have spread throughout civilizations and causing utter destruction, covenant relationships have an even greater power to restore, renew, redeem, reconcile, regenerate, and revive our civilization. This is a move toward Heaven on earth.

I am suggesting that the dynamics of covenant relationships is God's solution for redeeming a broken earth. Covenant relationships teach that you and I are not the center of the universe. God is the center of all relationships. And when He is not, they are prone to brokenness. How much of our life is lived just trying to survive?

Since embracing the themes of covenant relationships in all areas of living and with all people, I enjoy life on planet earth much more. Life in the wilderness with God is far better than life in the Promised Land without God. By the way, what is the Promised Land to Americans? Whatever it is, if it does not include God, it is a mirage, a lie from Satan right out of the pit of hell.

Covenant applied to earthly relationships wears a unique set of lenses. These lenses are not manufactured on earth. You can only get them from Heaven. God invented these unique lenses and the price is right. The instructions are in Ezekiel 36:26–27.

You and I do not wear them over the eyes of our face; rather we wear them over the eyes of our heart. A changed heart will lead to changed relationships. Changed relationships will lead to a changed earth. A heart wearing covenant lenses will see earth not as fallen, though it is, but rather as forgiven. A heart wearing covenant lenses will see earth not as failed, though it is, but rather as freed.

Indeed, covenant can become earth's best friend. Heaven and earth become a bead welded with covenant relationships that become stronger than ever before. I call it "Heaven's covenant with earth"!

CHAPTER 1

My Story and Covenant

I want to go to Heaven! I believe you want to go to Heaven too! This goal is what brings people together from all walks of life. We each travel a road that leads to eternity. The only way to our destination of eternal life is through a personal relationship with Jesus Christ. We each travel a different road in this life and have different views along the path we call our "journey." My journey is likely not your journey. Yet, our journeys desire the same destination: Heaven!

We each have a story that when put in the blender of time, it becomes the mosaic for human history. Be definition, my journey was quite ordinary up until January 6, 2003, when my journey was suddenly catapulted into dimensions unthinkable to my ordinary existence. That is where my story book begins: January 6, 2003.

This is my story. Like yours it is very personal. Ultimately, it is a story that came down to me from God. It is a story that left me half-dead—and certain the half that lived probably would be dead not long thereafter. It will appear my story is about a great personal loss. It is not. It is a story about great personal gain.

On January 6, 2003, my life was turned upside-down and inside-out. As had been my practice for the 18 years since Kristi, our oldest, had been born, I came home from work to be with my family. When I reached the place where I would normally greet my 16-year-old son Kevin, I found him unconscious in our bathtub. I jerked him out of the tub, screamed for Joanie and Kristi, and performed pathetic CPR. Time stood still. I rode in the ambulance to the hospital in total shock, praying, crying, and constantly asking the people caring for him if he was still alive! One hundred hours later my son was in Heaven. He never regained consciousness. A massive brain seizure had instantaneously ushered him into the presence of the Lord.

You may be left wanting the details. Sometimes details cloud the big picture. I desperately want you to embrace the big picture of my message for you. Besides, this story is not about Kevin. It is a story about my journey with God. It is a story about a surprising journey with God that I did not know was attainable this side of Heaven. My hope for you is that you experience life with God without traveling a journey of tragedy and grief. Tragedy is not necessary to discover life with God. But if your life does include tragedy and grief, perhaps my discoveries can be your discoveries too!

In the months that followed Kevin's death, I can honestly tell you that I never once felt anger toward God. However, I did believe that God deeply hurt me beyond human expression. I felt this way because I believed God could have prevented Kevin's death but chose not to. Thousands of people prayed. I prayed my heart out! It's a tough thing when you have been taught all your life that God answers prayer, and then the one time you put in the time and have the passion in your prayers, God chooses to be silent. Honestly, that sucks!

I never viewed my tragedy as God punishing me, but I was deeply hurt, simply because I knew God had the power to make my son live! Most of the time God doesn't make sense to me! However, I have never loved Him more than I do at this writing. God is faithful! God is good! God loves me! God loves you! I am experiencing these truths having lived life on the other side of the eye of the storm.

Every morning after Kevin's death I struggled to crawl out of bed and stagger into the shower, turn on the hot water, sit down, and just cry. That was my pattern for four months! I began noticing I was screaming out to God the same three questions over and over. I was able to unload my hurt to God in the shower, because it was the only place in the house where my wife and daughter could not hear my crying, my screaming, and my yelling out to God from the deepest anguish in my soul.

It is important for you to know a bit about my journey prior to January 6, 2003. I have been a pastor for 30 years. I grew up in the church. It is all that I have ever known. Since boyhood, the only thing I ever wanted to do in life was be a preacher. I never strayed far from God since I knew that would tick Him off. Besides, I had always been afraid of going to hell.

After a marvelous undergraduate experience at George Fox College and further study at Western Evangelical Seminary, my wife Joan and I embarked on a life of ministry together. In July of 1986, after having served two other churches in the early years of our marriage, we were assigned to the church where I serve to this day.

God had given me a near-perfect wife (most of the time), a near-perfect daughter Kristi, and a near-perfect son Kevin. I had a good job (most of the time) and a ministry that for 23 years saw God's blessing and anointing.

Our family went to Disneyland at least yearly; we bought annual passes based on our frequency in the Park. Our ministry and life was a Disneyland experience. Our family life was a Disneyland experience. I was truly a blessed man. I had come to believe this was the reward God gave to those who were faithful to Him.

It turns out God does not owe us anything. Everything we have in this life is a gift from God. These years were truly Heaven on earth for me. I am not a prosperity theology advocate as it is being taught today. I do believe God blesses His people. I do not believe it is owed to us. Our reward is waiting for us in Heaven, not on earth. I do believe God prospers His people, not as a universal law but as He sees fit.

Then I lost Kevin, and my morning showers became anguished talks with God. As I stated earlier, there were three questions I screamed to God every morning for the better part of four months. The first question I screamed at God through my tears and my pain was, "What were You thinking?" The second question I hurled at God was, "Is this the best You can do for me?" And the third question I barked at God in my despair was, "Do You really expect me to show up every Sunday and tell everyone how great You are?"

My theological world had been turned upside-down. My theology had been reduced to rubble. Have you ever thought you had life, God, and stuff figured out ... until tragedy strikes? Have you ever had a theology that one day was worth gold and the next day wasn't good enough to be flushed down a toilet? I became a pastor without a theology. My troubling question would become: Was I a pastor without a God?

I am learning that God is very patient with us. At least, He is very patient with me! I suspect that if you give Him a chance, you will experience His patience as well!

God is a gentleman. He never interrupts! God waited until I was through screaming, crying, and yelling at Him. In the silence, I began hearing the voice of God. The water drizzling out from the shower head became silent. Without any announcement, in my silence, God spoke to my soul. He had an answer for each of my three questions. God always has an answer for us. I don't always like His answers! Do you?

Friends tried consoling me over the months that followed my tragedy. I was given a multitude of books from people who were just trying to help. But it was God who ultimately spoke to me in the dark night of my soul. I am learning that whenever life is dark, God makes an appearance.

In my silence, God clearly addressed my first question. I asked God, "What were You thinking?" God answered, "I was thinking of what I experienced with My Son. We too, like you, had a perfect life together." I despised this answer at first because God got His Son back in three short days after His death. I hardly call the death of God's Son the same thing as what I had experienced!

I began to discover God would answer my other two questions in a similar fashion as well. Every time God spoke to me, He took me back to the cross. I didn't want to go to the cross! I wanted my son back! In grief, there is a silence and darkness of the soul that is more silent and dark than physical silence and physical darkness. Put another way, there is silence beyond silence, and darkness beyond the darkness of the soul. This is where my tragedy took me. All roads lead to the cross. While I was slowly gaining my sanity, I still could not see what God was doing in my soul. We rarely do at the time.

Likewise, God began giving me His answer to my second question, "Is this the best You can do for me?" He answered, "I was thinking of what I experienced with My Son." Again, this was not the answer I had hoped to hear. Honestly, I had no idea what I wanted to hear. Grief is like that. Not much makes sense. Yet, God's answer began to give me peace in my soul. All roads lead to the cross! I still was not interested in the cross as the answer to my broken heart. I wanted my son back!

God answered my third question the same as He did the first two questions I asked Him. I said to God, "Do You really expect me to show up every Sunday and tell everyone how great You are?" God answered, "I was thinking of what I experienced with My Son. That is what I expect you to tell them." God was making it clear to me that all roads lead to the cross. I didn't want the cross; I wanted my son back! I was gaining peace for my soul and healing for my broken heart, yet I still did not comprehend what God was saying to me. Sometimes, we don't understand what God is saying. The comfort comes not in the understanding, but in just knowing that God is there. That has been my experience.

Three months passed, and somehow we as a family lived our lives without Kevin. My cousin, a professor at George Fox University, told me that my college professor whom I majored under in college was releasing a book on Heaven. My cousin thought I might be helped by the book. Great, another book! With great doubt and a sense of duty, I called my former professor and asked about his new book. Dr. Arthur Roberts graciously asked if I would be interested in coming to visit him at his home on the coast. I accepted his invitation. I was a desperate man, and a broken father. Broken and desperate people are some of the most willing people in the world.

I arrived at his home on the central Oregon coast from my home in Salem, Oregon. I had no idea what to expect. We had not really talked in 25 years, though from the pulpit I occasionally mentioned his influence in my life. He and his wife warmly received me into their home. I listened to his every word, something I wished I had done 25 years earlier!

He spoke to me as the brilliant professor I remembered from college. More importantly, Dr. Roberts spoke like a pastor to my heart, as a father to my fatherhood, and as a friend to my soul. Needless to say, I read his book *Exploring Heaven*[1] as soon as I got back home to Salem. I have read it numerous times since our meeting together in his home that God-ordained day. All days are God-ordained! In our busyness we fail to see the hand of God in our daily lives

Shortly after my time with Dr. and Mrs. Roberts, a pastor friend told me about a class being offered at a seminary in Portland, Oregon, by a man named Randy Alcorn. Prior to this, I would have never attended the seminary where he taught since I did not agree with them doctrinally. I had never even heard of Randy Alcorn, but a strange thing happens when your

---

[1]Roberts, *Exploring Heaven* (New York: Harper Collins, 2003).

child dies; suddenly doctrine is no longer important. The class consisted of five days of intense lecture and study. I figured, "Why not?" So I signed up and showed up.

That week became a turning point in my life. By then, I had four new questions I began asking God that bugged me to no end. This time they were not questions about God, rather they were questions about God and my son.

The first question was, "Is Kevin safe?" The second question I asked—sometimes hourly—was, "What is he doing?" My third question was, "Is Kevin having fun?" And the fourth question racing through my mind on a daily basis was, "Could God really care for Kevin as much as I did?" This fourth question may sound silly and trite, but not if you knew the relationship we had. We were unbelievably close to one another. I was certain God did not have time for Kevin in Heaven the way I made time for Kevin on earth!

Three days into Randy Alcorn's class on Heaven, I sat in class and simply wept. I wept because I missed my son. I wept because I was learning how marvelous Heaven is. I wept because God was entering into the dark caves of my soul and was shedding light by His very presence. God was reassuring me that everything was fine. He was telling me, "You have not lost your son. He is safely home. He will be waiting for you." Wow!

The class with Randy Alcorn ended, but I had been given a lifeline to my son. I knew Heaven was real and that it is marvelous place to live. I knew that my son was in Heaven and there was nothing to worry about. Beyond that, I did not know much about Heaven. For me, it was a place I would enjoy someday, but just not now. Remember that sentence. It turns out to be the greatest lie in Christianity. I knew so little about Heaven.

This was yet another turning point in my journey back to life. Randy gave me Scriptures to study and books to read. I devoured everything I could get my hands on. I taught about Heaven in my church. I taught the book of Revelation for what it really is: a book about Jesus, not so much a book about the end of the world. I spent hours studying about the place where my son now lived and where I would one day join him.

During this season in my life of tremendous discovery, something was happening in my soul. I began getting closer to God as I shifted my attention away from Kevin and onto the subject of eternity. My message to those reading this book who are grieving: I discovered the best way to overcome grief is to look forward and stop looking backwards!

I e-mailed Alcorn and asked if I could meet with him, and he graciously agreed. A transformation was being birthed within my heart. The more time I spent thinking about eternity, the more healing came to my soul. In fact, for the first time in months, I felt I no longer needed artificial life support to sustain me. I was experiencing God. He became personal. I began to think thoughts I had never thought before. God was taking me on a journey from death to life. Real life!

Since then I have gone back to school and graduated with a degree that has helped me to articulate and experience my new theology. It is not really a new theology, just new to me. My dissertation explained how this new theology looks. This book is my explanation on how it works in everyday life. I call it "Covenant Theology."

Prior to January 2003, I had a theology that said, "I will see Jesus when I get to Heaven." My "new" theology says, "I will see Jesus when I get to Heaven, but I can also experience Him right now." This has been my experience since January 2003. In case God is not personal to you, and in case you are waiting until you get to Heaven for the introductions, I have some things for you to consider in the pages that follow.

In a book entitled *Studying Congregations*, the authors state: "Practical theologians will listen for the stories people tell most readily about themselves."[2] This book is about my story with God. It is practical and it really works. I thought people might gain insights into their journey with God through the lenses of my journey. If theology is not practical, universal, and timeless, I doubt it should even be called theology at all.

In another book I found helpful, *What Type Am I?*, the author, Renee Baron, states, "Midlife can bring about profound changes in people."[3] While secularists would say what I am experiencing is a midlife crisis, I would

---

[2] Ammerman et al, *Studying Congregations, a New Handbook* (Nashville: Abingdon Press, 1998), 33.

[3] Baron, *What Type Am I? Discover Who You Really Are* (Harmondsworth, Middlesex, England: Penguin Group, 1998), 153.

argue I am experiencing a transformation of my heart to the heart of God. If that sounds good to you, read on. If not, I will not be offended.

Buckingham and Clifton wrote in their book, *Now, Discover Your Strengths*, "Delusion plus denial is a lethal combination."[4] I would argue that I am neither experiencing delusion nor denial. No, I am going through what God calls "transformation."

I invite you to join me in this marvelous journey. You have your own story, your own journey. I trust my journey of transformation will motivate you to experience God this side of Heaven. For me, it has been a journey back to life! How about it? Wouldn't you really like to live life to its fullest this side of Heaven? Wouldn't you like to be in a relationship with God, one that isn't infested with rules, fear, and other church stuff, this side of Heaven? I invite you to join me on this journey with God. It is a journey about a really good relationship with God that is not theory but real. A covenant relationship with God really works with Him, within my life, and in others. Let's journey together with God!

---

[4] Buckingham & Clifton, *Now, Discover Your Strengths* (New York: The Free Press, 2001), 128.

Chapter 1 Reflection and Discussion: Creating Covenant

1. Identify the one or two big events in your life that were life-changing.

2. Did this (these) event(s) draw you closer to God or drive you away from God? Why or why not? (We either get bitter or we get better!)

3. What might be God's perspective in the big events in your life?

4. Have you used your big event(s) to help others?

5. Have you thanked God for these big events in your life?

6. Are you at peace? Why or why not?

7. Identify a verse in the Bible that is God's promise for you concerning these big events.

8. Find a story in the Bible that draws application to your story.

CHAPTER 2

MODERNS, POSTMODERNS AND COVENANT

There are many modern Christians who, like me, have experienced Christianity, but who have rarely experienced God. The modern church has maintained a steady diet of dos, don'ts, rules, lists, and "right doctrine." I know Moderns and the modern church well.

The message received from the modern church has been a constant message of living life through lists of propositional truth. Moderns have embraced *rational* Christianity over *relational* Christianity. The 200-year era of modernism (1789–1989) leaned heavily on reason and science. Unfortunately, it became the mantra for the church too.

I am a Modern. I am also a Christian. Today I am more Christian than Modern or Postmodern. The process of God transforming our hearts is not easy to calculate, yet it always adds up. Robert Mulholland, in his book, *Invitation to a Journey*, states, "We must give God permission to do the work God wants to do with us right there, because transformation will not be forced upon us."[5] God is a gentleman. He will patiently wait for you to invite Him into your space. My space needs to include God. Your space needs to include God.

Most of the time Moderns take the path of least resistance through propositional truth because it is easier than working through the tough issues of life that lead to covenant relationships. To this statement Joan

---

[5] Mulholland, *Invitation to a Journey* (Downers Grove, Ill.: InterVarsity Press, 1993), 38.

Chittister responds: "We cannot expect life to be without struggle, perhaps. We cannot expect life to be perfect. But we can expect to see life come from death."[6] This is precisely what happened in my journey. This is my prayer and hope for you and all Moderns who have found Christianity less than experiential with God.

I agree with the authors of *Posers, Fakers, & Wannabes* who say: "Christ is alive right now and death is dead for good."[7] God desires through His Son Jesus Christ to give life to those who are spiritually dead. Indeed, Robert Quinn has it right in *Deep Change*: "The problem is not 'out there' but inside each one of us."[8]

It is my desire to help you move into an arena of spiritual vitality. I like to compare covenant relationships to a baseball game in which every seat is a good seat based on what is happening on the field. If it is a great game, the excitement and the experience reach clear to the bleachers in the outfield.

A covenant relationship with God is the best game in town. Each seat in Covenant Stadium is a great seat. God is inviting us to His stadium! Experiencing God this side of Heaven is meant to be more exciting than any game, any drug, any vacation, any job, any amount of money, any relationship the world has to offer.

I hope to give you clues to unlocking the bondage your soul may be in because God is not real in your life. In each of our journeys we encounter a Mt. Everest where the goal is to make it to the summit where we will find God. A covenant relationship with God is not only about the summit, but also about the climb. You are not climbing alone. God is with you. C. Gene Wilkes, in *Jesus on Leadership*, states, "Jesus came to show us the heart of God."[9] The heart of God is to be with us.

The Bible says in Ezekiel 36:26–27, "Moreover, I will give you a new heart and put a new spirit within you; and I will remove the heart of stone

---

[6] Chittister, *Wisdom Distilled from the Daily* (San Francisco: HarperCollins, 1991), 191.

[7] Manning & Hancock, *Posers, Fakers, & Wannabes (Unmasking the Real You)* (Colorado Springs: NavPress, 2003), 118.

[8] Quinn, *Deep Change* (San Francisco: Jossey-Bass Publishers, 1996), 101.

[9] Wilkes, *Jesus on Leadership* (Wheaton, Ill.: Tyndale House Publishers, 1998), 168.

from your flesh and give you a heart of flesh. I will put My Spirit within you and cause you to walk in My statutes, and you will be careful to observe My ordinances." This passage captures the essence of this book. I want to flesh out a covenant relationship with God for you in everyday life. I want you to experience a covenant relationship with God.

In order for modern Christians to experience God, we must stop talking about ourselves. Modern Christians have failed to discern the voice of the Holy Spirit as guided by Scripture. This failure in discernment has left modern Christians with little more than propositional truths as their foundation for Christianity.

Moderns' mantels are lined with trophies of truth, yet the hearths of our hearts are vacant of God. Moderns own a hollow, sometimes shallow Christianity. Moderns only know Him as the God "up there." Moderns know Him as the God we will be with "some day." How very sad and how very unnecessary for us to live this sort of pathetic Christianity and pretend as though it is the greatest religion on the face of the earth.

Modern Christians have settled for a penal relationship with God—one based on punishment and penalties—when in fact God offers us a covenant relationship. A strict penal view of the atonement is an incomplete view on the atoning work of Christ.

God desires to reveal Himself to us. He likewise intends to have a relationship with us. Like the Israelites, we tend to focus on ourselves, and not Him. How many messages over the past 30 years have we heard about "how to"? Are we any better off? We are worse off! Kenneth Leech writes in *Experiencing God*: "The history of Israel is in a sense the history of God."[10]

As you read my personal story of tragedy, it was when I became silent and took the focus off myself that God put the spotlight on Himself. This book puts the spotlight on God—and we are the beneficiaries of that focus. This book is not about helping you find more of yourself. This book helps you and I find more of God!

I have made statements about Moderns. You may be wondering what that term means and if you are one such creature. Age is not necessarily what determines what you are. Modern Christians in the United States are

---

[10] Leech, *Experiencing God* (San Francisco: Harper & Row, 1985), 65.

products of both their environment and their heritage. In a time when "cultural relevancy" is the buzzword, there appears to be a desperate attempt to "get it right" with God. Moderns have jumped from fads to fashions to forms, all in an attempt to find a connection with God.

Yet there appears to be restlessness within the body of Christ. There is also division within the body of Christ. With the rise of postmodern Christians and the emerging church, modern Christians are left scratching their heads, searching for answers to questions that never existed a generation ago—at least, questions that were not as relevant and time-sensitive as they appear to be today.

We are in the midst of political uncertainty. We are in the midst of a financial crisis, the worst since the Great Depression. We are in a moral crisis, at least by some accounts. We are in a global crisis with the United States being a microcosm of what is happening on the world scene. Perhaps at the core of each of these crises is a crisis that has been overshadowed or overlooked by the masses. Is it possible we are in the greatest relationship crisis with God this earth has ever experienced? If so, then we are at the porch of the greatest reunion with God this earth could ever experience!

The problems for modern Christians are basic. They are not new problems; nevertheless, they loom large in churches today. Where did all the people go? They aren't all following Oprah, are they? Where did we go so wrong? Why isn't the church attractive anymore?

Moderns need a both/and approach rather than an either/or approach as modern Christians. Moderns panic as though they are in the all-or-nothing round of church history. Modern Christians need to make a paradigm shift, not find a new God! Moderns' emphasis on a 200-year-old penal relationship with God is not wrong, but it is incomplete. (Incomplete in the sense that it stops with "Jesus died for my sins." While that is true, it is nonetheless incomplete). This book offers solutions for modern Christians by introducing them to a covenant relationship with God.

Likewise, postmodern Christians need to approach God with a both/and approach. Postmodern Christians need to discover God not only in poverty, not only in the environment, not only in art, not only within community, but also within the pages of the Bible. This book offers solutions for postmodern Christians by showing them the possibility of a covenant relationship with God.

In this book I will share with both Moderns and Postmoderns what is meant by a covenant relationship with God in everyday life. You will see the relationship between God, yourself, and the stuff that happens in everyday life in a much different light. You may discover, as I am discovering, that it is possible to have a slice of God on earth this side of Heaven. As Holt puts it, "Go on a pilgrimage."[11] I invite you to go on a pilgrimage with me. A very exciting, worthwhile pilgrimage!

According to Thomas Merton, as we journey we will discover this about God: "He comes down from heaven and finds us."[12] This has been my experience. I sure hope you experience something similar. This covenant relationship I speak about can bring together Moderns and Postmoderns. Together, we are Christians.

Christians must stop fighting one another. According to Ray Anderson, God is always working from the future. "The Spirit that comes to the church comes out of the future, not the past."[13] In other words, God knows how our book concludes, so we are told to trust Him before our story comes to its conclusion. Boyatzis, Goleman and McKee write, "Tapping into that kind of insight can come more easily if a leader makes a habit of retreating to a quiet place to reflect on a regular basis."[14] Remember, I heard God in my silence. I saw God in my darkness.

The ultimate goal of this book is summed up by John R. Tyson, in his work, *Invitation to Christian Spirituality*, speaking about Meister Eckhart: "He sought, through various practices and reflections, to detach the soul from temporal things and affections, so that in stillness and silence, and in

---

[11] Holt, *Thirsty for God* (Minneapolis: Augsburg Fortress, 2005), 208.

[12] Merton, *New Seeds of Contemplation* (New York: Abbey of Gethsemani, Inc., 1961), 39.

[13] Anderson, *The Shape of Practical Theology* (Downers Grove, Ill.: InterVarsity Press, 2001), 105.

[14] Goleman et al, *Primal Leadership, Learning to Lead with Emotional Intelligence* (Boston: Harvard Business School Press, 2004), 205.

grace and love, the human soul could find union with God."[15] This book is a tool for your journey to find union with God.

You must be willing to have an open view on the work and role of the Holy Spirit. Raymond Brown states, "The Spirit emerges clearly as a personal presence—the ongoing presence of Jesus while he is absent from earth and with the Father in heaven."[16] This is a great starting point for transformation, which is what a covenant relationship with God is all about.

You must be accepting of an active role of the Holy Spirit in the world today, and more importantly, in your life. Henry Nouwen writes, "But I am also getting in touch with the mystery that leadership, for a large part, means to be led."[17] That is, I trust you are willing to be led by the Holy Spirit of God. Postmoderns are suspicious of authority. If you can't trust God, who are you going to trust? Moderns do not like being told what to do. Moderns need to learn to bow the knee to God instead of Pharaoh.

The second important starting point for a covenant relationship with God is to acknowledge the place for Scripture in the world and your life today. Sam Rima writes in his book, *Overcoming the Dark Side of Leadership,* "We must realize that consistent exposure to scripture will provide us with the most accurate self-knowledge available to us."[18]

I am in complete agreement with this statement. I trust you will give Scripture a fair chance in your life as you enter into a covenant relationship with God. In fact, it is a requirement. God does not work apart from Scripture. Everything He does in this world is supported with the pages of the Bible!

The higher your view of Scripture, the greater the opportunity you will have to enter into a covenant relationship with God. To negate the Word of God is to cut off the tongue of God! Yikes! Rima puts it even more bluntly

---

[15] Tyson, *Invitation to Christian Spirituality* (New York: Oxford University Press, 1999), 177.

[16] Brown, *The Church the Apostles Left Behind* (New York: Paulist Press, 1984), 106.

[17] Nouwen, *In the Name of Jesus* (New York: The Crossroad Publishing Company, 1996), 57.

[18] McIntosh & Rima, *Overcoming the Dark Side of Leadership* (Grand Rapids, Mich.: Baker Books, 2005), 191.

in another book he has written, *Rethinking the Successful Church*: "Either we believe the Bible or we don't."[19]

If you are a Modern, stop gloating. Moderns have done a pathetic job of making God real. If you are a Postmodern, set aside your disagreements with the Bible long enough to read this book. God is more than allegory, He is real. God is more than the God of the first century; He is the God of the twenty-first century too! While some Postmoderns are deconstructing the pages of the Bible, this book is an attempt to construct a relationship with God.

A Modern's problem is not a Postmodern. A Postmodern's problem is not a Modern. Our problem together is broken relationships. The Bible is a book; God is a person. God restores relationships. His Book is our guidebook on restoring broken relationships.

In a marvelous manual I read several years ago, *Studying Congregations*, the author states, "To paraphrase the prologue of John's Gospel, the vision must become flesh in the congregation's life, full (we hope) of grace and truth."[20] It is my hope that you experience God in the flesh as you read this book. I hope you will experience Him in His fullness. If so, you will have self-defined what it means to have a covenant relationship with the God of the universe!

---

[19] Rima, *Rethinking the Successful Church* (Grand Rapids, Mich.: Baker Books, 2002), 137.

[20] Ammerman et al, *Studying Congregations, a New Handbook* (Nashville: Abingdon Press, 1998), 187.

Chapter 2 Reflection and Discussion: Creating Covenant

1. Would you define yourself as a Modern or a Postmodern? In response to one another, you either interact on the level of: as, to, or with. This is important to identify.

2. What is your attitude and behavior toward those who are of the other persuasion in question 1? Cite some examples.

3. What is your common ground with people that are not like you?

4. What are your non-negotiables or core values? Do they match Scripture?

5. How can you begin loving in covenant those whom you like the least?

6. What will your church be like in three years if you do nothing to build a bridge? Something to build a bridge? Everything you can to build a bridge?

7. Identify a verse in the Bible that will help you love people you do not like.

8. Find a story in the Bible of people loving people they did not like.

CHAPTER 3

SCRIPTURE, THE HOLY SPIRIT, THE MIND AND COVENANT

Scripture and Covenant

Massive vandalism! It is the best phrase I know to describe how some Christians are treating the Bible. I am not a deconstructionist. I am a constructionist when it comes to the Bible. Deconstruct Scripture and you deconstruct God! Deconstruct God and you deconstruct a covenant relationship with God.

I no longer fear the atheist. I fear the Christian who views the Word of God as less than relevant. Vandals! The Bible is not broken. Relationships are broken. The Bible is a story—a true story—about redeeming relationships. The Bible does not need fixing. Humans need fixing. The Bible does not need an overhaul. Humans need an overhaul.

Deconstructing Scripture is spiritual vandalism! Leave it alone. It is God's authoritative word to all and for all generations, to all cultures, to all of creation. Reducing Scripture to mere allegory is to reduce Jesus to a myth and the Holy Spirit to Casper the Friendly Ghost. *Blasphemy*!

For those reading this book who consider themselves deconstructionists of Scripture, please consider the merits of this chapter. Consider the relationship between our view of Scripture and how we treat one another. If everyone would just chill out, we would discover at the heart of broken relationships is the heart of humankind, not the heart of Scripture.

While the Bible declares itself alive, the text has no heart; the Bible is not a person. The Bible is the inspired, written Word of God aimed at the heart of humankind. Its aim is redeeming the heart of humankind, not condemning the heart of the human race. The Bible has no heart. Leave it alone. You and I are the ones who have a heart disease, not the Scriptures. Sin cannot destroy the Bible, but sin is destroying the human race!

If you would be willing to look at the Scriptures from a constructionist point of view, you will have a better understanding of what I am writing about when I address a covenant relationship with God.

Covenant cannot be understood apart from Scripture. If you and I are to embrace the covenant model being described in this book, we must maintain a high view of Scripture. I see Scripture as more than allegory. I see Scripture as more than a narrative. I see Scripture as more than figurative. I see Scripture as more than symbolism. I see Scripture as literal. I see in Scripture that God is literally telling me He is literally inviting you and I to have a literal relationship with Him this side of a literal Heaven.

Kenneth Boa writes, "The Spirit of God uses the Word of God to guide, reprove, and teach the child of God."[21] For Boa, Scripture is foundational to covenant. Too many times we have assumed that when words such as guide and teach are used in Scripture, it is for purpose of correcting us or telling us yet again how we have strayed from God.

Oftentimes it is viewed only in light of sin. I believe Scripture is screaming out to our generation that there is more to Scripture than just telling us how wrong and how bad we are. Scripture is God's love letter to mankind. It is God interacting with you and I so we can know Him intimately.

Ultimately God wants to release you and I from the bondage of the flesh. Boa writes, "When believers do not respond to the warnings of conscience and scripture and to the conviction of the Holy Spirit, they are in bondage to the flesh."[22]

The reality of Christianity is that there is more to a relationship with God than simply atonement for our sin. Once sin has been atoned for, you and I are invited into a covenant relationship with God. "Jesus died for my sin" is foundational to the Christian faith, but it is an incomplete foundation. What about the resurrection? What follows atonement? Covenant relationships!

---

[21] Boa, *Conformed to His Image* (Grand Rapids, Mich.: Zondervan, 2001), 195.
[22] Ibid, 347.

Yes, I am a sinner. Yes, I am in need of a Savior, but, I am also in need of a friend! So are you! God is God, Savior, Friend and Dance Partner with us.

Richard Foster articulates the importance of Scripture by stating, "The one Spirit will never lead in opposition to the written Word that he inspired. There must always be the outward authority of Scripture as well as the inward authority of the Holy Spirit."[23] Foster's point is crucial: Progressive revelation outside of Scripture never trumps the Spirit speaking within Scripture.

I often hear people talk about doing what God told them to do. I am all for listening to the voice of the Holy Spirit, then, I discover that what someone says is the "voice of God" is completely contrary to Scripture, or no Scripture has been used at all. This is not how God speaks. God always speaks within Scripture. I agree with Johnston in making his case regarding postmodernism: "One task of the biblical communicator will be just getting people to take the Bible seriously again."[24]

This is not an overstatement by any stretch of the imagination. If you desire a covenant relationship with God outside of Scripture, then it is not a covenant relationship. A covenant relationship with God lives within Scripture, not outside of it, or in spite of it. In this, Scripture is relevant to the twenty-first-century church. What we do with the Bible determines what we do with God.

Boa articulates the need to be both Spirit-centered and Word-centered. He writes, "We need both the fire of the Spirit and the light of the Word, but many believers and churches have made this an either-or rather than a both-and by tending to be either Spirit-centered or Word centered."[25]

Clearly, covenant requires the reader to be both Spirit-centered and Word centered. Boa further states, "A more balanced perspective combines openness to the surprising work of the Spirit with discernment that tests experience in light of the Scriptures and the fruit that it produces."[26]

---

[23] Foster, *Celebration of Discipline* (San Francisco: HarperSanFrancisco, 1998), 188.

[24] Johnston, *Preaching to a Postmodern World: A Guide to Reaching Twenty-First Century Listeners* (Grand Rapids, Mich.: Baker Books, 2001), 54.

[25] Boa, *Conformed to His Image*, 295.

[26] Ibid, 292.

It seems that what is missing in our Christian culture is discernment. Perhaps we have secularized the biblical term of discernment using the term "common sense." I define it as godly wisdom, understanding and clear direction from God. Whatever term you choose to use, we need it in order to better embrace a covenant relationship with God.

Boa talks about evangelicals and their tendency to move away from covenant and slide back into a penal model of Christianity. Penal simply meaning that I am a debtor and Jesus has paid the price for my sin. Boa states, "But when evangelicals study Scripture, they typically look more for precepts and principles than for an encounter with God in the depths of their being."[27]

A covenant relationship with God is all about an encounter with God. It is not an isolated encounter that can be described as a mountaintop experience, but it is an experience in which our earthly dance takes place with God no matter where we are on the mountain.

Scripture is the tool that helps us accomplish this covenant relationship with God. Boa gives us a warning about Scripture, "Some students of the Word have come to love the content of truth in the Bible more than the source of that truth."[28] That is precisely what this book is about; it is about loving the source of truth more than the principles that govern truth. This is something all Christians must guard against, especially modern Christians.

I recall vividly the night of December 4, 1966. At 7:05 p.m. I gave my heart to Jesus Christ. I remember the evangelist Rev. John Kunkle (we knew him as "Uncle Kunkle") saying at the end of his message, "The greatest man to ever walk the face of this earth was Jesus Christ. There was never anyone greater than He, and there never will be anyone greater than He. I am asking you to invite Him into your heart before you go home tonight."

You must understand that I was seven years old. I had not heard a word he said during his entire message. That is how it is with seven-year-old boys. I was a cowboys-and-Indian sort of kid. I had holsters, cap guns and chaps. I was a "real" cowboy.

The number one show on the air in 1966 was *Bonanza*. My hero was Hoss Cartwright, a bigger than life cowboy. If this Jesus the preacher was

---

27 Ibid, 75.

28 Ibid, 192.

talking about was greater than my hero, then I wanted Him to come into my heart. So I made my way to the front of the church, knelt at the altar, began to weep under conviction, asked Jesus to come into my heart, and I was amazingly saved!

(By the way, when we got home *Bonanza* was airing; I put on my chaps, holsters and guns and my new friend, Jesus, and we watched *Bonanza* together that night. It was the best *Bonanza* ever!)

The bottom line when discussing the relationship between covenant and Scripture is to find out what God wants us to be. Leonard Ravenhill, states, "The Holy Spirit is looking for a body to indwell."[29] This is what Paul was talking about when he said, "Christ in you, the hope of glory" (Colossians 1:27). It is what is meant when Jesus says, "I am the way, and the truth, and the life" (John 14:6). We embrace God's Son, Jesus Christ, through the Holy Spirit and guided by Scripture in order to experience a covenant relationship with the God of the universe!

It is important to note that it is possible to know Scripture and not know God. The end is not Scripture. It is simply the vehicle God uses to introduce us to Him. He speaks through Scripture. I have a relationship with God, not with Scripture. My Savior is Jesus Christ, not the Bible. Jesus died on the cross, not the Bible.

However, without the Bible, I am limited in covenant relationship. For evangelicals, this is a tough pill to swallow. It is difficult for evangelicals to place Scripture under covenant just as it is for them to elevate the humanity of Jesus alongside the divinity of Jesus.

The Holy Spirit and Covenant

You may think we have adequately covered the Holy Spirit, unless of course you are Pentecostal or charismatic—in which case, I can never satisfy you. We seem to go to one of two extremes with the Holy Spirit. The first extreme is to ignore Him altogether because of the stigmas attached to Him historically. The other extreme is to be one-dimensional and only speak of the Holy Spirit, sometimes to the exclusion of Jesus Christ Himself.

---

[29] Ravenhill, *Revival Praying* (Minneapolis: Bethany House Publishers, 1984), 78.

Perhaps Boa, whom I have quoted freely, can give us a healthy balance on the subject. He helps us see how we can invite a visitation of residency of the Holy Spirit into our lives. Unlike putting together a model car where you can get away with leaving out a couple of tiny parts, this component in covenant is not optional. The Holy Spirit is not a tiny piece to covenant. He could well be called the engine that makes you run. Boa writes, "How do we seek the visitation of the Holy Spirit? While Scripture offers no step-by-step formula, the experience of the saints as well as biblical principles point to certain requisites that prepare the way.

1. Admitting weaknesses.
2. Surrendering our will.
3. Confessing our disobedience.
4. Sanctifying our desires.
5. Trusting God's promise to fill us."[30]

This is a powerful presentation by Boa to help us embrace the Holy Spirit. In fact, the word visitation is misleading. It makes it appear as though the Holy Spirit comes and goes in our lives. Not so. He desires to reside within our lives at our response to His invitation. Likewise, covenant is not about visitation or a short-term relationship. God is not a one-night stand! Covenant has eternal implications that begin here on earth this side of Heaven.

I recall the infamous board meeting all ministerial students had to endure before entering the ministry of our denomination. I remember being asked about "being filled with the Holy Spirit." In denominations, leaders are looking for the "right" phrases. I knew what to say, and I said it. I didn't lie; I just didn't know what I was talking about. I articulated a belief that was in my head, but it had not yet penetrated my heart. I did not know if I had experienced what I articulated in that board meeting. I just knew I wanted to be a minister, so I said what had to be said. Christians do this a great deal; they just say what they have to say, never really moving the belief in the head to an experience in the heart!

Johnston, writing about preachers hearing the voice of the Holy Spirit, makes this statement, "Either God has spoken and still speaks to the hearts

---

[30] Boa, *Conformed to His Image*, 320–321.

of people or preachers are to be pitied above all."[31] I wonder how many times the sermon is hollow because the church is void of the Holy Spirit. Could this be the reason why so many have fallen back on doctrine, dogmas, rules, rituals, propositional truths? It's easier.

A covenant relationship with God breathes life into people, churches, and sermons. This fresh breath from God will permeate culture. If culture is not affected, then it is not covenant. It is an imposter. It is not Christian if it does not touch all segments of society.

Jim Cymbala adds light to the connection between covenant and the Holy Spirit by stating, "I cannot say it strongly enough: When we seek God, he will bless us. But when we stop seeking him ... all bets are off, no matter who we are."[32]

A covenant relationship with God is like a free-flowing river, not a stagnant cesspool. In a covenant relationship with God, seeking is not a chore. It is a joy. I crave it like I crave strawberry milk, pizza and chocolate-covered cake donuts each night before I go to bed!

Johnston, on the subject of churches that God blesses, says, "Is it any wonder that churches emphasizing the presence of the Holy Spirit and the experiential outworking of God comprise some of the fastest growing churches around the world?"[33] My focus is not church growth. Covenant is not a code word for church growth. My focus is a covenant relationship with God. Church growth is the natural outflow of a covenant relationship with God. It is attractive. It is contagious. It is genuine. It is authentic. It works!

We, the church of Jesus Christ, are in need of the Holy Spirit. We need the Holy Spirit if we are to experience a covenant relationship with God. Ravenhill writes, "The world boasts of its atomic power; some cults boast of their satanic power; but where are those who boast of the Holy Ghost (Spirit) power?"[34]

---

[31] Johnston, *Preaching to a Postmodern World: A Guide to Reaching Twenty-First Century Listeners,* 62.

[32] Cymbala, *Fresh Wind, Fresh Fire,* ed. Dean Merrill (Grand Rapids, Mich.: Zondervan, 1997), 162.

[33] Johnston, *Preaching to a Postmodern World: A Guide to Reaching Twenty-First Century Listeners,* 123.

[34] Ravenhill, *Revival Praying,* 20.

I cannot explain covenant to you apart from the Holy Spirit. Foster writes, "In our day heaven and earth are on tiptoe waiting for the mergence of Spirit-led, Spirit-intoxicated, Spirit-empowered people."[35] This can happen if you and I will embrace a covenant relationship with God.

The Mind and Covenant

I want to say a brief word about the mind God has blessed each of us with. The mind is to be used for the glory of God just like anything else in our life. This aspect is often overlooked when speaking about the Holy Spirit and covenant. I fear we have at times reduced evidences of the Holy Spirit to emotional manifestations. There is a very real presence of the Holy Spirit when one chooses to surrender the mind to God.

Trueblood, whom I quote often in this book, believes that in every local church there ought to be a lay seminary. I have taken this into consideration, and am preparing myself, preparing materials, and preparing my congregation for such an adventure in the coming years.

Richard Farson, author of *Management of the Absurd,* writes, "Finally, and probably most important of all, education gives managers new ways of thinking, new perspectives."[36] If education is good for the business world, it certainly will not hurt Christians to move in this direction as well. Mark Noll says, "The scandal of the evangelical mind is that there is not much of an evangelical mind."[37]

A covenant relationship with God will move you in this direction with your mind. My mind was virtually in hibernation before experiencing a covenant relationship with God. Before covenant I was doing my job, loving God, and waiting until I got to Heaven before I would apply my mind. My mind is alert, active, productive, energized, all because a covenant relationship with God makes me more alive, not less alive. It is a great way to live life. How about you?

---

[35] Foster, *Celebration of Discipline,* 175.

[36] Farson, *Management of the Absurd* (New York: Touchstone, 1997), 156.

[37] Noll, *The Scandal of the Evangelical Mind* (Grand Rapids, Mich.: Wm .B. Eerdmans Publishing Company, 1994), 3.

I remember a trip I took with Stan, a dear friend who travels with me to the mission field sometimes. Stan is my prayer partner and a tremendous encouragement to my ministry. He knows Scripture better than I do! One time before taking off to Haiti, we were getting ready to board the plane in Portland, Oregon, and he said, "Watch this; I'm going to get on the plane before you."

I was very curious how he would do this. He went to the agent gathering the boarding passes for our flight and had a quick conversation with her. He looked back at me with a grin and boarded the plane with those sitting in first class. When it was my turn to board the plane, I made my way through the walkway to the plane, caught up with my friend and asked him how he did it.

"I told her I had lost my mind." Under federal law, she was not permitted to question his disability and had to let him board the plane.

I asked him how he had come up with that lame excuse.

"After I told her I had lost my mind, I asked if she wanted to know how I had lost it. Of course, she was curious. So I told her that as a believer I now have the mind of Christ. She smiled and said, 'Board the plane.'"

I advocate having the mind of Christ. I do not advocate using it the way my friend Stan did!

Making the Paradigm Shift toward Covenant

I am attempting to guide you toward a covenant relationship with God. Perhaps you will need to consider this relationship intellectually before you embrace it experientially. We all have a comfort zone. Ultimately, a covenant relationship with God is meant to be experienced.

This is not Christian window-shopping. It's time to buy and buy big! Boa writes, "The occupational hazard of theologians is to become so engrossed in the development of systematic models of understanding that God becomes an abstract intellectual formulation they discuss and write about instead of a living person they love on bended knees."[38] I am asking you to make a paradigm shift in your heart, your mind, and your soul. Join me in this journey. The water is warm, the Son is shining, and the angels are singing! What a great setting to dance with God!

---

[38] Boa, *Conformed to His Image*, 31.

One of the shows Joanie and I watch faithfully is *Dancing With the Stars*. I do not like the show nearly as much as Joanie does. However, it is time we spend together. I find myself "getting into the show" almost as much as she does some nights. That is embarrassing. However, I am amazed at how good some of the stars are at dancing. And of course, the professional dancers are amazing. I have observed as they dance that they really have a lot of fun together. That is what I believe God had in mind with us. He intended for the dance to be fun!

There is much to gain in experiencing a covenant relationship with God. This covenant model I am advocating may well be the only solution in a world that is lacking ethical values, moral integrity, and societal harmony.

I am tired of living in a world where people are always fighting with each other. I am tired of politicians fighting with one another. Worse than fighting in that arena, I am really tired of Christians fighting with one another.

It used to be that Wesleyans would fight with Calvinists. It used to be that Baptists would fight with everybody else. It used to be that Pentecostals and Evangelicals would rather kill each other than worship with one another.

These battle lines are no longer the front lines of spiritual casualties. It is now a war between Moderns and Postmoderns. It is now a battle between emerging churches and non-emerging churches. Stop it! Stop fighting with one another. We are not one another's enemy. Our enemy is Satan!

Howard Thurman writes, "The logic of the development of hatred is death to the Spirit and disintegration of ethical and moral values."[39] We must consider a covenant relationship with God for the good of the body of Christ, for the good of culture. A covenant relationship with God resolves ethical and moral tensions.

The problem in America is our self-centeredness. Robert N. Bellah, in a fascinating read, *Habits of the Heart,* writes, "Individualism lies at the very core of American culture."[40] Little has changed in the 23 years since Bellah wrote this statement.

Boa writes, "It is easy and comforting to reduce God to a set of biblical propositions and theological inferences rather than a living person who

---

[39] Thurman, *Jesus and the Disinherited* (Boston: Beacon Press, 1996), 87–88.

[40] Bellah, *Habits of the Heart* (New York: Harper & Row, 1986), 142.

cannot be boxed in, controlled, or manipulated by our agendas."[41] I want to remind us that covenant is not our idea; it is God's idea. It is not our invitation to God; it is God's invitation to us. It is not centered on us; it is centered in God. Just be glad you have been invited to the dance!

The ones who struggle most with this paradigm shift to a covenant relationship with God are Moderns. It is not natural. In fact, it is very foreign. It shows how far the enemy has taken us from Scripture and God's original design for us. Darrell Guder writes, "Modernity is the story of this struggle to create society on the basis of objective scientific truth and the construct of the autonomous self."[42]

The modern Christian is in crisis. So is the postmodern Christian, just in a different form. Both need God! I am offering a solution to our crisis. I am offering an explanation and solution to what Satan has hidden from Christians in Scripture.

Vigen Guroian has it correct when he says, "Modern people need to be reminded that our humanity is an indivisible oneness of body and soul and that our salvation is no less of the body than of the soul."[43] Through a covenant relationship with God, God is bringing together both body and soul. Covenant makes us whole!

Leech adds, "Most of all we need to see that the essence of sin lies not in the infringement of moral rules but in the fact that it separates us from God."[44] A covenant relationship with God turns our brokenness into wholeness.

Plato taught that the body is bad and the soul is good. Plato never experienced a covenant relationship with God. In God, I am made whole: body, soul and spirit. God is not broken. Mankind is broken. God's solution is covenant.

I remember one afternoon coming home from school. I was in my early grades, though I do not remember which grade. I was bored, wishing I had

---

[41] Boa, *Conformed to His Image*, 295.

[42] Guder, *Missional Church* (Grand Rapids, Mich.: William B. Eerdmans Publishing Company, 1998), 25.

[43] Guroian, *The Fragrance of God* (Grand Rapids, Mich.: William B. Eerdman, 2006), 108.

[44] Leech, *True Prayer* (San Francisco: Harper & Row, 1980), 144.

someone to play with. I had quite an imagination as a child. I loved playing baseball. I played first base and pitcher on my Little League team. Wanting to get in some batting practice, I came up with a brilliant idea. Our property had faucets about the height of my waist. What a perfect object to place baseballs on and swing away! I was having a blast until I swung a little low. I broke the faucet handle off clean as a whistle. I knew that if Dad found out, when he got home I would be in trouble. I did what any little boy would do, I glued it back on.

Dad came home several hours later. He would always water the grass soon after getting home from work. That night was no exception. Of course, as he turned the handle it fell off. He knew who to blame. When asked, I told him what I had done—sort of!

That faucet is an example of what we do with broken relationships. We hide them from our Heavenly Father. We pretend that everything is fine, when in actuality we are broken. By the way, I did not get into a lot of trouble on that one. Dad fixed the faucet and everything was fine again. That is what God wants to do with us: fix our faucet so we can play ball again!

Richard Foster sums up our need in terms of the Disciplines. He states, "The Disciplines allow us to place ourselves before God so that he can transform us." [45] This is God's ultimate goal for us: transformation. Transformation happens when we live in a covenant relationship with God.

Anthony de Mello makes an important contribution at this juncture: "You don't change yourself; it's not me changing me. Change takes place through you, in you. That's about the most adequate way I can explain it." [46] This is why I say it is not about you or me. It is all about God. God is our change agent. We are simply the invited vessel.

Wouldn't you agree that in the most recent years of church history in the United States, we have made it about us with such an emphasis on being user-friendly and seeker-sensitive? We seem to care more about what each other thinks than what God thinks.

I make occasional trips to Haiti. Their problems are not our problems, at least on the surface. They are concerned about where their next

---

[45] Foster, *Celebration of Discipline*, 7.

[46] de Mello, *Awareness* (New York: Doubleday, 1990), 167.

meal is coming from or if the next storm is going to destroy their fragile dwelling place. They are concerned about if their children will make it to age five.

Christians in the United States are consumed with food too. We are thinking about how angry we are because the preacher has gone five minutes over and we will not beat the people from the church down the street to our favorite restaurant.

We are consumed with our homes too. We rush from church to the nearest store to buy more stuff to decorate our homes. We are consumed with our kids too. We see another child in church who has something our child is without, so we rush to the store and buy stuff to keep up with the other children in church.

In Haiti they are concerned about survival. They very much care about what God thinks. Christians have much to learn from our brothers and sisters in Haiti.

A covenant relationship with God defines purpose and meaning. It gives clear direction for living. I would take it one step further than the great catechisms of old by adding: man's purpose in life is to glorify God as we live in a covenant relationship with Him!

I conclude this chapter by suggesting that modern Christians move toward covenant in order that we might have something to celebrate once again. This was the pattern of Israel. They moved toward God in covenant. Then they would move away from God in religion. Then they would move toward God in covenant. Then they would move away from God with rituals. Then they would move toward God in covenant.

The reason why there are eight identifiable covenants in Scripture is not because God offered up an incomplete invitation the first time. Humankind chose not to live in covenant. I would suggest to you that the eight covenants in Scripture are all the same covenant. They simply represent a different time period in history.

I fully understand the new covenant as being the fulfillment of all the other covenants. Nonetheless, it is still the same covenant between God and humankind. The dynamics of the relationship have never changed. It has always been and still remains today God's invitation to you and I to live in union with the God of the universe in perfect harmony.

Foster writes, "Ancient Israel was commanded to gather together three times a year to celebrate the goodness of God."[47] This pattern of celebration takes place within a covenant relationship with God. God was forever moving the Israelites from ritual to relationship; from religion to relationship. Is God doing any less with us? No! A covenant relationship with God will change your focus. You will begin to care less about style and more about substance. Ninety-nine percent of the division in the church is over style.

If you ever attend the church I work for on a Sunday, you would likely see me in a black suit. If you came back the following Sunday, you will likely see me in that same black suit. I have never been too concerned about style. For the past five years, I have worn that black suit to church on Sunday. I recently got a second suit. One suit is my chubby suit; the other is what I wear when I lose a little weight during the year.

Very little of our time is spent concerned about substance. How sad. How true. How unnecessary. Let's change it. Let's move toward covenant! Let's move away from selfish styles and move toward celebrating a covenant relationship with God. Let's move away from consultants and move toward celebrating a covenant relationship with God. Let's move toward experiencing God. Let's move toward an interpersonal, intimate relationship with God. Why wait for the party to begin in Heaven when God has offered an invitation to you and I this side of Heaven to live with Him in a covenant relationship.

Alcorn states: "More important than leaving your children an inheritance is leaving them a spiritual heritage."[48] We cannot give to our children what we do not have. Let's model covenant to them and for them. It is the single greatest legacy we can leave them. What we leave our children and friends in our wills is not nearly as important as what we leave them from our hearts.

Ron Post, founder of Northwest Medical Teams (now Medical Teams International), writes in his book, *Created for Purpose*, "The conductor is calling all those who can hear to get on board. The train is never full. There is always room for more. The cost of the ride is a willing heart. The ride is not always comfortable, but the experience is always rewarding, meaningful,

---

[47] Foster, *Celebration of Discipline*, 192.

[48] Alcorn, *The Treasure Principle* (Sisters, Ore.: Multnomah Publishers, 2001), 70.

and satisfying."[49] Ron Post is my friend. I have watched him live out this marvelous invitation from God.

I had the privilege of traveling with Ron several years ago to Oaxaca to conduct three pastors' conferences and to preach in some local settings. Oaxaca is a beautiful part of God's creation. The people are even more beautiful. Ron has been ministering in this part of the world for well over twenty years and has many friends in Oaxaca. I watched him interact with the people of Oaxaca. I watched him exude great joy over the work that has been accomplished to make life better for the people of Oaxaca. I watched Ron experience the things he writes about in his book. God is our conductor. He is calling to you and I, "All aboard!"

[49] Post, *Created for Purpose* (Eagle Creek, Ore.: Coffee House Press, 1999), 179.

Chapter 3 Reflections and Discussion: Creating Covenant

1. What needs to happen in your life for Scripture to be your final authority?

2. Does the Holy Spirit have complete control of your life? Why or why not?

3. Has your mind been renewed by the Holy Spirit as you have been guided by Scripture within the past three months?

4. What single area in your life needs the most spiritual attention?

5. What is the role of the Holy Spirit in Scripture?

6. When was the last time you memorized a verse in the Bible? Develop a Scripture memory program. Perhaps encourage others to join you in this venture!

7. Identify a verse in the Bible that will help you love Scripture, listen to the Holy Spirit, and surrender your mind fully to God.

8. Find a story in the Bible that draws application to a relationship with the Holy Spirit.

CHAPTER 4

SPIRITUAL FORMATION AND COVENANT

"Spiritual formation is in."[50] This statement by Evan Howard in a *Christianity Today* article is right on the money. At least we can say that *spirituality* is in. He has observed what others have as well: Spiritual formation is very popular today in religious circles. In this chapter, I draw together words that define spiritual formation as a covenant relationship with God. Information reaches the mind. Spiritual formation as covenant reaches the heart, the soul, and the mind. It reaches the whole person. Spiritual formation is more than a reduction to just rational thought. It reaches into the relationships of the soul.

Modernism has vandalized spiritual formation. Modernism is concerned with reason and science. Spiritual formation as covenant is concerned with experience and faith. Spiritual formation is conforming to the likeness of Christ and leading others to this likeness too.

I define spiritual formation with language used by Dallas Willard, who states: "Here's an amazing truth: spiritual transformation is the process of forming our inner lives to take on the character of Jesus Himself."[51] Howard expounds the subject this way: "Christian spiritual formation is not simply fostering the experience of the Spirit but rather a radical formation, a

---

50 Howard, "Three Temptations of Spiritual Formation," *Christianity Today,* December 9, 2002, 46.

51 Willard & Frazee, *Renovation of the Heart* (Colorado Springs: NavPress, 2005), 150.

shaping and molding of the believer into conformity with Christ through the Spirit."[52]

This is the context of this chapter when thinking about covenant in terms of spiritual formation. Dr. Shelton, whom I will cite in the following chapter, calls this form of spiritual formation a "covenant with God." Guroian writes, "Where spirit and earth mix, God and man meet."[53] This chapter defines covenant with God.

Ultimately, covenant is a here and now, permanent and eternal relationship with God that is intended to be almost as good as when we get to Heaven. That is what this book is all about. It is about knowing God almost as well right now as knowing Him one day in Heaven. Let the party begin!

Covenant Is a Relationship

The very essence of covenant is a relationship. It is not a contractual relationship as much as it is a communal relationship with God. Covenant is very intimate and personal. I love the way Dr. Elton Trueblood states it in *The Yoke of Christ*: "The end is the complete losing of ourselves in the love of God."[54] This is the essence of covenant. It is nothing more because it does not need to be anything more.

Covenant is all about relationship. To be in a covenant relationship with God is to loose ourselves in His love. Relationships are core to Postmoderns. Truths are core to Moderns. Relationships need to become far more important to Moderns! Truth needs to become far more important to Postmoderns. Remember, I said I am a both/and Christian. The *truth* is Jesus Christ. We live in covenant in a *relationship* with Jesus Christ.

Francis Schaeffer, in *The Church before the Watching World*, states, "We are at this moment the bride of Christ. And what does our divine bridegroom want from us? He wants not only doctrinal faithfulness, but our love day by day."[55]

---

[52] Howard, "Three Temptations of Spiritual Formation," 49.

[53] Guroian, *The Fragrance of God*, 43.

[54] Trueblood, *The Yoke of Christ* (New York: Harper & Brothers, 1958), 57.

[55] Schaeffer, *The Church before the Watching World* (Downers Grove, Ill.: InterVarsity Press, 1976), 59.

The modern Christian has made doctrinal faithfulness the centerpiece of Christianity. Spiritual formation as covenant calls the modern Christian to make a paradigm shift from doctrinal faithfulness as the centerpiece to covenant, defining love not in theory, but as love in action. Doctrinal faithfulness will still remain important for the modern Christian. The difference is doctrinal faithfulness no longer is the engine driving the Modern's train. It is now the caboose. The engine driving the train for all Christians ought to be found in a covenant relationship with God.

In *The Mark of the Christian*, Schaeffer writes, "What is the final apologetic? 'That they all may be one; as thou; Father art in me, and I in thee, that they also may be one in us: that the world may believe that thou hast sent me.' This is the final apologetic."[56] This "oneness" with God is the essence of covenant. It is not theology I am describing. I am describing a relationship.

A covenant relationship with God makes great theology. It is a great relationship. This has been the problem for the church over the years; we have been more concerned about theology than relationship. People who frequent bars have better relationships with one another than most people who go to church! People in politics have better relationships with one another than people who go to church! Why is that?

I grew up on nine acres with only a few friends to have over since we lived in a marvelous country-type setting. It was a great place to grow up as an adventurous boy. For fourteen years I had a German shepherd named Tammy. We hunted together. We played ball together. Every place I went, Tammy went. I loved that dog. Our driveway was two-tenths of a mile long. Tammy walked with me each morning to the bus stop where we would stand together across from the old red barn. When I came home from school, Tammy was there waiting for me at the end of the driveway, across from the old red barn. I loved that dog.

God has a sense of humor too. When Tammy finally died at the age of fourteen, she died at my grandma's house, which was next to ours. Tammy died on her back door step. Why do I mention this? Grandma did not love

---

[56] Schaeffer, *The Mark of the Christian* (Downers Grove, Ill.: InterVarsity Press, 1970), 15.

Tammy! Like I said, God has a sense of humor too! Oh that Christians would treat one another half as good as dogs treat human beings.

Perhaps Christians have cared more about being right than being in love. Covenant is about being in love with God. You and I have been invited by God to have an intimate relationship with Him this side of Heaven. In Hebrews 12 we read, "Therefore, since we have so great a cloud of witnesses surrounding us, let us also lay aside every encumbrance and the sin which so easily entangles us, and let us run with endurance the race that is set before us" (Hebrews 12:1).

The next verse tells us to "fix our eyes on Jesus." You and I must find ways to keep our eyes on Jesus in a world that is filled with so many attractions and distractions. I quoted Hebrews 12:1 because it must be noted that a covenant relationship with God does not include sin. In fact, covenant moves the Christian so far away from sin that you may forget what it smells like. It never is far away, just blocked by covenant!

In *The Scandal of the Evangelical Mind*, Mark A. Noll declares, "The gospel properly calls the whole person."[57] Covenant with God is the deepest of all commitments because it is the deepest of all loves. It leaves little room for cheap grace.

Trueblood articulates covenant using marriage as a metaphor to help the reader understand the relationship between God and man. "The point of all this is that marriage is not a contract. If it were a contract, it would cease to be in effect for one party once the other party failed to keep his side of the bargain. Instead of a contract, it is a commitment and thus is intrinsically religious, since commitment is the crucial step of religious experience."[58]

I must admit there are days when relationships are governed by duty. That is how I view my assignment of taking out the garbage. I rarely think about it in terms of love. I usually think about it in terms of duty. We are all human. I wished I were better at it, but I am not. Thank God for grace.

In *Revival Praying*, Leonard Ravenhill writes, "To be much for God, we must be much with God."[59] Covenant as spiritual formation calls you and

---

[57] Noll, *The Scandal of the Evangelical Mind*, 46.

[58] Trueblood, *The Common Ventures of Life* (New York: Harper & Brothers, 1949), 42.

[59] Ravenhill, *Revival Praying*, 60.

me to a commitment of time with God. Time not spent out of duty, but out of love. Not theoretical love found in the pages of theology but rather love that comes from the heart, which yields the very best in us behaviorally.

I am reminded of a date Joanie and I went on together before we were married. Early on in our relationship we went to a worn-down amusement park. I hate rides, but I love Joanie. Joanie loves rides and was deciding at the time if she loved me, so I did what any guy would do who was trying to "catch" his girl. I swallowed my fear, got on the ride with her and was going to show her how much I really loved her.

The place where I sat on the ride had previously been occupied by someone who had left part of his lunch on the ceiling directly above my head. They strapped me in as if I were going to the moon. Joanie was laughing. I was crying. It was horrible. It was one of those rides where you could twist a wheel to make the ride more nauseating. Joanie had us in orbit. I begged her to stop. I promised her Japan, trips, cars and anything else that came to my scrambled brain enduring those moments of hell on earth. I call this "love from the heart." What I did that day was not theory. It was love in the flesh.

There are numerous ways to articulate the desired outcome of spiritual formation as covenant. In *Preaching to a Postmodern World*, Graham MacPherson Johnston writes, "Religion speaks of rigidity, structure, and institutionalism; whereas, spirituality is about personal growth and wholeness."[60] Personal growth and wholeness become the foundation for a relationship with God that is covenantal in form and function.

Another way to define covenant as relationship is with words from Brian McLaren: "In God we live and grow and have our being. In God's wind we sway and our leaves dance."[61] I have never been to a dance. I passed on the prom because I knew there was not a girl in my high school that would go

---

[60] Johnston, *Preaching to a Postmodern World: A Guide to Reaching Twenty-First Century Listeners*, 122.

[61] Brian D. McLaren, *A Generous Orthodoxy: why I am a missional, evangelical, post/Protestant, liberal/conservative, mystical/poetic, biblical, charismatic/contemplative, Fundamentalist/Calvinist, Anabaptist/Anglican, Methodist, Catholic, Green, incarnational, depressed-yet-hopeful, emergent, unfinished Christian* (Grand Rapids, Mich.: Youth Specialties Books by Zondervan, 2004), 283.

with me. Besides, I felt it was a terrible waste of my time and money. That is how you rationalize it when you are a nerd!

I was blown away the day I got my invitation from God to go to the heavenly prom with Him. I call it, "the eternal dance with God." I'm dancing! This is another way to describe what it means to live in covenant with God. So, when I invite you to covenant through spiritual formation, the result is dancing with God. It is a life filled with freedom and joy. But it is not a license to sin. That would go against everything covenant stands for with God. It is the life God intended all believers to experience. Have you?

For the Modern, this is foreign. Admit it. I have! But once you understand the God of covenant and embrace His invitation, you will abandon your fear and will come alongside me and countless others in "the eternal dance with God"!

This is not a new invitation. It is an invitation as old as the Bible. God has invited you and I to the dance. He wants us to experience covenantal love. Covenant removes the fear! Boa writes, "Philippians 3 affirms that true spirituality is not concerned with rules, regulations, and rituals but with the person of Jesus Christ."[62] This is God's generous invitation to you and I. Let's dance!

It is important to understand the covenant relationship I speak about is Trinitarian. McLaren writes, "The generous orthodoxy explored in the pages ahead assumes, for example, that the value of understanding the Trinity is to love and honor and serve the Trinity, and that allegedly right Trinitarian opinions that do not lead to divine adoration are worth little."[63] I agree!

Covenant, when I make reference to God, is that I am referencing God the Father, God the Son, and God the Holy Spirit simultaneously. I see them as one! This covenant relationship is with the Holy Trinity I call God.

Many Christians are waiting for this relationship I am describing to happen immediately following their death. I am not. You should not. Leech writes, "The heart of the Gospel is the fact that God in Christ has forgiven us our sins, has restored us to fellowship, and has brought us into his kingdom."[64]

---

[62] Boa, *Conformed to His Image*, 219.

[63] McLaren, *A Generous Orthodoxy*, 14.

[64] Leech, *True Prayer*, 129.

You and I have been taught over our many years of being in church that "the best is yet to come." That is true, but it does not negate getting started right now. Why are so many Christians so miserable? Why are so many Christians lacking joy? Why are so many Christians so defeated in daily living? Perhaps it is because they are waiting, waiting, waiting. I call this "stupid waiting." Why wait? The music is playing. Your partner is ready to dance with you. Get up out of your seat and quit feeling so sorry for yourself and start dancing. You might actually find joy and victory on the dance floor!

A covenant relationship with God seems foreign because far too many Christians are uncomfortable with intimacy. It is foreign. It is far easier to be rational, play it safe, keep our distance, and pretend we love God and others.

Likewise, it is easier to save the environment than to have an encounter with God. You can have an encounter with the environment and never have an encounter with God. When you really get to know God in a covenant relationship, then you can help the environment through a relationship with God.

Randy Alcorn writes, "Christ's emphasis isn't on making new things but on making old things new. It's not about inventing the unfamiliar but about restoring and enhancing the familiar."[65] I invite you to roll the dice! Live a little! Loosen up! It's not like you're being asked to smoke pot and down a case of Coors! Good night nurse, the God of the universe has invited you and I to experience an intimate relationship with Him this side of Heaven.

I remember the first time I went to a drive-in. It was with Joanie in her hometown of Madras, Oregon. We watched *101 Dalmatians*. I grew up being taught that theaters and drive-ins were "the devil's den." As the movie plot unfolded, sweat began pouring from my brow as conviction set in to my troubled soul. I was in a strange town, I was with a girl I didn't know very well, and I was in the devil's den! I endured the movie. When I got back to my room I got down on my knees and repented of doing such a terrible thing.

I share this story because this is how some people live their Christianity. My response then to that night of watching a bunch of spotted canines

---

[65] Alcorn, *Heaven* (Wheaton, Ill.: Tyndale House Publishers, Inc., 2004), 383.

is called bondage and legalism. Since then God has set me free from such a mind-set. Do you need to be set free?

Have you ever noticed there are three kinds of people when it comes to swimming in a swimming pool? There are those who sit beside the pool with no intention of ever getting into the water. Then there are those who dabble in the water, and if everything is right they venture into the shallow end of the pool. There is a third group of people who simply jump in! God is inviting you and I to jump in with Him. The water is warm. The company is good.

Of the twelve disciples, only one jumped in. (See Matthew 14:25–31.) We criticize Peter for sinking. At least he got out of the stinking boat. I invite you to get out of the stinking boat and really start enjoying your relationship with God.

My mentor, Arthur Roberts, speaks of covenant relationship in terms of redemption. He states, "Believers see human redemption as a key to recreating the universe. Redemption is the trigger mechanism for renewal, at least as far as human beings are concerned."[66] Roberts adds, "The covenant dream includes earthly distortions. I see heaven as a blending of the natural and artificial according to a divine blueprint."[67]

I close this chapter on covenant as spiritual formation with a quote from an insightful book, *Spiritual Traditions*: "In the same vein we are accustomed (simplistically) to equating being moral or 'good' with adherence to a set of rules arbitrarily set forth either by God or the church. Seldom do we remember that the rules are in fact the content of a covenant relationship between God and Israel and that the context of this Divine-human relationship was a prior act of divine deliverance. The Ten Commandments are not rules for the sake of rules; they instruct us in an appropriate lifestyle for a delivered people."[68]

Jim Cymbala, pastor of The Brooklyn Tabernacle, states it bluntly: "If we don't want to experience God's closeness here on earth, why would we

---

[66] Roberts, *Exploring Heaven*, 161.

[67] Ibid, 163.

[68] Maas & O'Donnell, *Spiritual Traditions for the Contemporary Church* (Nashville: Abingdon Press, 1990), 167.

want to go to heaven anyway."[69] Perhaps for you it is not that you don't want the closeness; it's that you may have thought it was not possible to attain closeness with God this side of Heaven. I hope you are beginning to think otherwise.

---

[69] Cymbala, *Fresh Wind, Fresh Fire*, 58.

Chapter 4 Reflections and Discussion: Creating Covenant

1. Between 1 and 10, with 10 being the highest or best, rate your relationship with Jesus Christ.

2. What do you need to do in the next six months to move that number from where it is to one higher?

3. What life events can move that number one lower?

4. What do you do best with God?

5. What is your greatest struggle as a Christian?

6. Do you have a spiritual plan? Spiritual goals? Identify a specific plan using specific goals?

7. Identify a verse in the Bible that will motivate you to be a stronger Christian.

8. Find a story in the Bible that is relevant to your life that will motivate you to be a stronger Christian.

COVENANT AND COVENANT

This chapter is the technical chapter that will give specific definition to what I mean by a covenant relationship with God. This theme is not original with me. I credit the theme to Dr. Larry Shelton, who was a major influence in my doctoral work at George Fox Evangelical Seminary several years ago. He encouraged me to put flesh on the covenant relationship I wrote about in my dissertation.

Dr. Shelton has written a landmark book named *Cross and Covenant*. My work is the fleshing out of his hours of research. His work gives credibility to the subject through scholarly research. Mine gives credibility in the fleshing out of the application of a covenant relationship in everyday life. The remaining chapters of this book are areas of life that I articulate in light of a covenant relationship with God. Beyond what I have already stated so far, I will give specific examples of how a covenant relationship with God is transformational in everyday life.

I began this book with my personal story of the tragedy with my son Kevin. I shared how God used tragedy in my life to give me an experience and understanding of what it means to live in covenant with God.

Shelton's book is a foundational book on the subject of covenant relationships. In fact, Dr. Shelton instructed me to refer to a covenant relationship with God as the Covenant Renewal Model. From this point on in the book, I will use these two phrases interchangeably. I urge you to read beyond my book and read Dr. Shelton's book if you want the scholarly version on this subject.

To give my book clarity, I have chosen to pull from Dr. Shelton's work citations that will complete my definition of the Covenant Renewal Model.

I have done so with his blessing! The remainder of the book will be given to practical application. I am not only interested in whether or not it is true but also in whether or not it works. Moderns are interested in truth. Postmoderns are interested in application. I am interested in both!

I claim that discerning the voice of the Holy Spirit guided by Scripture will move you, the reader, toward this Covenant Renewal Model. It is a tremendously exciting paradigm shift. Some may already be there but you have not been able to give it a name. I trust this book will help you to that end. For the vast majority, there is a hunger for God. I trust the Covenant Renewal Model is the equivalent of prime rib. For you vegetarians reading this book ... tofu!

Shelton's premise for his book is found in a Scripture I have already cited in this book taken from Ezekiel 36:26-27. It is worth quoting again since it is the theme verse for the Covenant Renewal Model. "Moreover, I will give you a new heart and put a new spirit within you; and I will remove the heart of stone from your flesh and give you a new heart of flesh. And I will put My Spirit within you and cause you to walk in My statutes, and you will be careful to observe My ordinances" (Ezekiel 36:26–27).

Shelton writes on the subject of covenant within the context of community, "The numerous references to these different ministries of God express the covenant concept in the form of community, which finds expression in the community of Israel and its spiritual life of covenant obedience, seen in both personal piety and community religious expression."[70]

This becomes a point of difficulty in grasping the Covenant Renewal Model because if you are not of a minority race or are not tribal in nature, grasping community is much more difficult. I do not belong to a minority race in this country. Consequently, I am not naturally in tune with tribal traditions.

Most white people living in the United States are in my boat. This is one reason so many Anglos in the United States see the Bible in such a different light from its first century audience. This is why so many Moderns have missed a covenant relationship with God. By nature, non-tribal people

---

[70] Shelton, *Cross & Covenant, Interpreting the Atonement for 21st Century Mission* (Tyrone, Ga.: Paternoster, 2006), 27.

groups are independent, isolated in their individualism, and very selfish. Our creed is "every man for himself." This is not the creed of Scripture at all!

When I was in college, I thought I would be doing God a favor by becoming the Protestant version of a monk. I had no intention of getting married. I was going to give God every hour of every day of every week of every month of every year of my life. To say college students can be naïve is a gross understatement. I was just plain stupid.

I was on track with this plan for my life (notice it was my plan, not God's plan) until one night in January of 1980. I noticed a girl in my law class, and in less than five minutes of careful thought I decided to scrap my plan of being a monk. I made the right choice. That girl I first saw in 1980 is the same one I have been looking at for 30 plus years.

Shelton sheds more light in the community aspect of covenant by stating, "The covenant between God and Abraham is what constituted the community in the first place."[71] Some further thoughts on the development of community and covenant are, "It is all about interpersonal obedience, social community and spiritual intimacy."[72]

Many Christians accept interpersonal obedience—at least in theory. They also would acknowledge spiritual intimacy, albeit a watered-down one. The one causing heartburn is the "social community." As long as it is a church potluck, count me in. As far as going outside the walls of my church, I mean really going outside the walls of church, which is where the rubber meets the road with covenant, count me out.

It is not only about getting it right with God; it is also about getting it right with others. Covenant is vertical and horizontal. But it is vertical first and horizontal second. And when everything is going the way it should, they both happen at the same time, like a beautiful symphony.

I am not talking about the sounds of a sixth-grade music recital (no offense intended—everybody has to start somewhere). A sixth-grade music recital is a little bit like a child's first year of baseball. The helmet is bigger than the child's head. The bat is usually heavier than the child swinging it. And the distance to each base might as well be to the moon. Humorous, if

---

[71] Ibid, 35.
[72] Ibid, 38.

we are talking about Little League baseball. Not so humorous when we are talking about our response to a hurting world that is in desperate need of people who could be living in a covenant relationship with God.

Shelton then develops covenant as God's idea not so much as payment for sin, but as a desire to restore a broken relationship. Shelton states, "Thus the main idea of covenant renewal was not to demand a particular payment to God, but to repent of the behavior that brought estrangement to the covenant relationship and to humbly and in faith seek God's forgiveness."[73]

I think you can begin to see the problem with this theology. As a Christian, I spent the vast majority of my time repenting. My question is, "What happens after I have repented?" Is there not a point in which I am to live in victory and joy and enjoy friendship with God? I say there is. This is what covenant has done for me. Covenant can do the same for you! When I stop repenting after I have repented for the same sin for the tenth time, I also start living without as much fear. Far too many Christians are plagued with fear. Fear-based Christianity is never what God had in mind. God is love. "Perfect love casts out fear" (1 John 4:18).

I remember growing up in a marvelous church. I loved the pastor and his family. His children and I played together often as part of that small rural church. There was, however, one moment each week when I would break out in spiritual hives.

When the preacher preached, I felt like he was talking right at me. Each week he invited people to the altar. The denomination I grew up in had a strong emphasis on losing your salvation. Naturally, as a child scared to death of going to hell, I went to the altar often, thinking I had lost my salvation every time I had sinned, which was often!

I got saved about 52 times a year just to make sure I wasn't going to hell. I know what I am talking about when I speak about fear-based Christianity. I don't blame the preacher. I blame a doctrine that was cruel and intimidating. I still belong to that same denomination, but I do not preach that fear-based doctrine. I preach a covenant relationship with God. God does not beat the tar out of His kids when they break the faucet, He fixes the faucet and says, "Let's play ball."

---

[73] Ibid, 67.

On the subject of sacrifice, Shelton makes this claim: "The penal substitutionary interpretations of the sacrifices are based on the forensic equality of value between a sacrifice and the life of the person offering it (the punishment must fit the crime").[74] A premise of Shelton's book is to show there are no ways you or I can accomplish this. We owe a debt we cannot afford. God has paid for a debt He did not owe!

Shelton moves us in another direction: covenant. To this Shelton adds, "Thus the concept of covenant reflects an interpersonal relationship rather than an objective impersonal statement of law."[75]

In other words, the focus is not about our sin; the focus is restoring a broken relationship. In fact, is that not what the entire Bible is all about? I believe from cover to cover it is about restoring a relationship that we broke in the Garden of Eden. The Bible is about a God who in His infinite love and grace has done everything but force His love and grace upon us. It took the cross of Christ to really get our attention.

I remember playing golf with my dad one Saturday as part of a weekly men's club group at Top O' Scott golf course. I was in high school, with aspirations of being a professional golfer one day. (That is what many high schoolers think in the sport they play.)

I birdied the first hole and the second hole. I stood on the tee of the third hole, a short par five easily reached in two. I addressed my ball, took a swing at it and hit the ball straight up in the air. In frustration, I immediately slammed my new $138 driver (in 1974 that was a ton of money) into the ground, snapping it at the head where it had been connected to the shaft.

I felt horrible. My dad never said a word. That is how I picture God in His infinite love and grace. When I fail Him, I look at Him and He does not have to say a word. Rather, His love and grace comes upon me like a baby in need of its blanket and bottle.

Covenant stripped down is about redemption, restoration, reconciliation, renewal, and what I call "recovenanting." The dictionary says this is not a word. It is now!

---

[74] Shelton, *Cross & Covenant, Interpreting the Atonement for 21st Century Mission*, 71.
[75] Ibid, 79.

Shelton then does a masterful job showing us God's relationship to His Son, Jesus Christ. He states, "When God acts in Christ, he offers himself not an experience or a legal standing."[76]

Do you see Shelton teaches us that the work of the Son is the work of the Father? Thus Shelton ties together my comments on the Trinity earlier in the book by putting it this way, "The Father initiates the covenant, Christ empowers and seals it, and the Holy Spirit administers it."[77] Once again, perfect harmony. The Trinity has perfect pitch, playing a melody that is attractive to the soul of mankind. Like me, Shelton sees the absolute necessity to present a Trinitarian sort of theology when speaking on the subject of covenant.

Shelton addresses the mind-set of the modern Christian and the mind-set of Western Christianity by stating, "Indeed, the tendency of Western Christianity to transform the ideas of righteousness and justification into exclusively legal categories seriously threatens to suppress the biblical covenantal relational aspects of salvation language."[78]

He also says on this subject: "The penal view sees the death of Christ as payment of a penalty, thereby enabling God to forgive."[79] For 200 years, the atonement has been viewed through the lenses of a penalty. Covenant looks beyond the penalty and sees the relationship! Covenant does not negate the penalty and the price paid for our sin, but it does not stop there either. Covenant frees us to live beyond our sin. It allows you and I to actually experience redemption in the soul and not just on paper or in our heads. Big difference!

Shelton continually drives home the theme of restoration. He says, "The renewed relationship with the covenant God is a real restoration of the covenant union."[80] As you and I begin to come to grips with the depth of love demonstrated by God to bring us back into union with Him, one wonders what would keep you and I from such a marvelous invitation. God wants

---

[76] Shelton, *Cross & Covenant, Interpreting the Atonement for 21st Century Mission*, 86.

[77] Ibid, 90.

[78] Ibid, 120.

[79] Ibid, 131.

[80] Shelton, *Cross & Covenant, Interpreting the Atonement for 21st Century Mission*, 132.

union with us far more than we want it with Him. He really loves us. He does not call us scoundrels! He calls us sons and daughters!

It is amazing what we will do in the name of love. During the break, I dated Joanie long-distance our first summer away from each other. She lived two hours away in Madras, Oregon, and I lived in Clackamas, Oregon. Driven by love, I worked 16 hours each day on Monday and Tuesday and then from 4 a.m. until noon on Wednesday so that I was done putting in my 40-hour week by noon on Wednesday.

I would run to my 1973 AMC Hornet and race to Madras (from driveway to driveway was 1 hour, 58 minutes) for the remainder of the week just to be with Joanie. That's the way it is with God and us. He is racing to get to us.

My dad lives about an hour away from me. He lives in Portland, Oregon, and I live in Keizer, a suburb of Salem, Oregon. For years now, my dad has driven to my church in Salem every Sunday to listen to me preach. He drives by one hundred great churches on the way, including his home church, which is five minutes from his house. God is always the one who will drive to where we are no matter how far from Him we are living. That is just His nature! He can't help Himself! Aren't you glad?

If you have ever been abused or treated improperly by another human being, I have great news for you. A covenant relationship with God can bring healing to your scarred life. Covenant heals! Covenant heals from the inside out!

On the subject of contracts and broken relationships, which is what most people think of when they think about the term covenant, Shelton states, "The problem Christ confronts in his sacrifice is one of broken relationships that need healing, not simply a breach of contract that needs legal redress."[81]

The modern Christian—I am one—has had a steady diet of the latter rather than the former. These days I am more a covenant Christian than a modern Christian. The modern Christian has been pounded with the contract concept that says, "I did something really bad and there is nothing I can do to fix it, so I will just beg for mercy. And 'thank God, Jesus decided to die on the cross.'" While this is true, and while I am eternally grateful to God for this unbelievable act of love, the cross does not stop at my sin. The

---

[81] Ibid, 141.

cross cares about healing a broken relationship with God. The cross is not only about sin; it is also about restoring a covenant relationship with God. This is amazing love!

On a similar note, Shelton offers the reader a historical perspective back to the Latin view: "The Latin view, with its penitential system, has allowed sin to become substantialized, or materialized. Salvation is thus reduced to the removal of guilt, rather than understood as the transformation of the person of Christ." [82] In fairness to the modern Christian reading this book, this mind-set has been around for a long time. Shelton and Postmoderns are bucking two hundred years of church history.

I am a Modern who deeply loves my heritage, but I love God far more, and I have moved from penal Christianity to covenant Christianity. This move to a covenant relationship moves me away from modern Christianity, which I believe is a very healthy move to make. For Postmoderns this is more of a natural move.

My caution to Postmoderns is not to ignore the issue of sin. It still remains an issue this side of Heaven. Remember, for Moderns and Postmoderns to come together, a covenant relationship with God is a unifier, not a divider. It is a both/and theology, not an either/or theology. This is critical to remember.

On the subject of sin, Shelton writes, "The forensic theories thus see sin as the primary problem and death as a secondary problem, since it is the penalty of sin. They focus, therefore, on how to pay the penalty." [83]

By now, you are beginning to understand that covenant goes beyond penalty and lands in relationship. I never ignore sin. I never write sin off. However, the fear of sinning is no longer my focus. Likewise, my focus is not to live a form of cheap grace by living in sin either. The more I live in union with God, the more my thoughts are concentrated on Him and not the lusts of my mind.

Shelton makes five consecutive statements on the Covenant Renewal Model in his book. "First, the covenant perspective thus overcomes the debate between imputation and impartation of righteousness because the

---

[82] Ibid, 169.
[83] Ibid, 170.

righteousness of God is expressed as covenant relationship."[84] This greatly simplifies the different categories theologians have used to articulate the work of Christ on the cross. Shelton simply reduces the categories down to covenant. I like it!

Second, Shelton states: "The reconciled relationship of sinners being 'rightwised' with God is in fact a functioning 'righteousness' relationship made possible by mediation of Jesus Christ in bringing two alienated parties together in himself. This is atonement."[85]

Shelton sees atonement as a process whereby two parties are brought back together in union with one another. He calls this, "covenantal union,"[86] which is a third major statement. Covenant by itself is powerful. Union by itself carries with it strong imagery. Covenantal union carries with it the weight of Heaven to bind on earth what humankind has broken. Thus we see *Heaven's covenant with earth*!

His fourth conclusion addresses the subject of holiness: "Holiness consists of living out the reality of this restored covenant relationship."[87] I was a modern Christian, raised in the holiness tradition. To have my heritage reduced to this statement is both mind-boggling and very freeing. It would be easy to fight it and lean back on the comforts of a list of do's, don'ts, and propositional truths to carry the day. As I have fought through a quagmire of doctrinal bondage, I urge you to join me and break through to the other side in a covenant relationship with God.

I vividly remember my fourth-grade year of school. My teacher, Miss Sogn, was beautiful, at least to my fourth-grade eyes. She had a program where she handed out red slips and green slips. Students got red slips if they were talking and being bad. Students got green slips if they were being quiet and doing their work.

I was a fourth-grade boy with a big imagination and loved to play more than to sit at a desk. Guess how many red slips I got compared to green slips? I got so many red slips I could have stretched them from sea to shining sea!

---

[84] Ibid, 223.

[85] Ibid.

[86] Ibid.

[87] Ibid.

God has a lot of green slips. He has some red slips too. But since coming to Him with my life, I get far more green slips than red slips from God. A covenant relationship with God is not about getting red slips; it is about gaining green slips. I have since discovered His red slips are red with blood from the cross!

Fifth, Shelton addresses further his own heritage in the holiness tradition and states: "Holiness is the obedience of love, not the coercion and guilt-motivated obedience of the Law. The latter leads to legalism and externalism. The former leads to relational intimacy and obedience out of love for God. It is motivated by gratitude versus duty, freedom versus bondage, grace versus guilt." [88] Herein lies the difference between two hundred years of penal Christianity versus covenant Christianity.

I have made a paradigm shift from the penal substitution model to the covenant renewal model. I do not hate where I have come from, I just like where I am now a whole lot better! Why do so many Christians make loving God so complicated?

Professor Shelton once said in a lecture on the subject of covenant: "This (covenant model) is second grade, people. How did we get away from it?" With that said, I now invite you to read on and watch how covenant works in everyday life as it relates to all the stuff you and I encounter.

---

[88] Ibid.

Chapter 5 Reflection and Discussion: Creating Covenant

1. How was your life transformed at conversion?

2. Since conversion, what transforming works has God been doing in your life?

3. Forecasting your future to the finish line, what transforming work do you trust God for in your life?

4. Are you an "all or nothing" Christians or a "something is better than nothing" Christian?

5. How is your relationship with God affecting your relationship with the people in your life?

6. Who are the people in your life who pick you up and dust you off when you fall spiritually?

7. Identify a verse in the Bible that speaks of your love for God.

8. Find a story in the Bible of someone who loved God more than his or her peers.

HEAVEN AND COVENANT

There are many days when Heaven seems so far away, so far removed from being a reality. Some days Heaven is hard to imagine. With all the hell on earth, Heaven seems like an unattainable destination. Heaven seems to be a place reserved for old people. I am imagining that at that stage of my life I will be either too old to care or too senile to know the difference. These are the sort of thoughts I used to think before being introduced to material on Heaven.

You would think that material about Heaven would be taught in seminary. Not a word that I can remember was said about Heaven during my years in seminary. What do you specifically know about Heaven? And is there a relationship between Heaven and a covenant relationship with God this side of Heaven?

I believe there is a connection, a very strong connection. I want you to see how practical and necessary living in covenant is when it comes to the subject of Heaven. I also believe it is important for you to see that had I not had grounding in Heaven theology, I doubt I would have arrived at a covenant theology.

We have all looked forward to a special vacation. As I said in an earlier chapter, our family used to go to Disneyland every year. Part of the experience was to put the four of us in our small Neon along with plenty of pizza from our favorite local pizza parlor and everyone's favorite junk foods.

Did I mention we only stopped for fuel, at which times the other three members of the family went to the bathroom while I pumped the gas? Our fastest pit stop was just under seven minutes. A ten-minute pit stop was not allowed. It was all part of the magical experience.

We usually left our house by 4 a.m. so we could be in the Disneyland Park for dinner and the fireworks show at 9 p.m. We had the fifteen-hour drive down to a science. Our memories are vivid.

If you feel like you're not connecting with your children, especially if they are teenagers, put them in a Neon (one of the smallest and most uncomfortable cars ever designed!) and drive fifteen hours with two stops totaling less than fifteen minutes! (Did I mention we did not use the air-conditioning since it was my goal to get forty miles to the gallon?) This type of travel I refer to as "acute family therapy." If interested, I can give more details. Simply e-mail me at my address in the back of this book.

Once in Disneyland, Kevin and I always tried to find the best spot for watching the fireworks show. One night, on our last trip to the Park the summer before Kevin joined the Lord in Heaven, he found the most amazing spot in the Park for us to watch the fireworks—near the trinket stand by the entrance to the "It's a Small World" ride. (This is a great ride to take a nap on if you are tired.)

On a hot day, the surface of the ground is warm and the nighttime southern California air is equally warm. If you lie down near the trinket stand and look straight up, you get a great view the fireworks. What an awesome place to see the show! I remember saying to Kevin, "Just think: Heaven is better than this." I remember his excitement knowing the best was yet to come.

Is it possible to live so close to God this side of Heaven that many days you see shadows of Heaven while on earth? Is it possible to have such a close walk with God while on earth that you are able to better visualize Heaven?

I have discovered two realities since the temporary separation from my son. The first reality is a covenant relationship with God. The second reality is the reality of Heaven, knowing that Heaven is closer to us than many realize. Allow me to describe Heaven so I can ignite your desire to live closer to God this side of Heaven in a covenant relationship with Him.

I have come to appreciate deeply the writings of Randy Alcorn. He has written some outstanding books on numerous subjects, including Heaven.

On that subject he states in his book, *In Light of Eternity,* "Living in light of eternity means being prepared for the day of your death."[89]

Alcorn is the first author I have read who puts death in perspective for the Christian in a way that I can accept. Living in a covenant relationship with God is the best way I know to prepare for Heaven. Covenant always looks to the future.

One of the truths I learned shortly after my son went to Heaven was that if I was to regain my strength, I would need to look forward not backward. I would encourage anyone who is grieving to apply this principle I discovered. My healing came more quickly the more forward I looked. That is one reason why Heaven and covenant are such a perfect match for one another.

To live in a covenant relationship with God is to think about Heaven, and to think about Heaven is to live in covenant with God. Death is our focus on earth. Death is but a brief transition. Death is not the end, but a door from which we pass from covenant with God on earth to covenant with God in Heaven!

It seems quite a few people are trying to beat death. You can't beat it; you can only prolong it. Isn't that what diets are all about? Like many, I have tried lots of diets to try and get into shape. (I am in shape; it looks like a two-liter bottle of soda. Some have a six-pack; I have a two-liter bottle!) You can't beat death. So let's learn to deal with it in a positive manner.

In an article written by Alcorn on the same subject, he says: "If you lack a passion for heaven, I can almost guarantee it's because you have a weak, deficient, and distorted theology of heaven ...A robust, accurate, and biblically-energized view of heaven will bring a new spiritual passion to your life."[90] Living in covenant unlocks the realities of Heaven, and studying Heaven in Scripture unlocks the realities of living with God in covenant this side of Heaven. The two almost become interchangeable.

A central verse for Alcorn's definition of Heaven theology is Revelation 13:6. It states: "And he opened his mouth in blasphemies against God, to blaspheme His name and His tabernacle, that is, those who dwell in heaven" (Revelation 13:6).

---

[89] Alcorn, *In Light of Eternity* (Colorado Springs: WaterBrook Press, 1999), 150.

[90] Alcorn, "Overcoming the Myths About Heaven," review of Reviewed Item, *Eternal Perspective Ministries* (1999), 3.

Alcorn states, "Our enemy slanders three things: God's person, God's people, and God's place—heaven."[91] Alcorn exposes three lies Satan has held over Christians down through the centuries: First, Satan wants us to have an incorrect view of God. Second, Satan wants us to have an incorrect view of Heaven. And third, we fail to understand that Satan hates Christians because we get to have a relationship with God in the place where God dwells, which is called Heaven.

Satan gets none of these, ever again! That is the bottom line. So, Satan deceives us into thinking that Heaven may not be real, we are losers, and we cannot have a covenant relationship with God this side of Heaven. These are the three primary lies from Satan from whence all other lies exist.

Alcorn writes, "We have the very answers the world cries out for, yet our wrong views of God's person and God's place silence and distort our message."[92] I wish I could tell you which light bulb came on first for me: covenant or Heaven. I actually think God gave them both to me at the same time because I believe the two are inseparable. Alcorn states it in a similar way: "Our passion for God and our passion for Heaven should be inseparable. The more I learn about God, the more excited I get about heaven. The more I learn about heaven, the more excited I get about God."[93]

I get very excited about food. I love eating food. My favorite restaurants have two qualities: price and quantity. These two qualities are not my wife's, they are mine. The cheaper the food, the better it tastes to me. Likewise, the bigger the plate of food, the better it tastes to me. Consequently, my favorite type of restaurant is a buffet. I believe buffets were first created in Heaven, at the least the part of Heaven that I plan on living in! I pray God will help us to be more excited about Him than the things that excite us on this earth, including buffets!

Alcorn painstakingly walks his readers through the Scriptures, showing them how marvelous Heaven is going to be. He continually brings our focus back to God and the place God dwells: Heaven. Alcorn writes, "We may imagine we want a thousand different things, but God is the one we really long for. His presence brings satisfaction; his absence brings thirst

---

[91] Alcorn, *In Light of Eternity*, 2.

[92] Alcorn, "Overcoming the Myths About Heaven," 2.

[93] Alcorn, *In Light of Eternity*, 5.

and longing. Our longing for heaven is a longing for God—a longing that involves not only our inner beings, but our bodies as well." [94]

There is a growing number of people who in recent time have begun to recognize the strong connection between Heaven and covenant. In fact, I can say Heaven is the ultimate in covenant!

Moderns must move away from theology that states God as propositional truth and a person to be enjoyed when we get to Heaven. God is to be enjoyed this side of Heaven. God is not a proposition; God is truth! And in truth, we live in an interpersonal relationship with God. God is not so concerned about our theology. God is far more interested in relationships. Jesus did not die on the cross to give us good theology. Jesus died on the cross to give us good relationships!

Likewise, Heaven affects life on earth as it relates to sin as well. There is a correlation between sin and Heaven. Thus, there is a great deterrent to sin: covenant. Alcorn writes, "When I meditate on Jesus and my future in Heaven, sin is unappealing. It's when my mind drifts from that person and that place that sin seems attractive." [95]

So we can discern from this statement by Alcorn that Heaven theology may be the foundation for a realistic covenant theology so that we can have a proper response to a sin theology. In other words, my understanding of Heaven impacts my behavior this side of Heaven. As I grow in the Lord, my propensity toward sin decreases.

Alcorn talks about the connection between Heaven and holiness: "Thinking that Heaven leads inevitably to pursuing holiness, our high tolerance for sin testifies to our failure to prepare for heaven." [96]

Holiness is what God longs to see in you and I. Holiness brings us closer to God rather than farther away. Holiness takes us away from sin and moves us toward a stronger union with God. The motivation here becomes Heaven because Heaven is central to a covenant relationship with God. In other words, my relationship with God has a direct impact on my sin, my Christianity, and my future for all of eternity!

---

[94] Alcorn, *Heaven*, 165.

[95] Alcorn, *50 Days of Heaven* (Carol Stream, Ill.: Tyndale, 2006), 269.

[96] Ibid.

Growing up, I went to old-fashioned "camp meetings." I loved going to them because it gave me something to do and I generally really loved church stuff except that one part when I thought I was going to hell every week. At camp meetings a special speaker would preach. He was different than my weekly preacher. This guy would yell louder, stomp harder, and point all ten fingers at me. Who needed horror films—I went to camp meetings!

Often the emphasis was on "death to self." So I killed my soul over and over and over. I was so dead that funeral homes would seek me out! The problem I had with this preaching was that after I killed all that bad stuff in me, I never was told about what comes next.

Another perplexing problem was that each time I killed it, it always came back to life, so I am not too sure what that was all about anyway. In my third-grade mind I had simplified it down to: sin separates, and the cross is the bridge to a restored relationship with God.

Alcorn excites his readers with the possibilities that exist once we get to Heaven. He has strong themes on continuity and connection. Alcorn uses multiple Scriptures to show there is continuity between what we do on earth and our life once in Heaven. Further, Alcorn shows the many connections that exist from this life to the next. He discerned these truths from the Holy Spirit as he studied the Scriptures. He writes, "Since none of us learns everything on earth that God would desire us to, rather than abandon the lessons he wanted to teach us, he might allow us once in heaven to review our lives on earth and this time learn everything he intended."[97] If any portion of this quote is true—and I believe it to be all true—then this supports the need and advantage of living with God in a covenant relationship as I have outlined in this book.

Our life on earth with God is a shadow of the life we will enjoy on the new earth with God, but without the presence of sin and death and Satan. Alcorn writes, "That we'll forever enjoy a resurrected life on a New Earth isn't true because we want it to be. It's true because God says it is. Paying attention to context and taking other scriptures into account, we need to draw God's truth from the text, not superimpose our preconceived ideas into it."[98]

---

[97] Alcorn, "Rethinking Our Beliefs About Heaven," 3.

[98] Alcorn, *Heaven*, 476.

Alcorn also talks about this love relationship we can have with God. "No wonder Satan doesn't want us to learn the truth about Heaven. If we fall in love with the place and look forward to the future that God has for us, we'll fall more in love with God, and we'll be emboldened to follow him with greater resolve and perspective."[99]

I believe Alcorn likely would support the Covenant Renewal Model. His writing gives tremendous support to my claim that covenant and Heaven are a marriage made in Heaven … literally! Alcorn states, "We need a generation of heavenly minded people who see human beings and the earth itself not simply as they are, but as God intends them to be."[100]

I believe as does Alcorn that having an eternal perspective in this life makes for a better life. Once again, it is the idea of looking forward. It will give you and I a more productive life this side of Heaven, not a less productive life this side of Heaven. What a tragedy it would be to get to Heaven and realize the party and the dance could have started with God while on earth. I do not want to miss out on one minute with God. I trust you feel the same way. If there is a way to experience anything on earth that I can experience in Heaven, I want to live accordingly. Who wouldn't?

Friedman in his book, *Generation to Generation,* states, "Death is the single most important event in family life."[101] I am in full agreement with this statement. I am convinced that a covenant relationship with God is the absolute best way to face death … and win!

One of the best ways to face death and grieving is to understand death as Alcorn understands death from Scripture. He writes, "Five minutes after we die, we'll know exactly how we should have lived. We'll know how we should have given, prayed, shared our faith, meditated on Scripture."[102] The more willing we are to accept and live in a covenant relationship with God, the more we will know how to please God this side of Heaven. This is another reason to embrace a covenant relationship with God.

---

[99] Ibid, 156.

[100] Alcorn, *50 Days of Heaven,* 7.

[101] Friedman, *Generation to Generation* (New York, London: The Guilford Press, 1985), 168.

[102] Alcorn, *50 Days of Heaven,* 256.

Alcorn writes, "The Bible tells us that while men may not remember or care what our lives here have been; God remembers perfectly and cares very much—so much that the door of eternity swings on the hinges of choices made here and now."[103]

I doubt Alcorn was advocating covenant when he wrote his material, and I doubt Shelton was writing about Heaven when he wrote his material. I have the privilege of bringing these two together. It is a perfect fit for twenty-first century Christians. It is a perfect fit in that it is not doctrinal or theological. Neither is it a program, a denominational thing, or anything else that could ruin it. A covenant relationship with God is the perfect solution for the individual and for the community of believers.

Dr. Arthur Roberts, in *Exploring Heaven,* puts it this way: "So, then, earth is a province of heaven, albeit a sin-laden one."[104] While a covenant relationship with God is but a shadow of what we will enjoy in Heaven, nonetheless it is a marvelous alternative to all the other choices out there in religion and particularly Christianity. My security in God used to be "being right." Now my security in God comes in being in relationship. Big difference! God intends for us to enjoy relationship with Him without interruption. Sin is the interruption this side of Heaven. Combining Heaven and covenant is one way to combat that horrible interruption between God and man.

Alcorn writes, "May God give us the grace to live today as citizens of heaven, ambassadors to this foreign soil called earth. May we live today with the perspective that will be ours one moment after we die."[105] That is yet another way of describing a covenant relationship with God; we are citizens of heaven, on assignment for God, with God on planet earth.

Those of us who fly the friendly skies under the clouds of terrorism know the airlines have reduced the amount of weight we can have in our luggage. Likewise, the airlines have limited the number of items you can carry on your flight. Actually, the airlines have done us all a favor by lightening our loads. A covenant relationship with God is a lightening of our

---

[103] Alcorn, *In Light of Eternity,* 141.

[104] Roberts, *Exploring Heaven,* 169.

[105] Alcorn, "Heaven: Our Certain Hope," 4.

load. We are just passing through this town we call earth. Our wardrobe, our "new robes," are awaiting us at home: Heaven.

The Bible says in 1 Corinthians: "But just as it is written, 'Things which eye has not seen and ear has not heard, and which have not entered the heart of man, all that God has prepared for those who love Him.' For to us God revealed them through the Spirit; for the Spirit searches all things, even the depths of God" (1 Corinthians 2:9–10). God wants His people to know there is a better way to live on planet earth. The better way to journey through life is not through religion, but by relationship. That is the invitation God gives us today. His Spirit is revealing this better way to live in union with God. It is very personal. It is very practical. It is very pragmatic. It is perfect!

I discovered in 2003 that my journey had two very important signs along the road. Neither is my own, yet I own them both. First, life is a wilderness. My wife Joanie taught me this in 2003. I had grown up knowing the Bible story about how the Hebrew people were delivered from Egypt, only to experience 40 long years in the wilderness. In fact, the "promised land" was so far removed from their reality that the first generation that left Egypt never stepped foot in the "promised land." Moses was only permitted to see it from a distance. Some promise. Some God. Maybe the Hebrew people were right in wanting to go back to Egypt. Do you ever feel like going back to a place you remember as safe, secure, predictable? Of course you do. Why not go all the way back to our mother's womb? At least there, there is no memory of pain!

I had spent my life creating a promised land for myself, my family, and everyone else I cared about. Like the Etch A Sketch I grew up playing with as a child, you shake it up and the image is gone forever. My life was an Etch A Sketch. My world had been shaken to the core and the image I was drawing had been erased forever. The new image in my life could be titled, "LOST." However, it was in the wilderness that I found God.

By the way, that is how we Christians like to view the finding God thing. We like to think we are the ones that find Him. It gives us a greater sense of control. However, if the truth be known—and I am making it known—God finds us!

I tripped over God. You see, when we are planning our lives, we rarely run into God unless there is a problem. We humans are so predictable. In the wilderness, you do not plan anything. You stumble. I stumbled over God. In other words, God was always with me.

It seems that God, in His patience, waits for us to take our hands off the dials of the Etch A Sketch. Then He begins to draw an image that can only be described as extraordinary. All mosaics are created in the wilderness.

I am still in the wilderness. But my title has changed from "lost" to "found." I found a covenant relationship with God. It is so good I never want to leave the wilderness this side of Heaven. The wilderness with God is better by far than the Promised Land without God. Imagine the Promised Land with God! Indeed, a covenant relationship with God is Heaven on earth. It is *Heaven's covenant with earth.*

I said there were two signs I read from 2003. The second reality I discovered was "thy kingdom come." That phrase in Scripture is not only for later, it is also for right now. We serve a right-now God who lives in the here and now. God is not abstract. God is tangible, solid, real, and really good. I have found Him so.

When does Heaven begin? And what is the definition of Heaven? Heaven is about being with God. Heaven is all about a reunion of relationships. Is it possible Satan has deceived the church into thinking that a covenant relationship is not possible this side of Heaven? Satan is a LIAR! Covenant relationships do exist this side of Heaven. I am in one. I am inviting you to join me in one with God.

I have had the privilege of learning much about Heaven in the past five years. I consider Randy Alcorn the premier authority on the subject. The more you know about Heaven, the closer you will be to God on earth. The closer you are to God on earth, the closer to Heaven you will find yourself thinking and living. The closer you are to God, the closer you are to the loved ones who have died and are with God right now. I am closer to my son who is in Heaven because he is literally with God. The closer I am to God, the closer I am to my son.

I like to put it this way: To think about Heaven is to think about God. To think about God is to think about Heaven. Therefore, to live with God in a covenant relationship on earth is to live with God now in a covenant relationship very close to the gates of Heaven. Putting it another way: To be close to God is to be close to heaven. To be close to Heaven is to be close to God.

Covenant has a multiplying effect on all relationships. I begin with God. I move to myself. I then move to others. Covenant and Heaven are connected. It is a connection worth embracing. Again, God has issued you and I the invitation to dance with Him.

So while there is a literal Heaven that every Christian longs for, there is likewise a piece of that literal Heaven on earth right now. That is what the covenant relationship is all about!

Chapter 6 Reflection and Discussion: Creating Covenant

1. Describe Heaven.

2. What elements of relationships on earth will be in Heaven?

3. What elements of relationships on earth will not be a part of Heaven?

4. How does life on earth prepare us for life in Heaven?

5. How close can you live to Heaven while living on earth?

6. Discuss/describe life on the new earth (Revelation 21) as it relates to relationships.

7. Identify a verse in the Bible that excites you about Heaven.

8. Find a story in the Bible that best describes Heaven on earth for you.

CHAPTER 7

MARRIAGE AND COVENANT

"Till death do you part?" We have no clue what we're getting ourselves into when we get married. We have no clue what the long-range implications of our vows mean. We make lofty promises all in the name of "love." What a joke! The divorce rate within the Christian community is staggering. It should be "0." We Christians have an epidemic on our hands, with absolutely no cure in sight.

It has been stated that insanity is doing the same thing over and over and expecting different results. We have never had more counselors available for marriages, more books written on the subject of marriage, more seminars aimed at marriage, more insurance money to pay for it all than what we have right now in 2011. Are we better off? Of course not! I am not a pessimist. I also am not stupid. I am a problem-solver. Christians have a practical problem: broken relationships.

Imagine the social implications if Christians would "get along" and would "work it out." Imagine what would happen within Christianity if we could completely end divorce! The thought of such a thing is staggering to the mind. Pastors specializing in singles' ministry would be unemployed. Divorce recovery workshops would be put out of business. We would be one generation away from blended families becoming an extinct dinosaur. Those of you in the divorce industry can relax; you are safe.

Imagine what would happen to welfare in this country if divorce were eliminated. Imagine what would happen to the divorce lawyers of this country if Christians stopped getting divorced. Imagine what would happen to learning in the schools if children came from happy homes with a mom and a dad who actually liked one another. Imagine how we Americans could redirect our energy toward solving other problems in our society if the communicable disease of broken relationships were ended.

The ramifications of zero divorce within the Christian community would ignite our faith and we would have people coming to Christ by the millions. We could usher in the kingdom of God in one generation if we could model for the world healthy, happy marriages. Imagine.

Why do we accept broken relationships as inevitable? We have been deceived by the enemy (Satan) once again. I know there are some people reading this book who think I am out of touch. I am a believer in the Bible. I believe God has given us what we need to be holy, happy, and successful this side of Heaven. This side of Heaven, sin will not be eliminated, nor will pain and suffering.

God has given us a way to weave into our lives holiness, happiness, and success. This includes marriage. I am inviting you to read this chapter with renewed hope in God and the relationships He desires to transform. I am convinced that a covenant relationship with God will literally transform the sickest marriage if both people will enter into a covenant with God. Entering into a covenant with God is the starting point. Entering into a covenant with your spouse is the outflow of a covenant with God.

In *Hopeful Imagination,* Walter Brueggemann writes, "We build low-roofed churches which foster horizontal fellowship but which have brought the sky down to human proportion."[106] This is the single largest mistake the church has made in the past 30 years. We have taken the focus off a relationship with God and we have focused on relationships with one another. Wrong. Whenever human beings are the focus, relationships will decay. God needs to be our focus. Get it right with God and we will get it right with one another. Simply put, healthy souls lead to healthy marriages. Covenant relationships address the condition of the soul.

On one of my trips to New York City, my friend and I rode the elevator to the top of the observation deck on one of the Twin Towers. I will never forget the view. It was magnificent. America has lost her view when it comes to marriage relationships. Marriages are collapsing as tragically as did the Twin Towers. The winds of compromise are knocking over marriages with

---

[106] Brueggemann, *Hopeful Imagination* (Philadelphia: Fortress Press, 1986), 54.

far less force than the jets that hit the Towers on that fateful day.

We have forgotten what the view looks like from the observation deck. We have settled to cluck with chickens when our marriages were made to soar like the eagles. How can we stop the daily destruction of the Twin Towers of marriage? Covenant applies to every area of life, which includes marriage. Again, the solution looks like this: Heal the soul, you heal the person. Heal the person, and you heal the marriage.

Stanley Hauerwas writes, "The problem does not focus so much on the notion of 'mythical union' with Christ, but rather on the inability to characterize the human side of that union."[107] Clearly, we have talked about, written about, theologized about union with Christ. Obviously, that is all we have done. We know Him, but we don't really know Him. We love Him, but we don't really love Him. The same can be said in our marriages. We pretend to have something better than what we really do. We live much of our lives behind a mask in constant denial of being honest. This does not give license to give up on marriages; rather it is incentive to get it right.

Hauerwas put it this way, "My only interest has been to try and show that we as men who are loyal to God's act in Jesus Christ cannot think unimportant the way we as agents act and the kind of persons we become as a result."[108] I am of the belief that when we better develop our relationship with God, we then have a greater foundation upon which to build a marriage. Christians must demonstrate a better response to marriage than what we have been showing.

The truth of the matter is we are sicker than we think. There are many reasons why marriages get sick. What must be acknowledged are the sources from which the sickness comes. Brennan Manning and Jim Hancock wrote a great little book entitled, *Posers, Fakers, & Wannabes*. In this revealing work they write, "We are sicker than we think. We're dying and, crazily, running from the healer because we're ashamed, because we hate ourselves for all we are and all we're not."[109]

---

[107] Hauerwas, *Character and the Christian Life* (San Antonio: Trinity University Press, 1985) , 193.

[108] Ibid, 228.

[109] Manning & Hancock, *Posers, Fakers, & Wannabes (Unmasking the Real You)*, 25.

A covenant relationship with God is an attempt to become all that we are and move away from all that we are not. Covenant is about becoming complete in Christ. It understands that I can have what God says I can have with Him this side of Heaven. It understands Satan is a liar and a deceiver and he has hidden the truth from Christians. We have bought into his lie. It is time Christians start claiming, living, and receiving what is rightfully theirs—a covenant relationship with God.

Perhaps we should look at models that work in relationships other than marriage and try applying those models to marriage. Take for instance a book by Peter L. Steinke, *How Your Church Family Works*, which teaches us principles in relationships. He states, "Put people together and inevitably anxiety will arise."[110]

This would be a good starting point for all marriages: When two people are together, there will be anxiety. Marriage assumes when a married couple is together, problems will vanish. Not so. Steinke's principle on anxiety seems more realistic. It helps us to lower our expectations of one another. Failed expectations are a big reason why marriages crumble.

He also says, "The truth is that we constantly influence each other, that we leave our mark on each other's souls, that we either *hurt* or *help* each other."[111] This is not a principle he considered in the context of marriage, but what if it was? What if each day we who are married consciously thought about our spouse in terms of their soul and recognized that each word and each motion of the body was either hurting or helping the one we ought to love more than anybody else in the world? This sheds a different light on marriage, doesn't it?

I mentioned earlier about the summer Joanie and I dated long distance. Over the course of our courtship we wrote many letters and cards to one another. On our honeymoon we burned them. We no longer needed them as reminders of our love for one another. The words we had put on paper were now on the pages of our hearts.

Third, Steinke states, "No family or relationship can change and heal

---

[110] Steinke, *How Your Church Family Works* (Herndon, Va.: The Albin Institute, 2002), 13.

[111] Ibid, 37.

when focused on damage and blame."[112] Wait a minute, isn't that what we do though in marriage? Of course it is! We focus on what is wrong, not on what is right. We do the same thing in most areas of life; that is, we focus on what is wrong, not on what is right.

What would happen if our focus shifted from the problem to not even the solutions, but to the covenant aspect of the relationship? What would happen if marriages stopped dwelling on the ruins of the Towers and looked for the good that is hidden in the rubble of the destruction? We would first see a change of attitude.

Second, we would see hope renewed. Third, we would start thinking positively instead of negatively. Fourth, we would become a more pleasant person to be with. Fifth, we would discover that a covenant relationship is the only solution for marriage failure.

Later in this chapter I will give specific instructions on how to move from where you are to a covenant relationship with your spouse. Before that, though, the pages in between are important foundations, so read them first!

Fourth, Steinke says, "We need, therefore, to see forgiveness more as a process than an event."[113] Building a marriage is a process. A part of building a marriage includes forgiveness. Unfortunately, it takes much longer to build a marriage than it does to tear it down. We need to see forgiveness in the context of marriage as a process rather than an event.

Men often see forgiveness as an event. They are ready to kiss and make up and go watch football. Women have a different DNA than men. Women, let me caution you at this point: Do not use your DNA to frustrate your spouse. Forgiveness is a process, so don't milk the cow dry and expect to keep getting milk! Process yes, but an excuse, never!

Each marriage has role players. It is both/and, not an either/or in marriage. I think we have made grave errors in spiritualizing our problems, which usually leads to blame-casting in relationships, especially marriages. Stacy Rinehart in his work, *Upside Down: The Paradox of Servant Leadership,*

---

[112] Ibid.
[113] Ibid, 124.

states, "Leaders exist in order to serve."[114] Let's not make more of this than what is there, and let's not make less of what Rinehart is stating. Serve. To the one serving, it is not a one-way street. And to the one being served, don't push your luck. Remember, in a covenant relationship, it works both ways.

Rinehart also states, "A leader cannot demand what he has not earned. And earned authority in God's economy is based on humility—a spirit of brokenness before God and man."[115] We have focused on the wrong elements when talking about serving and leading. Rinehart gives us a window into the workings of covenant relationships. Our focus ought to be brokenness before God and spouse. Our focus ought to be on developing humility.

What would happen if we reversed the emphasis on serving and leading and just led and served without keeping score or worrying about who had which role in the relationship? What would happen if our focus was brokenness and humility? Wow! Revolutionary!

One of the vivid memories I have from our children's growing-up years are the many games of Monopoly we played together. We played that game so much we had to buy a new one because we wore out the old one. We played every version of Monopoly known to man. By the way, Monopoly is a great tool for teaching your kids simple math, simple economics, as well as sociology.

We had our most fun when we stopped playing by the rules. By the time you have played that game for the hundredth time in a year, creativity becomes necessary. We devised a way to play without really keeping score. It added creativity and enjoyment to the game and our time together. Apply this to relationships. Lead and serve without keeping score. If you keep score, it will seem longer than a game of Monopoly!

One of my favorite theologians, Dietrich Bonhoeffer, in *Life Together,* writes, "Human love is directed to the other person for his own sake, spiritual love loves him for Christ's sake."[116] Imagine with me what would happen if in a covenant relationship with God we started loving people for Christ's sake. Do you see the root of the problem? We are selfish! It is that

---

[114] Rinehart, *Upside Down: The Paradox of Servant Leadership* (Colorado Springs: NavPress Publishing Group, 1998), 37.

[115] Ibid, 51.

[116] Bonhoeffer, *Life Together* (New York: Harper & Row, 1954), 34.

simple. Deny it, avoid it, disclaim it all you want, but it is so true. It means we are human. That is what makes a covenant relationship with God revolutionary and transforming. It moves us out of our selfishness and into loving the way God loves us. It works!

At this point, I must add an element that is obvious and necessary, but missed by many Christians: The need to be filled completely with the Holy Spirit every hour of every day. Short of this filling and indwelling, a covenant relationship with God or anybody else is not likely.

Geoffrey Nuttall, in his work, *The Holy Spirit in Puritan Faith and Experience*, writes, "In so far as the New Testament remains the ideal for the life, if not for the letter of Christianity, it is imperative that the doctrine of the Holy Spirit should receive attention in theology, and that the presence of the Holy Spirit should, above all else, be sought in Christian faith and experience."[117]

Nuttall is writing about a time in Christianity in which the Puritans sought after a pure faith. It would not hurt modern-day Christians one bit to embrace some of the teachings of the Puritans. In order for the Covenant Renewal Model to work, a strong theology embracing the Holy Spirit in our lives is mandatory.

Let me also say to those who have strong doctrinal bias concerning the Holy Spirit; apply what I have said as you see fit. I am not making a doctrinal statement about the Holy Spirit. I am talking about a covenant relationship about the Holy Spirit. No more and certainly, no less.

In our premarital counseling, Joanie and I were told never to go to bed with an unreconciled difference in our marriage. If that were the case for some who are reading this book—given at the state of their marriages right now—they would not be going to bed for quite some time. Precisely my point, fix it! Bonhoeffer states, "It is perilous for the Christian to lie down to sleep with an unreconciled heart."[118]

Why do we continue living in misery? Do we think the problem will just go away? It will only get worse. The problem with burying problems alive is that they are alive. They never go away until crucified.

---

[117] Nuttall, *The Holy Spirit in Puritan Faith and Experience* (Oxford: Basil Blackwell, 1947), 176.

[118] Bonhoeffer, *Life Together*, 74.

There is one point I must make that is crucial in covenant relationships, the point of single-mindedness. When Joanie and I got married on June 27, 1981, there is one phrase that stood out to me above all the others. Part of the marriage vows includes this question: "and keep yourself only unto her so long as you both shall live?"[119] This phrase is at the heart of covenant.

When a relationship is sour, this statement is a chore, a mandate, a plague. When the relationship is sweet it is a joy, a blessing, a gift. When things are sweet, it is also very easy to keep this vow. When things are going sour, it is almost impossible to keep this vow. It is simple: Live in covenant and keep this vow; live outside of covenant and break this vow!

Walter Brueggemann, another favorite theologian of mine, writes in *Hopeful Imagination* concerning the people of Jeremiah's day: "In different moments, he indicts his people of both stupidity (4:22) and stubbornness (18:12)." To reconcile any marriage is going to require being neither stupid nor stubborn. Both are children of selfishness. Neither is related to covenant. Enough said.

I am keenly aware that when marriages are hurting, there is no single answer, counseling session, verse or prayer that can immediately change the relationship. We must keep thinking in terms of process. That is one of the meanings of the word "journey" that I used earlier in this book. Journey is process, and to process is to journey.

I love the way Brueggemann states it in *Hopeful Imagination*: "In God's attentive pain, healing happens. Newness comes. Possibilities are presented. But it all depends on being present with God in the hurt, which is incurable until God's hint of healing is offered."[120]

Look for God's hint. In a covenant relationship with God you will find the hint. It will be obvious. God wants very much to be a part of all your relationships, especially your marriage!

What I am advocating is not new to Christian thought; it is new though to our generation, thanks in large part to the work of Dr. Shelton whom I referenced earlier. Great preachers of the past like Charles G. Finney focused on

---

[119] Evangelical Church of North America, *The Discipline 2002* (Minneapolis: Commission on the Discipline, 2002), 192.

[120] Brueggemann, *Hopeful Imagination* (Philadelphia: Fortress Press, 1986), 47.

covenant too. Timothy L. Smith, in his book, *Revivalism and Social Reform,* writes of Finney, "Because of such convictions Finney became the first to elaborate clearly the doctrine that the Christian covenant was supreme in human affairs."[121] Finney declares covenant must be supreme in human affairs. Can we do any less? If we do not get a covenant relationship with God happening, there will be more marital affairs within human affairs!

One of my favorite books of all time is by Kenneth Boa, *Conformed to His Image.* My summary on this section of this chapter is a direct quote from his book:

"What does it take to finish well? I have arrived at a set of seven such characteristics:

1. *Intimacy* with Christ
2. Fidelity in the spiritual *disciplines*
3. A biblical *perspective* on the circumstances of life
4. A *teachable,* responsive, humble, and obedient spirit
5. A clear sense of personal *purpose* and calling
6. Healthy *relationships* with resourceful people
7. Ongoing *ministry* investment in the lives of others"[122]

Each of these is a part of a covenant relationship with God that is to happen simultaneously within the context of your marriage. Covenant relationships do not exist in compartments; they flow from one area of life to another. Covenant relationships flow—and by nature overflow—especially into marriage.

Helping Marriages Move into Covenant

In this chapter I have connected covenant relationships to marriage relationships. Perhaps you are wondering where to begin. The following are some things I have written over the years concerning marriage. I now give them to you in print. The first is a sequence on love: when love is no more, qualities necessary to restore love, and keeping a good thing good.

---

[121] Smith, *Revivalism and Social Reform* (New York: Harper and Row, 1957), 156.
[122] Boa, *Conformed to His Image,* 451.

When Love Is No More

1. God can restore any broken relationship.
2. The will to obey must be exercised vigorously.
3. Behavior must change and be consistently consistent.
4. The past must not dictate today in order to change tomorrow.
5. Feelings will lag behind will and mind.
6. Forgiveness must be the rule of covenant, not the exception.
7. "I can't" means "I won't."
8. Apart from a covenant relationship with God, restoration is rare.
9. Restoration begins within my heart.
10. Many barriers are exaggerated or untrue.
11. Satan's desire is to break up and ruin.
12. Human failure must not be the final chapter.
13. Negative voices are no form of support.
14. If it once was, you can have it again.
15. It takes two to live in a marriage covenant. Start within.

Qualities Necessary to Restore Love

1. Be trustworthy.
2. Be honest.
3. Be accountable.
4. Reevaluate priorities.
5. Have integrity.
6. Be consistent.
7. Be transparent.
8. Have sensitivity.
9. Have covenant check-ups.
10. Be positive and encouraging.
11. Be nice.
12. Have a covenant relationship with God.

Keeping a Good Thing Good

1 Work hard.
2. Be humble.
3. Don't make a move without checking with God first.
4. Pray.
5. Compliment.
6. Remember what got you where you are.
7. Keep weaknesses before you.
8. Laugh every day.
9. Keep growing the vision.
10. Never compare.

Another tool that I developed some years ago was a non-traditional method for rebuilding severely damaged relationships. Most people who need help with marriage usually come to me after seeing counselors. I am usually the last stop before seeing the lawyer (just in case the preacher has a miracle up his sleeve). I trust this tool will be a help to some.

A Non-Traditional Method for Rebuilding Severely Damaged Relationships

1. Both sides must admit complete failure. (Humility)
2. Both sides must confess, repent, and forgive one another and reconcile with God the entire past. (Peace)
3. Both sides must rebuild, using nothing from the past. (Freedom)
4. Both sides must structure a daily covenant hour by hour. (Discipline)
5. Both sides must allow room for repeated failure without punishment. (Grace)
6. Both sides must set expectations, and then cut them in half. (Growth)
7. Both sides must demonstrate only praise and positive reinforcement. (Covenant Love)
8. Both sides must build on each other's strengths ... ignore, forgive, leave alone weaknesses. (Compassion)
9. Both sides must follow biblical authority. (Both husband and wife are under God's authority)
10. Both sides must read and obey the Bible every day. (Instructions)
11. Both sides must journal what God is teaching you each day. (Accountability)

12. Both sides must regard punishment as unacceptable. (Kindness)
13. Both sides must change their lifestyles and spend large blocks of time together throughout the week. (Covenant Bonding)
14. Both sides must stop analyzing and lecturing … simply live and just be. (Building)

Premise #1: Manipulating and controlling do not build relationships.

Premise #2: Fighting and arguing do not build relationships.

Premise #3: Negative reinforcement does not build relationships.

Premise #4: Only the principles of covenant relationships build relationships.

One day I was asked if I would marry a couple who asked me to do their pre-marital counseling separately. The guy was in the military and it would be impossible for me to counsel them together before the weekend they were to be married. I agreed. This forced me to put in writing the things I had been saying for years in premarital counseling. This is one of five sections I use in my premarital material. These are things I have been saying for years but had never put in a book for the public to view. I thought they might be helpful for some in light of covenant relationships.

1. *Laughter*
   a. Laughter ought to happen every day when you're together. If it doesn't, you know for sure something is very wrong.
   b. Laughter represents the ability to have fun, even if there are dark clouds overhead.
   c. Laughter opens up great opportunities to visit with one another.
   d. Laughter is very normal, natural and healthy.
2. *Work*
   a. Marriage takes a daily effort.
   b. A happy healthy marriage doesn't just happen. It takes a lot of intentional work.
   c. You ordinarily get out of a marriage what you put into a marriage.
   d. Work narrowly defined will always include sacrifice.
   e. Hard work always pays off.
   f. Work and a work ethic are very much different.
3. *Forgiveness*
   a. If you don't forgive, you'll never have a healthy marriage.

     b. Forgiveness and trust are not always connected to one another.

     c. Keeping score is not forgiveness.

     d. Your attitude will always tell if you forgave or not.

     e. Forgiveness should be accompanied with sweetness and kindness.

     f. Forgiveness with God's help can heal any hurt.

     g. The heart of forgiveness is in Ephesians 4:29–32.

4. *Expectations*

     a. Don't unfairly change the expectations once married.

     b. Make sure you help your spouse succeed.

     c. Make sure expectations don't become legalisms.

     d. Make sure you remember that failure is inevitable, but need not be final.

     e. You can't change people. What you see is what you get (so choose wisely on the front end).

5. *Communication*

     a. Debrief every day.

     b. Go over tomorrow's plans and schedule.

     c. Always share your emotions and your heart with your spouse before anyone else.

     d. The evidence of a best friend is the desire to communicate.

     e. The most important piece of communication is to listen (which is probably why we have two ears and one mouth).

6. *God*

     a. God makes a positive difference in every marriage, if you will obey Him in covenant love.

     b. It is a mistake to think you need to be spiritual only when things are rough.

     c. God hates divorce. (Malachi)

     d. God created marriage to be wonderful.

     e. If you do not read and obey His Word, God is really not much a part of your marriage.

     f. God has shown us through His Son two great models: servant-hood and forgiveness.

7. *General Information*

     a. The one who keeps score will never win.

b. Marriage takes more work than a career.

c. A clean slate requires careful communication every day.

d. When cared for, marriage is the best of the best. When it is neglected, ignored, and assumed, it becomes the worst of the worst.

e. Marriage is supposed to be very rewarding and a lot of fun.

f. Goals, goals, goals. If you aim at nothing, you will hit it every time.

g. If your spouse is not your very best friend, your marriage will suffer.

h. Tired people are grumpy people.

i. When dealing with children, remember who is in charge.

j. Marriage teaches us not to be selfish.

k. Do the things in your marriage that got you to the marriage altar.

l. An unkind word can always be forgiven, but not always forgotten.

m. You will get out of your marriage exactly what you put into it.

8. *Anger*

a. Get professional help.

b. Read your Bible more.

c. Get more rest.

d. Pray more often.

e. Pretend you're being recorded.

f. Stop taking it out on people you love.

g. Be disciplined.

h. Recognize how counter-productive you are when you're angry.

i. Anticipate.

9. *Money*

a. Credit debt shows a lack of control.

b. Each month spend less than you make.

c. Honor God with at least 10%.

d. Save something each month.

e. Financial freedom from debt takes pressures away from the marriage.

f. Live within your means.

g. Percentage breakdown of a covenant relationship related budget: 10% tithe, 10% savings, 10% debt reduction, 80% living expenses to include mortgage.

10. *Conflict*
   a. Is it a hill worth dying on?
   b. Is it a repeat?
   c. Get some help.
   d. Discover if the issue or your approach to it is the real source of conflict.
   e. You can be right and still be very wrong if your tone is not sweet.
   f. Your spouse is your friend, not your enemy.
   g. Put yourself in the other person's shoes.
   h. Apologize first.
11. *Boundaries*
   a. Boundaries are easily ignored-—be careful.
   b. Boundaries provide security and safety.
   c. Boundaries are not meant to be broken.
   d. Boundaries develop love and trust when abided by.
   e. Boundaries take away a lot of worry and trust issues.
12. *Vows*
   a. Promise.
   b. Commitment.
   c. Nobody plans on divorce on their wedding day.
   d. Neglect—the big problem in life.
   e. The grass always looks greener on the other side of the fence. But weeds grow on both sides. The green grass isn't the problem; it's the weeds.

I really owe this following piece to Pastor Bob Zachary, who married Joanie and I. He was her pastor. Together he and I worked on the message for our ceremony. I have changed it somewhat and added to it. I use it often with couples.

How to Have a Happy Marriage

1. Saturate your marriage with love.
   a. You can't describe it; you should only display it.
   b. Sacrifice.

  c. Compromise.

  d. Show compassion.

 2. Continually renew your commitment.

  a. Avoid ruts.

  b. Date one another.

  c. Be alone with one another.

  d. A good happy marriage takes work.

 3. Continually communicate.

  a. Speak nearly forgotten phrases (I forgive you, I love you, I am wrong).

  b. Speak well of one another.

  c. Build each other up.

  d. Refrain from old arguments.

  e. Control your own emotions. (Not, "he makes me mad," but "I let myself get mad.")

Another little tool I have used is a study in the book of Proverbs. I have noted ten simple statements that help with turning struggles into peace and also instruct us in how we should treat one another.

How to Turn Struggles into Peace

  a. Proverbs 1:8 – Listening is essential.

  b. Proverbs 3:1–2 – Discipline is essential.

  c. Proverbs 20:20 – Respect is essential.

  d. Proverbs 22:6 – Training is essential.

  e. Proverbs 29:15 –Authority is essential.

How the Bible Says We Are to Treat One Another

  a. Proverbs 4:24 – Speak well of one another in the home.

  b. Proverbs 5:15 – Build a strong marriage.

  c. Proverbs 14:17 – Be very patient with one another.

  d. Proverbs 15:29 – Always be in prayer about all family matters.

  e. Proverbs 22:1 – Maintain a good reputation.

I trust these tools will help make covenant more practical for you. There are many places to start. The important thing for you is to start. Find a place where you can be alone and spend some time with the Lord. Seek Him in a covenant relationship and ask Him to help you with the covenant you have made in marriage. God bless you.

Chapter 7 Reflection and Discussion: Creating Covenant

1. Which parts of your marriage are as good as the first day you were married? Which parts are better? Which parts are worse?

2. What has gone wrong (if anything) in your marriage to date? What do you have going for you in marriage?

3. Is your marriage more contractual or covenantal? Analyze it.

4. If trust is gone in your marriage, consider the strength of love and forgiveness. How might you strengthen these to regain some trust?

5. Review and renew your wedding vows. I encourage you to even have your pastor conduct a renewal ceremony for you!

6. Men: Describe ways you can serve your wife. Women: Describe ways your husband can serve you. (The rest will take care of itself.)

7. Identify a verse from the Bible on serving.

8. Find a story in the Bible that you can use to strengthen your marriage.

CHILDREN AND COVENANT

My intent in this chapter is not to compete with the likes of James Dobson. My intent is not to give you one hundred ways to win your children over to you and God. My intent is not to fix your children. My intent in this chapter is twofold: to paint with broad strokes the potential in our children under the effects of the Covenant Renewal Model. Second, I wish to share some thoughts from me to you.

I am writing this chapter on Christmas evening, 2008. I had a marvelous time with my wife, daughter and her husband this morning in our home. I cherish every moment I have with them. However, this was my sixth Christmas without my son Kevin.

We live life as though our children are going to be around forever. They are not! When I was a young parent and the days seemed long at times as we raised our children, I was told what every young parent hears: "Enjoy them, because before you know it they will be grown and gone and you will wonder where the time went." I was not expecting to be shortchanged as I was with Kevin, so, the second portion of this chapter is from a father's heart to yours.

Tom Brokaw refers to the generation that lived through the Great Depression as "The Greatest Generation." He cites examples in his book of what made that generation so great.

We live in a different day, a different era. Is it possible to create a generation of children that one day, short of the tragedies of war, disease, and financial loss could be termed "The Greatest Generation of the 21st Century"? I would like to believe this is attainable. However, it is not attainable at the rate we are going.

What if Christians would apply the rules of covenant relationships with our children? What if we could reverse the trends we are seeing in children as it relates to God? Is it possible to break the cycle of chaos our children are experiencing? The first thing that needs to change is parents! Parents need to stop fighting with one another! Is there any part of this you do not understand at this point in this book?

There is a passage of Scripture in Isaiah 61 that talks about becoming "oaks of righteousness." Is it possible for us to lead our children in this direction? We call the children of our church "acorns." We call them this because all mighty oaks of righteousness begin as tender acorns. All children start out as tender acorns!

Isaiah 61:1–3 says, "The Spirit of the Lord GOD is upon me, because the LORD has anointed me to bring good news to the afflicted; He has sent me to bind up the brokenhearted, to proclaim liberty to captives and freedom to prisoners; to proclaim the favorable year of the LORD and the day of vengeance of our God; to comfort all who mourn, to grant those who mourn in Zion, giving them a garland instead of ashes, the oil of gladness instead of mourning, the mantle of praise instead of a spirit of fainting. So they will be called oaks of righteousness, the planting of the LORD, that He may be glorified."

I recognize this was a prophetic word for the nation of Israel. I believe it is a prophecy for all people. I believe God does not discriminate His covenant against people groups. I believe covenant relationships with God and one another are for all people groups. I believe it is time for the church to rise up and start claiming ground in the name of Jesus on behalf of our children. It is time we start telling them who they are in Christ. It is time we start telling them that for such a time as this they are created to become oaks of righteousness to the glory of God.

As I have defined and described a covenant relationship with God, an oak of righteousness is a perfect image for what I have been writing about with covenant. A covenant relationship with God produces strong healthy people. Covenant relationships are God's cure for the cancer in the Church, in Christianity, in the world!

It says just a few verses later on Isaiah 61: "For I, the LORD, love justice, I hate robbery in the burnt offering; and I will faithfully give them their recompense and make an everlasting covenant with them. Then their offspring will be known among the nations, and their descendants in the midst of the peoples. All who see them will recognize them because they are of the offspring whom the LORD has blessed." (Isaiah 61:8–9). I believe this is something every Christian wants for their children. God is waiting to grant this to our children, but we must lead them into it. Let's be the generation that rediscovers the everlasting covenant with God!

God makes numerous promises in the Bible, most all of which are conditional promises. I have discovered that every conditional promise requires two elements on our part: relationship and obedience. What an amazing discovery, an amazing connection. Covenant requires a proper relationship with God: obedience!

Imagine with me a generation of children who love their parents because their parents are in covenant with God, are at peace within, and really do love other people. Imagine with me a generation of children that grew up knowing only of a church where there is love for all people. Remember, covenant touches three areas of relationships: First, with God; second, within; third, with others.

If you would be willing to evaluate your relationship with your children and strip away all the clutter, you will discover once you get past the passion to give them every name brand known to Americans, and once you remove all the time spent trying to make them professionals (to include all sports, dance, music, drama, tiddlywinks, and anything else I may have left out that turns parents into taxi drivers 24/7 and leaves our children tired, worn out, and void of imagination), you discover relationships.

You will discover the most important part of any vacation is time spent with your children. You will discover Christmas is not the gift from the store that makes it a great Christmas, but the gift of time. (And if it is the gift, a sure sign the type of covenant relationship I have been talking about is not present as it should be.)

Gifts follow time. Time makes relationships, not the gifts. Ask your children; they will tell you. By the way, this battle between quality time and quantity time, that is a pile of manure! Tell your children you only have five minutes to play with them because you have to go to the club to work out and maintain your gut. As you leave, tell them that the five lousy minutes you just spent with them was quality time. They will smile, give you a hug, and tell you they love you as you walk out the door to work on your gut. What else can they do? Nothing takes the place of the time you spend with your children. I will address this later in this chapter when I speak from a father's heart on Christmas day.

Sometimes, stripping it all down and recognizing that it is all about relationships is a tough thing for many people to do. Stop defining the relationship you have with your children by what you buy them. I recently reflected back on the years we had our children in the home. I thought of the ways I might have been able to buy them more stuff to make them happier. My daughter tells me time and time again she had everything. I know she did not have everything. In fact as a daughter of a pastor she did not have much in the way of material things. My greatest regret in life was that we could not afford the monthly dues at the nearby golf course so my son could play golf like the rest of his friends.

Kevin loved playing golf and was on the varsity team. He got a job at the golf course so he could play golf without paying. That came just several months before January of 2003. I have to trust my daughter when she tells me the things I gave them were of far greater value than a membership at a golf course.

Many times it is difficult to afford for our children what others can afford for theirs. We can be poor in the world's eyes, yet millionaires in relationships! If you turn me off at this juncture, you will never understand covenant relationship. It is not about materialism at all. It is about the time we invest in the lives of others. It is that one component you cannot assign a dollar value for. It is that one component that is absolutely priceless: time.

A covenant relationship is about union. Unions take time. When we have union, all else becomes very insignificant in comparison. The Covenant Renewal Model, I believe, stands the test of all cultures, all generations, and all social levels because God transcends all cultures, generations, and all social levels. Covenant relationships have their existence in God. God does not need help from Walmart!

From a Father's Heart on Christmas Day 2008

Cherish your children. They are a gift from God. Life is so uncertain. One thing I am certain of is that my son was with Jesus today to celebrate

Christmas! I will never forget what Joanie told me when our children were very young. She had to have a talk with me because when we got married I enjoyed golfing at least two times a week with practice in-between, hunting, softball leagues, and lots of football games on TV. You get the idea.

I remember the words, reflecting on them as I write tonight as though they were said to me tonight, yet they were said some twenty years ago: "You get one chance with our children. You can play all you want when our children are grown and leave our home."

It is interesting that I was not given a choice. But then again, when God talks, it is best not to debate. It is best just to obey. On that occasion, God had a name: Joanie! By the way, I say that with the greatest of appreciation. I am eternally grateful Joanie had the courage to see something I was missing. She was right.

I am so thankful I listened and made the necessary changes in my life. By the way, it wasn't difficult. If it is difficult for you to give up your personal selfish events and feel like your children are in your way, you need help! The best advice ever given to me was those words from Joanie.

Allow me to suggest how our family lived in covenant relationships before I even knew about the terms I am writing about in this book. The first home we owned as a family was less than 1,100 square feet. The four of us shared one bathroom. Limited space is a blessing when developing covenant relationships because there is less to separate us from one another. Limited space is a blessing. Sometimes the more room you have in a home, the more hindrances you have in developing covenant relationships. Allow me to share some of the things I did with my children rather imperfectly, but nonetheless consistently.

1. Be a part of your kids' lives by having at least one meal a day together all the way until they are grown and out of the house. (You learn more over a meal than in a counselor's office.)

2. Watch television with your kids. (Watch what they want to watch. You will learn much about your children watching what they watch.)

I learned this from my daughter Kristi one evening when I visited her in college. We were both in school at the same time and I thought it would be cool if we studied together. We were on the campus of George Fox University in the Commons area. I was studying away and noticed she was doing a lot of laughing. I wondered what subject she was studying on her computer that made her so happy. I asked her and she said, "I'm not studying; I'm watching *Friends*."

That night I learned more about relationships than I could have learned from any professor. For my daughter it was about the experience. If the relationship does not include a meaningful experience, then time together is meaningless. I realized that night that as a Modern, I could learn from a Postmodern: Develop the relationship. I learned that success follows relationship.

Moderns see it just the opposite. Moderns believe that if you go out and become successful, then relationships will follow. They are dead wrong. My daughter has it right. (By the way, I asked her about the show since I had never watched it because I thought it was meaningless. Why would I waste my time watching six people engage in nothingness? They weren't accomplishing anything in the show. They were just "friends.")

Then I realized something profound: What I was learning from books on the subject of covenant, my daughter learned from a sitcom. This is the point of a covenant relationship with God: We are "just friends." I hope you are catching the spirit of the law rather than the letter of the law. Covenant relationships are all about the time we spend together in union.

3. Help them brush their teeth.

4. Pray with them (every night) until they leave your home.

5. Play a game with them every night. (There are ways to make a game of Monopoly shorter. That will be in my sequel.)

6. Tuck them into bed.

7. Read to them. (Joanie did this to perfection.)

8. Ask them about where they are in their relationship with Jesus at least once every six months. (This can be done most effectively at a meal.)

9. Do something with them one-on-one every single day.

10. Tell them you love them and are praying for them. I did this for my daughter from the first day of first grade to the day she was married. (I still do it, but I don't tell her all the time. She has an awesome husband who is caring for her needs now.)

11. Require them to live by your rules. As long as they are under your roof, they follow your rules.

12. Remind them that you are the parent and they are the children. They are not in charge.

13. Discipline your children. This takes tremendous energy.

14. Hold your children every single day.

15. Affirm your children every single day.

16. Pray for your kids every single day.

17. Know their friends and you'll know what your child does.

18. Require church attendance. Not going is not an option. They go when the doors are open.

19. Model Christ.

I gave you 19 so you would better remember them. Conformity to rounded numbers like 10 or 20 makes no sense to me.

One point to follow up on item #18—requiring church attendance. I am not a legalist. But when I find something that works, I stick with it. I say this not because I am a pastor but because my parents and Joanie's parents modeled this for us when we were children. When the doors are open, have your children in church. I know what I am about to say next is not popular (but then again, neither was Jesus—they killed Him!): Church is more important than sports for your children.

I have found that a covenant relationship with our children is the most fun and rewarding of all the relationships God gives to us. If raising your children is a pain in the rear, or you see them as a nuisance, you have yet to grasp the concept of covenant. If on the other hand, you desire to grasp covenant relationships, starting with your children is the easiest of all places and a great way to get started!

Chapter 8 Reflection and Discussion: Creating Covenant

1. Losing a child is unthinkable. Take time and thank God for your children. Don't just do something special for them once in a while; do something special for them every day!

2. In what ways are you demonstrating Christ to your children?

3. How much time each day are you spending with your children? Remember, there are no do-overs!

4. How much time do you spend in prayer for your children?

5. How many meals a week does the entire family have together? It ought to be at least one per day!

6. Have you hugged your child today? My daughter is 26; I hug her every time I am with her!

7. Identify a verse from the Bible on raising children.

8. Find a story in the Bible that you can use to become a better parent. (Remember: good parenting leads to covenant relationships, being their friend does not!)

CHAPTER 9

CHURCH HISTORY, 95 THESES AND COVENANT

This is a very important chapter for me. It defines covenant in a way that is not like any of the other chapters. I have always been fascinated with church history—both the triumphs and the tragedies of the church. I have tried to learn from 2,000 years of recorded history, recognizing I am a part of the book on church history that is being written in our day. To me, that thought is both daunting and humbling.

For many, history and hives go together—to be avoided at all costs. The challenge is to view church history as one big story that still does not have a final chapter this side of Heaven. One can either vandalize church history, or one can redeem it. I choose to redeem it.

There are church leaders today who would say the church has been one giant failure to humanity. That view is a pathetic view of God's work over the past 2,000 years. It presumes God has really messed things up. To do this is to deny the sovereignty of God. I cannot and will not do that to my God! He has redeemed humanity for the last 2,000 years in spite of us.

The goal of this chapter is not to review history, but to write it. Someone has to do it, and while I know little of all that has been written, I have not seen a new posting of 95 theses for 500 years!

My concern in this chapter is our place in church history. What has been written thus far over the past 2,000 years cannot be changed. It can be interpreted, but it cannot be changed. Let's write a clean draft for the chapter God has given us to write in the scheme of eternity. Let's bring people back to a covenant relationship with God, both within themselves and with others.

I am not particularly a Star Trek fan. My wife is. Part of our covenant relationship requires me to be an armchair fan of Star Trek. (By the way, a phrase in the Star Trek theme music is "to boldly go where no man has gone before." This may be the path of the Covenant Renewal Model.)

The first Star Trek movie featured a story line where the crew of the Enterprise was on a mission and discovered a ship that has been lost for years. They discover it by a transmission that keeps repeating the word "vger." They could not understand what this meant until they found the lost starship. The name on the ship had been damaged and the only four letters left on the side of the ship was V, G, E, and R. The actual name of the ship was "Voyager."

Perhaps our problem in Christianity is that we have lost track of the ship. Over the years we have forgotten her name. We have reduced her name to "Covet." We have lived accordingly. Maybe God is leading us to a place of rediscovery. It turns out we have been living out "Covet" when all along God intended for us to live out "Covenant." The question in this chapter is: How do we get back to God's original plan for us?

Imagine with me an era in church history when a generation actually got it right. Imagine with me a church where all the people actually like each other. I do not see another model that can effectively do what the Covenant Renewal Model is capable of producing.

I am a student on revivalism. I love to research, read, and study the great revivals of church history. I will refrain from citing such examples. The intent of this chapter is to look forward, not backwards.

The 21st century church is very sick. The problem is not the people outside the four walls of the church; our problem is within. There is not enough love. It is available, but we are not looking to God to get more of Him. We keep surrendering our lives to God, looking for noble deeds to do for others, and have bankrupted ourselves of God in the process. We have become God-poor! Our need is more of Him!

When Luther posted his 95 theses in a small German town called Wittenberg, I truly doubt he foresaw his impact on church history. He simply

wanted to make right, according to Scripture, what he saw as wrong practices by the church.

I do not claim even that. I just know from personal experience that
there is more to this relationship with God than what I see in people. I have
a name for it and want to share it with as many people as I can. In Acts
chapter 4, the Bible says, "For we cannot stop speaking about what we have
seen and heard" (Acts 4:20). This too, is my personal testimony.

History records Luther as being an outcast of the church. Some 500
years later, I am proposing 95 theses centering on a covenant relationship
with God. Each thesis is intended to bring definition to what I have meant
by covenant relationship. If I am criticized for these theses, then so be it. (It
is a guarantee I will be criticized).

We are lukewarm. We need a good stirring. We need to be jolted out
of our apathy. We are in a war. We act like there is no war going on at all.
We are living in the spiritual realm much the same as Americans are living
today in society. Though we are at war in at least two countries, unless we
know someone in Iraq or Afghanistan, our lives go on without even a hint
of war. We are at war. Our enemy is Satan. He is more subtle than the radical Muslims who hate us and all we stand for as Americans.

The following are meant to bring the church closer to God, not drive
people away. The purpose of the following 95 theses is meant to bring unity,
not division, within the body of Christ. The purpose of the 95 theses is to
bring freedom, not legalism and bondage. My goal is for all in Christ to find
a covenant relationship with God. My goal for all outside of Christ is to get
it right at conversion and know the God of covenant union.

The purpose of this chapter is to stimulate thinking and conversation toward the Covenant Renewal Model. Given the deep roots of the
penal substitution model within the modern church, the following 95
theses are intended to be starting points, talking points, not necessarily
conclusions.

The Scriptures stated are starting points, not exhaustive. They are
intended to stimulate further thought and development of the Covenant Renewal Model. If even one of the 95 theses leads you to the Covenant Renewal Model and a covenant relationship with God, then I have
succeeded.

95 Theses for Christians in a Postmodern World
Section 1: Factionalism

Factionalism is a quarreling spirit that divides. Dogmatism, denominationalism, and doctrine have all fed into defining factionalism. Church styles, primarily over music, have caused divisions. The Covenant Renewal Model is an attempt to bring Christians together. It is an attempt to bring together Moderns and Postmoderns. The common ground for both groups is God. Covenant brings people groups together.

1. Factionalism, by default, pits Christians against one another. (Ephesians 4:3, 13)
2. Factionalism limits the work of the Holy Spirit with dogmatic restrictions. (Acts 1:8; Romans 1:6)
3. Factionalism uses Scripture to manipulate discerning the voice of the Holy Spirit. (Psalm 119:11, 105)
4. Factionalism restricts free worship to God, limiting the leading of the Holy Spirit. (John 4:23–24; Acts 2:15–21)
5. Factionalism dulls perceptions about a literal Heaven and a literal hell. (John 14:1–6; Luke 16:19–31)
6. Factionalism leads to untenable creedal preferences of one doctrine over another. (Acts 17:24–25; 1 Corinthians 9:19–23)
7. Factionalism is ritualistic to a fault and relevance-blinding. (Isaiah 1:10–15; Genesis 4:3–7)
8. Factionalism ordains ritualism over the leading of the Holy Spirit. (Ezekiel 37:1–6; Luke 5:38)
9. Factionalism is exclusive by nature with membership privileges. (Matthew 5:33–37; 23:16-22)
10. Factionalism has life in the flesh, yet lacks life from the Holy Spirit. (2 Chronicles 1:8–13; Revelation 3:8)

Section 2: Christians

Christians are those people who have received Jesus Christ into their heart and life. They have confessed their sins, repented of them and intend to live life now in Jesus Christ, with Jesus Christ, according to the Bible.

11. Christians ought not to rely more heavily on political beliefs than on Spirit-led beliefs. (Matthew 22:15–22; John 3:16)

12. Christians have one enemy ... Satan! We must stop fighting within! (1 Peter 5:8; John 13:34)

13. Christians frequently value psychology more than the counsel of the Holy Spirit. (John 14:26–27; Philippians 4:7)

14. Christians sometimes complain about the absence of God in the public arena, yet say little about the Holy Spirit being ignored within the church. (Acts 4:20, 32-37)

15. Some Christians seem to be more moved by the prayer of Jabez than the prayer of Jesus. (John 17:11, 13, 15, 17, 21, 24)

16. Some Christians have walked away from the authority of God's voice. (Exodus 3:14; Hebrews 4:12)

17. Some Christians have embraced purpose-centered thinking over Christ-centered living. (Philippians 3:7; John 21:15–19)

18. Some Christians show little interest in Heaven. This is not of God; it is of Satan! (Revelation 13:16; Matthew 24:36–41)

19. Some Christians have relativized morality by diluting Scripture. (2 Timothy 4:3–4; Mark 12:24)

20. Some Christians seem more concerned about their pensions than about Christ's provisions. (Matthew 24:10, 12)

Section 3: Ministers

While there are numerous definitions for the noun "minister," I use the following definition: Ministers are men and women who by profession oversee and shepherd a local church congregation.

21. Ministers ought to preach in light of eternity each time in the pulpit. (John 3:16; 2 Timothy 4:8)

22. Some ministers have embraced materialism; it ruins passion for souls! (2 Timothy 3:1–5; 4:5)

23. Ministers ought to accept suffering as much as they do prosperity! (2 Corinthians 1:3–7; Acts 9:16)

24. Ministers ought to accept the sick and suffering more readily than the rich and popular! (2 Corinthians 12:9; 1 Corinthians 2:1–5)

25. Ministers ought to consider praying far more and playing far less! (1 Thessalonians 5:17–18; Ephesians 6:18)
26. Ministers ought to seek fervently a revival of their soul and the souls of their congregation! (Psalm 42:1; 51:10–13)
27. Ministers should grasp images of Heaven and hell to see as Christ sees the world! (Revelation 20:14—21:7)
28. Ministers ought to rely more on the Holy Spirit and less on consultants! (Acts 4:5–12; Matthew 17:21)
29. Ministers need to consider that worship includes silence before God! (Exodus 20:4–6; John 4:19–26)
30. Ministers ought to recognize that spiritual warfare is not defined by the church board! (Ephesians 6:12; James 4:1–10)

Section 4: The Church

I define the church in two generalizations. First, I define the church as any group of believers who gather together as a community. Second, I define the church as the body of Christ, which is made up of believers around the world. In this section I am referring specifically to the first definition.

31. The church must reinstate Jesus as Lord. (Revelation 22:13; Acts 2:14–27)
32. The church must become generous givers as the people of God. (Malachi 3:10; 2 Corinthians 9:6–7)
33. The church must reinstate the cross; it leads toward covenant renewal. (1 Corinthians 1:17; Galatians 6:14)
34. The church must reinstate the altar since it unifies man to God. (1 Kings 18:20–39; Revelation 8:3)
35. The church must vigorously elevate a trinitarian paradigm. (Genesis 1:26; John 16:13–15)
36. The church must vigorously elevate corporate prayer. (Luke 19:45-46; 2 Chronicles 7:12–26)
37. The church must view itself as a hospital, not a country club. (Hebrews 10:19–25; Matthew 11:28–30)
38. The church must uphold a high view of marriage. (Malachi 2:16; Mark 10:2–9)

39. The church must lift the Bible to a level of complete and total authority. (I2 Timothy 3:16–17; 2 Peter 1:20–21)
40. The church must hold up Jesus Christ as Lord. (1 Peter 1:25; Malachi 3:6)

Section 5: Theology

I define theology as the study of God and His relationship to humanity. Theology and doctrine are very different though they are oftentimes used synonymously. They are not synonymous. They are very different.

41. Theology must be Holy Spirit-empowered and inspired. (Romans 1:16; 5:5)
42. Theology must be grace-centered and justice-centered. (Ephesians 2:8–10; 1 John 1:9)
43. Theology must include relationships both with God and with man. (Mark 12:28–31; John 13:34)
44. Theology must always have as a goal the new heavens and the new earth. (Revelation 21:1–6; 22:1–5)
45. Theology must move away from government-centered to throne-centered. (Revelation 4:1—5:14)
46. Theology must reaffirm the Ten Commandments. (Exodus 20:1–26; Mark 10:17–22)
47. Theology must unify the community of believers, not divide it. (Acts 15:1–35; Matthew 9:36–38)
48. Theology must become important to the church again. (1Timothy 1:17; Ephesians 3:14–21)
49. Theology must revolve around God as the center of all things. (Matthew 6:24; John 1:1–5)
50. Theology must put greater weight on thinking than on feelings. (2 Peter 3:1–2; 1 Peter 1:13)

Section 6: The Holy Scriptures

By the Holy Scriptures I am referring to the 39 books of the Old Testament and the 27 books of the New Testament. There are other writings that are considered sacred, but they do not meet the criteria for canon. You may have noticed that I capitalize the word Bible or Holy Scriptures. I do this out of respect for the Word of God.

51. The Bible is a book of redemptive love—all 66 books. (Job 19:25–27; Ephesians 1:7–8)

52. The Bible will outlast trends, movements, fashions, and fads; it is eternal. (1 Peter 1:24–25; Revelation 20:15)

53. The Bible has no equal; preach the Word! (Acts 17:22–23; 1 Kings 18:19–29)

54. The Bible must be the central text from every pulpit, for every church! (Mark 16:15; Romans 10:14–17)

55. The Bible must be read often by Christians, and it must be obeyed by all! (Matthew 21:42; Ephesians 3:4)

56. The Bible must dominate over all other writings so covenant can thrive. (2 Thessalonians 1:8; 1 Peter 1:22–23)

57. The Bible is sacred and holy. (Romans 1:2; 2 Peter 2:21)

58. The Bible is a direct threat to Satan! (Matthew 4:1–11; Revelation 20:10)

59. The Bible has every answer for every problem in life. (Philippians 4:19; Matthew 6:25–33)

60. The Bible is absolutely true! (Psalm 119:160; Galatians 2:5)

Section 7: Christian Culture

By Christian culture I mean the way we live and behave as believers. Culture is made up of the standards, practices and norms of everyday life that define a group. The Christian culture is a subset of the larger culture in which we live. The goal is to impact the larger culture in which we live.

61. Life is sacred and it begins at conception! (Psalm 139:13–16; Exodus 20:13)

62. Drinking alcohol is a slippery slope. It hurts more than it helps. (1 Thessalonians 5:22; Daniel 1:8)

63. Gambling is a slippery slope. It hurts more than it helps. (1 Thessalonians 5:22; 1Timothy 6:9–11)

64. Cussing hinders relationships. It never edifies relationships. (James 3:9–10; Exodus 20:7)

65. Pornography is an evil and an enemy of all Christian culture! (Galatians 5:16; 1 John 2:16)

66. Children should obey their parents. This promotes covenant unity within the family. (Ephesians 6:1; Colossians 3:20)

67. Our bodies have become the golden calf of the 21st century. (1 Corinthians 6:19–20; Matthew 6:25)

68. Busy schedules are destroying families and hurting relationships. (Ecclesiastes 1:2–3; 2 Corinthians 11:3)

69. Overeating is a god the church cannot ignore much longer. (Proverbs 23:21; Matthew 6:25)

70. Christians amusing themselves to death are missing out on a covenant relationship with God. (Revelation 1:12–20; Isaiah 9:6–7)

Section 8: Non-Christians

By non-Christian, I am referring to the opposite of what I wrote defining what a Christian is. A non-Christian is oftentimes a good person who does good things. However, non-Christians are just that: non-Christians. They do not have a personal relationship with Jesus Christ. They have not invited Him into their heart and life. They have not asked for forgiveness of sin. They have not repented of their sins. Believing in God is not the same thing as being a Christian. The demons believe in God but certainly are not considered Christian. I love non-Christians. They are a great motivation in my life.

71. Non-Christians are constantly watching Christians interact with God. (Acts 1:8; John 13:35)

72. Non-Christians need Jesus right now! (Matthew 7:13; Luke 19:10)

73. Non-Christians may actually be in part spiritually dead Christians! (Revelation 2:4; 3:14–22)

74. Non-Christians are skeptical of Christians; it's our problem, not theirs! (James 1:8; 2 Timothy 3:5)

75. Non-Christians have religion; everybody has religion, especially Christians. (Matthew 5:20; James 1:26)

76. Non-Christians are sometimes more moral than Christians. (Mark 10:17–22; 1 Corinthians 5:1–2)

77. Non-Christians are running out of time. Christians need to wake up! (Matthew 24:22; 1 Peter 3:15)

78. Non-Christians are the enemy. NOT TRUE! Satan is the enemy!
    (Ephesians 6:12; 1 Peter 5:8)
79. Non-Christians are loved by God the same as Christians—maybe
    more! (John 3:16; Romans 5:8)
80. Non-Christians need Christians! Christians need non-Christians!
    (Matthew 5:43–48; 22:36–39)

Section 9: Christian Common Ground

By Christian common ground I mean things that we should agree on,
things that historically we have agreed on from time to time. If we cannot
come up with some basic common ground, covenant relationships are hin-
dered. Every relationship requires common ground.

81. Heaven and being with Christ is better by far. (Philippians 1:21–23;
    Revelation 21:3–4)
82. Hell is a literal place! (Matthew 10:28; 13:41–42)
83. The Christian must define sin as it is defined in Scripture.
    (Romans 6:1–4; 1 John 1:9)
84. Jesus is the centerpiece of our faith! Any alternative other than
    Christ is unacceptable! (John 1:12; Philippians 2:9–11)
85. Salvation is the only way to get to Heaven! (John 3:3; Acts 4:12)
86. Sanctification is manifested through covenant. (1 Thessalonians 4:3;
    5:23)
87. Evangelism is not optional for the Christian—or for the church!
    (Proverbs 11:30; Matthew 5:13–16)
88. Missions are not optional for the Christian—or for the church! (Mat-
    thew 28:18–20; Revelation 7:9–10)

Section 10: Scripture on Christian Unity

I use Ephesians 4:1–6 as my central text on unity: "I … implore you to
walk in a manner worthy of the calling with which you have been called,
with all humility and gentleness, with patience, showing tolerance for one
another in love, being diligent to preserve the unity of the Spirit in the bond
of peace. There is one body and one Spirit, just as also you were called in one

hope of your calling; one Lord, one faith, one baptism, one God and Father of all who is over all and through all and in all."

I believe that in order for there to be covenant relationships manifested within Christianity, there must be unity in the body of Christ. I believe the following theses are what will bring us together under the umbrella of the Covenant Renewal Model.

89. One Body. (Ephesians 4:4; 1 Corinthians 12:12)
90. One Spirit. (Ephesians 4:4; 1 Corinthians 12:13)
91. One Hope. (Ephesians 4:4; Colossians 1:5)
92. One Lord. (Ephesians 4:5; John 14:6)
93. One Faith. (Ephesians 4:5; Galatians 2:20)
94. One Baptism. (Ephesians 4:5; Matthew 3:11)
95. One God. (Ephesians 4:6; Exodus 20:3)

TO GOD BE THE GLORY!

I invite you to use these theses as discussion starters to draw you closer to the Lord. They work wonderfully in a class setting, in a Bible study setting, or for your own private time with the Lord. They can be used in numerous ways.

I invite you to find other Scriptures that will lead you toward covenant with the particular thesis(es) of your choice. First, study the ones you disagree with. Then study the ones that upset you. Finally, study others as the Lord lays them on your heart.

This is the only chapter with a Bible study built into it. I have an appendix of considerable length with many applications too! This Bible study is unique in its subject matter in light of the Covenant Renewal Model. Don't just read the 95 theses; look up the Scriptures as well. I trust this chapter will move you closer to a covenant relationship with God.

Chapter 9 Reflection and Discussion: Creating Covenant

1. Who in church history is a positive role model for you and why?

2. If you were to write five theses on a covenant relationship with God, what would they be?

3. What would future generations say about a generation of Christians who loved God and each other through thick and thin?

4. What have we learned about humanity throughout history as it relates to war?

5. In what ways can the covenant model lead to world peace?

6. Inner peace precedes world peace. What model would you like to leave for your children regarding peace?

7. Identify a verse in the Bible that addresses peace.

8. Find a story in the Bible that closest resembles a world at peace.

SPIRITUAL WARFARE
AND COVENANT

This chapter is critical in battling Satan! Covenant is practical. A covenant relationship with God equips us for everything life can throw at us. The stronger your relationship with God, the more powerful you become in defeating Satan in your life. It is not a matter of praying the right prayers. It is not a matter of quoting the appropriate Scriptures. Spiritual warfare requires knowing God in an intimate interpersonal way. It is having the mind of Christ—in order to know the will of God, in order to hear the voice of the Holy Spirit, in order that we might have what we need to defeat Satan.

I grew up in church and never heard the phrase "spiritual warfare." In fairness to the two pastors from my childhood, they may have talked about it on one of those Sundays I was not paying attention. In fact, I don't remember anything being mentioned about spiritual warfare while in seminary either.

In defense of my pastors and the seminary I attended, I do recall one Sunday morning as a child when I didn't pay attention in the morning church service. Our church had very hard wooden pews. (I think they may have been manufactured in Hades!)

The Sunday school office was directly behind the left-hand side of the sanctuary where I was sitting. There was a small window where teachers would get supplies from a person working in the little office. Nobody was in that office during church.

Each week, during the service (you could set your watch by it), the pastor prayed the "pastoral prayer." It always seemed longer than the sermon, but at least I didn't feel like I was headed to hell during his prayer. We always stood for that special weekly prayer. I got an idea!

I went to the office, grabbed a small box of thumbtacks and proceeded to carefully place one under each person who was standing in the row in front of me. When the preacher finally said, "Amen" and added "you may be seated," I figured I was in for the show of a lifetime.

Everybody sat down and the people in the row in front of me showed signs of being very charismatic. They jumped, they shouted and they screamed. It was awesome! I don't think anyone had ever jumped, shouted or screamed in that church, ever!

It was great for about ten seconds. Then my dad took me out of church and it was my turn to jump, shout, and scream! My point is that whatever I may have missed in church and school was my fault.

It is interesting that as pastor I often deal with themes like eternity and spiritual warfare and other critical subjects. I wish I would have learned more about these subjects while in seminary, which I now realize never completely prepares you for the ministry. It gives you the training wheels to get started, and the rest is up to you.

If you're heading to seminary, I want you to have realistic expectations. I did not study spiritual warfare until years into my ministry. The heritage I come from does not use that kind of language. We should! I was already in ministry when I recognized I needed to know more about spiritual warfare.

As Christians we oftentimes treat spiritual warfare like we do the attacks of 9/11 or the Iraq war or the war in Afghanistan. We live life in denial that there is a war going on with the United States. If it doesn't affect me, it must not be that bad.

That is very wrong thinking. That is precisely the thinking Satan wants us to have. He wants us to downplay his role in our lives. He wants us to let down our guard. Christians often ask me, "How could this have happened?" My answer is, "Neglect." When we neglect to keep our guard up, we give Satan an opportunity to penetrate our souls.

The human soul makes every human being a spiritual being. Thus, every human being is in a war, albeit oftentimes a silent war. The church is at war. Christians are at war. (And I'm not talking about among themselves—though that is sadly often true.)

We dare not reduce the cross to a 2,000-year-old fairy tale and the resurrection of Jesus Christ to a nice bedtime story we get tired of hearing. The cross and the resurrection of Jesus Christ provide us the empowerment we need and are the foundation on which we build our covenant relationship with God. In that respect, it is the New Covenant. Our foundation is Jesus Christ. My point: *Wake up; we are at war!*

The Christians' enemy, Satan (Devil, Evil One, Slewfoot, Scumbag) has a game plan. While you're sleeping, he's planning how to steal your soul. By the way, stop looking at life as a game. It is a war. You and I are in a war zone.

I am a chaplain for my town's police department. One night, while on patrol with an officer, we got a call about suspicious activity. We arrived on scene (I just love police jargon); the officer went around the house with a flashlight and of course a belt full of protection. Chaplains carry only flashlights, no weapons but our pocketknives!

The officer told me to stand in front of the house and wait for him to come around the other side. So I stood by a bush in the front yard with only the moon lighting the yard.

I heard the front door open, and a man with a pistol aimed at me came outside. He was only fifteen feet away. All of a sudden, my bulletproof vest felt like jelly. It was dark enough that he couldn't see if I had on a uniform and a badge. At that moment, the officer came around the corner and ordered the man to drop his weapon. The situation was de-escalated and everyone was safe.

That was the first time I had ever had a gun drawn on me. It is not a good feeling. I don't know what it is like to experience war. That experience was close enough for me.

However, the reality is that Satan has a bazooka aimed at each one of us. In our blindness of busyness we fail to see his weaponry.

This is yet one more reason why you and I should be connected with God in a covenant relationship. Even though we are at war, God gives us peace within. The deeper the covenant relationship is with God, the greater the peace within our souls. Satan comes at us by placing doubt, fear, and discouragement in our minds. This is his game plan for you, your marriage, your children, your church, and your friendships. A covenant relationship with God addresses doubt, fear, and discouragement. I will talk more about these three in chapter 15 when I speak about spirit, soul, and body.

I offer a counterattack to Satan's attacks on you and I: covenant relationships. I believe every word in Ephesians, chapter 6 is true. Covenant is supported by Scripture as a solution to the warfare described in Ephesians 6. The imagery of the protective armor we are to put on to fight off Satan is in actuality a covenant relationship with God.

It has been said that educators take the simple and by virtue of their vocation make it complex. On the other hand, communicators take the complex and by nature make it simple.

Simply put, covenant relationships are a simple solution to the complexities of life. Remember the words of Dr. Shelton and how covenant is as simple as second grade. Do not be over-educated by Professor Satan. He is a teacher—a false teacher!

The covenant I write about in this book is not broken down like the covenants in Scripture. For me, covenant is covenant. The covenant I speak about is not the Edenic Covenant, nor the Adamic Covenant, nor the Noahic Covenant, nor the Abrahamic Covenant, not the Mosaic Covenant, nor the Deuteronomic Covenant or the Davidic Covenant—not even the New Covenant. I view covenant in Scripture as a single act of God from start to finish.

I view covenant not as anything new to God, only new to us. Covenant takes on a different form in the person of Jesus Christ, but it still remains God's desire to have a relationship with you and me. That has never changed in Scripture. The different names of covenants simply recognize the different eras and people for whom God offers a relationship within the narrative of Scripture.

The Bible is a single story about God and us. It is a story that is always adjusting to our sinful nature. God never changes. He does not have to. The problem is not with God; the problem is within us. Scripture screams out statements about the "New Covenant." It is new to us. Jesus is not new to God the Father!

I believe that the same desire God had with Adam in the Garden of Eden, He has with us. Today, God is asking the same question He asked in the Garden of Eden, "Where are you?" We often mistake that question as one of condemnation. God is not looking to spank us. God wants to walk with us. God desires a covenant with you and I far more than we with Him. If that does not blow your socks off, nothing will.

I remember yet another highlight in my childhood career. One warm day as I came home down that long driveway I mentioned in an earlier story, I got the idea to fill my lunchbox with grasshoppers. I thought it would be funny to watch my mom open my pail and have a million grasshoppers jump out at her. My plan was executed to perfection. There was only one little problem with my plan: my mom did not think it was funny. I do not recall getting spanked, though Lord knows I deserved one. I do recall my mother having a weird smile on her face and just shaking her head at me.

On another occasion in my childhood career of troublemaking, I was three years old, as the story goes. I have absolutely no recollection of this story. I only have the memory of my parents to rely on. My dad, at 73, is still an amazing golfer. He plays on the Oregon seniors' tour each year in weekly tournaments. He had high hopes that I would be a great golfer one day. That never happened.

Early in my golfing career, at the age of three, I took the plastic driver Dad had bought me, and in one short afternoon while Mom was at the store, I evidently knocked down every single flower she had planted around our home. (And you thought Bill Murray in *Caddyshack* was an original!) I don't recall being punished; at least I have no scars on my bottom.

I find it fascinating that while I got spanked for things I did that were wrong, I don't recall the spankings as much as I recall my parents' love for me. Yes, there are spankings in life, but a covenant relationship with God is not about the spanking; it's all about God's love.

The covenant God seeks with you and I has each of our names on it. As God has made His plan known to me more clearly in recent years, I have embraced my covenant relationship with God and named it "Randy's Covenant" (short for Randy Butler). It is personal and not a contract. That is the real point of this entire concept when I talk about a covenant relationship with God. It is all about a relationship with God and absolutely nothing else. It is *Heaven's covenant with earth*! It is God's covenant with humankind. I attempt to take the chains off covenant.

The commentaries confuse me on the subject of covenant. My goal is not to create a doctrine or to articulate a theological position. My goal is to communicate my experience to you so you can experience with God what I am experiencing. It is revolutionary! It is fresh! It is not modern. It is not post-modern. It is bigger than these. It transcends these. It is not a movement or a fad or a fashion, or a program. It is a relationship with the God of the universe this side of Heaven; and I am excited about it and want you to experience it too! A relationship takes two, and given the fact that I am not in Heaven yet, God is with me right now! That is the reality of the Covenant Renewal Model.

The first key in defeating Satan is recognizing that God is greater than Satan. We are not greater than Satan, therefore a covenant relationship with God makes perfect sense. It is the only way we can defeat Satan.

The second key is to know the ways of God over the ways of Satan. You never have to have a class on how to sin. That comes very naturally. You never have to have a class on how to have an affair. You never have to have a class on how to become an alcoholic. You never have to have a class on how to hate. These come very naturally. You never have to have a class on how to fight with your brother or sister. That is easier than breathing air.

I remember one summer vacation when my sister and I were playing in our front yard on the second day of summer vacation. The weather was gorgeous, and we were having fun. My sister Cindy is two and one-half years younger than I am. I had a great idea that fateful morning of summer vacation. I thought it would be fun to see how high I could get my sister up in a tree. I grabbed a rope from the garage and tied it around my sister. I threw the rope over the highest limb I could and began to hoist her up the tree. (Whenever trying an exercise like this, always use a tree that is not dead. That was my first mistake of the morning.)

I had almost hoisted her to where the limb held her weight. Suddenly, the limb broke, sending my sister falling to the ground. She began to scream and cry.

My first thought was of myself and the trouble I would get in. Cindy got up and we discovered her screaming and crying were justified—her arm was broken. I held her down and begged her not to tell Mom. That would be at least the second mistake of that fateful morning. She ran into the house and we made a trip to the doctor's office that morning.

Brothers and sisters don't need classes on how to mess with one another. (By the way, I recalled this story to my sister just before writing this chapter.

She remembers it well. She has also forgiven me and has found a place in her heart to still love me. However, I don't recall her letting me sign her cast!)

We know Satan better than we think we do. We need to learn more the ways of God. We do this by being filled with His Holy Spirit, by reading and obeying the Word of God each day, and by being in a covenant relationship with God each and every day. Again, this means I talk with Him, and I acknowledge His presence in my life as though He were physically with me. People do this all the time with dead people. Why is it so hard for us to do with the living God of the universe?

A covenant relationship with God will stabilize your life, not dismantle it. I consider divorce to fall under the category of spiritual warfare. Imagine a battle in which God is victorious in our lives and there is never another divorce this side of Heaven.

Imagine God being victorious in your life and the lives of your children, as well as over the habitual temptations each of us faces (often our loved ones never know what they are until it is too late). Imagine God being victorious in your mind and your entire being in the area of spiritual warfare. Living in a covenant relationship with God is the only way I know this can be accomplished. Again, I invite you to enter into a covenant relationship with God, within and with others. I call this "trinitarian covenant." As long as we are united in trinitarian covenant, Satan cannot win!

Jesus came to the earth to accomplish many things. Most would say it was to redeem mankind by His work on the cross. What if that was only part of the story? What if I told you there is another part of the story we keep leaving out? Consider the model Christ gave to us, not in dying, but in living. Consider with me the model Christ gave to us not in His divinity, but in His humanity.

We do well to talk about the death of Jesus Christ. One of the most famous phrases in all of church history, especially in the last century is, "Jesus died for my sins." That is very true, but when was the last time you heard someone say, "Jesus lives for me to know Him"? We rarely hear that one. A covenant relationship with God is both of these. It is both/and rather than either/or.

Very few emphasize the concept that Jesus lives for us to know Him. It is the left-out component in our theology. To leave it out is to leave out covenant relationships. Covenant is about relationships that are alive and well. Yes, I am a sinner, but I am a forgiven sinner. Once we embrace this theology, Satan has less of a hold on our lives, and spiritual warfare becomes a battle we can win!

Jesus came in the flesh to provide a model for us to follow in defeating Satan. He showed us in the flesh how to live in covenant with the Father, and in so doing defeat Satan. We see this marvelous model in how He lived in relationship to His Father, how He lived in this relationship with Himself, and how He lived in covenant relationship with others. There was no room left for Him to give Satan any allegiance or alliance.

In the arena of spiritual warfare, may God give us the desire to copy the life of Jesus Christ by living in covenant relationships. Total union with God is total and complete separation from Satan. That is how you and I defeat Satan.

Appendix to Spiritual Warfare

Over recent years I have heard people say, "I am a follower of Jesus Christ," or "I am a disciple of Jesus Christ." I have been troubled by these statements when I don't see covenant working in their lives, so I thought I would take a closer look at the life of Christ, and as I scanned the gospels, I began making notes of the things Jesus showed us and told us.

There is an appendix in this book outlining a study I did in response to the comments I have heard from so many Christians. Sadly, I have not seen the connection between their comments and what I read in the gospels supporting covenant.

I found 731 statements Jesus either showed us or told us. There may be a few more. I have used these statements in a study at my church and in a college setting with wonderful results. I have also used it as a tool in a seminary setting where I taught a hermeneutics class. This study is one of the more powerful tools I have ever used in my ministry.

I have included it because you can use it topically or thematically, or any other way you choose. It is a great tool. I boiled down the life of Christ into two categories. Study them, using inductive Bible study methods: observation, interpretation, and application. This has helped me tremendously to capture the Covenant Renewal Model. With this tool, I am able to see the Covenant Renewal Model in the life of Christ more sharply. (I am indebted to my friend Mel Hurley, who took my handwritten notes and compiled them into the format you have in the appendix).

Further Help on Spiritual Warfare

There are many good books on the subject of spiritual warfare. My purpose is not to duplicate their work. My purpose is to bring in the dimension of covenant and its relationship to spiritual warfare.

However, there is one excellent book I recommend for further reading. I have already used it in this book on several occasions. Kenneth Boa, in his book, *Conformed to His Image,* is the best work on spiritual warfare I have ever read. You would be wise to buy his book; it will give you practical helps in the area of spiritual warfare.

Chapter 10 Reflections and Discussion: Creating Covenant

1. Define and describe the war you are in with Satan.

2. How can covenant help you in spiritual warfare?

3. Can Satan penetrate a covenant relationship you have with God? If so, how? If not, why not?

4. Is the full armor of God effective without a covenant relationship with God?

5. Describe specific ways you need to distance yourself from Satan.

6. Reflect on the peace of God as described in Philippians 4:6–7.

7. Identify a verse in the Bible that will equip you in your fight against Satan.

8. Find a story in the Bible where a relationship with God defeats Satan.

CHAPTER 11

MORALITY, TEN COMMANDMENTS AND COVENANT

Morality

By nature, covenant is a move away from legalism. This should be appealing to postmodern Christians. In fact, it should be appealing to all Christians. Morality is at the heart of covenant relationships. Covenant relationships are at the heart of morality.

Subjective relativism exists because covenant relationships do not exist. Covenant relationships always move us from the edge of doing what is wrong and bad in a relationship to the center of doing what is right and good in a relationship. Immorality is weakness in a covenant relationship.

The authors of *Now, Discover Your Strengths,* write, "Our definition of a weakness is anything that gets in the way of excellent performance."[123] A covenant relationship with God is all about moving away from weakness and moving toward excellent performance in the relationship. Our world has always been in a morality crisis. The church is no different from the world.

What would happen if we could change the motives behind morality and immorality? What if the Covenant Renewal Model changed behavior? It does! I no longer do what God asks only because I am commanded by Him to do so. Instead, I obey based on my interpersonal relationship with Him. And I go beyond the command to obey and respond out of love—not just obedience.

---

[123] Buckingham & Clifton, *Now, Discover Your Strengths,* 148.

Where there is sin, there is a clash with morality. Therefore, it should be obvious that a covenant relationship with God does not eliminate sin; rather a covenant relationship with God is about restoring the sinner. Donald Miller writes in *Blue Like Jazz*: "Christian spirituality begins by confessing our sins and repenting." [124] I spoke about the connection between spiritual formation and covenant earlier in the book. Spiritual formation comes as we work through our sin and are restored back to a covenant relationship with God. Spiritual formation is about keeping us in covenant and out of sin. When in sin, getting out of it as quickly as possible and going back to living in covenant with God is an important piece in spiritual formation.

The Latin phrase "lex rex" means "law is king" and is the title of a book by British theologian Samuel Rutherford. When the law is king, you and I are free because we live within the boundaries of law. We do not live within the boundaries of law because we have to, but rather because we want to. I know that for some desiring to live within the law is hard to imagine.

Let me give you an example. Because I am so in love with my spouse, I do not need to be reminded of the seventh commandment. I don't go anywhere near adultery. I stay away from it, not because I have to, but because it isn't even close to my heart. My spouse is close to my heart. We commit adultery when we no longer keep the one we love in our hearts. A covenant relationship with God is about keeping God in our heart.

When God is in my heart, He is in my thoughts. When He is in my thoughts, He comes out in my behavior. It is inconsistent to say that God is in my heart and still make room for adultery. It has to be one or the other! That is how morality works with covenant relationships. The law does not go away; it just becomes something that is not an issue at all! When we live within the boundaries of a covenant relationship, we also naturally live within the walls of the law. It is not a big deal. It is total freedom. A covenant relationship with God is the cure for legalism!

Rutherford states that any time a civilization reverses "lex rex," there is chaos. To reverse lex rex is to say, "the king is law." The problem is that this is not referring to God. It is referring to man. The Bible speaks of this in a similar fashion: "In those days there was no king in Israel; every man

---

[124] Miller, *Blue Like Jazz*, 117.

did what was right in his own eyes" (Judges 17:6). That is the same mistake some Christians are making today in Christianity. To get away from legalism, they are doing what is right in their own eyes. This kind of theology will eventually take us away from God rather than draw us closer to Him.

The Covenant Renewal Model is the absolutely perfect solution to legalism. Likewise, it is the ideal response to subjective relativism. It is quite the opposite of legalism. In his book, *Exploring Heaven,* Arthur Roberts writes, "Exploring Heaven actually begins on earth. This is where we live, so we start the journey from where we are, in the here and now." [125]

There are no laws in Heaven. Our relationship with God this side of Heaven is practice for our relationship with Him on the other side of earth. In other words, we start with a covenant relationship with God. He takes us as we are, but He loves us too much to leave us the way we are, so He transforms our hearts and draws us close to His heart. In this transforming process, the law does not go away. The law is still there; however, it is no longer seen as our foe. Keeping it within a covenant relationship is our way of saying to God, "I love You with all my heart."

As a police chaplain I have been on a fair number of calls involving fatalities on the road. I remember early in my training when my boss said to me, "That is the worst one I have ever seen." The next fatality we had, he uttered similar words. That happened to us four calls in a row. Todd, my boss and friend, served as a relief chaplain at "ground zero" after the 9/11 attacks. He has seen the worst of the worst. So when he made those statements, I realized I was seeing some pretty bad stuff.

Without exception, each fatality had taken place because a law had been broken, oftentimes multiple laws. Laws are for our protection. God's laws are for our protection. It is as simple as that.

As Gerald May puts it in *Addiction and Grace:* "Grace always invites us forward." [126] Grace is God's icing on the covenant cake. Grace always moves us forward toward Heaven. The closer you and I are to God, the closer we are to Heaven. The closer we are to Heaven, the further we are away from sin. The Bible is a huge help in this process.

---

[125] Roberts, *Exploring Heaven,* 11.

[126] May, *Addiction and Grace* (San Francisco: HarperCollins, 1988), 155.

Boa states, "The key to overcoming the values of the world is renewing the mind with the truths of Scripture."[127] The way I stay in a covenant relationship with God is to stay in the Scriptures. There is a direct correlation between the two. Let me put it another way by quoting Robin Maas talking about the spiritual traditions of monks and nuns: "Monks and nuns lived within the silent world of the enclosure in order to sharpen their ability to hear the Word of God."[128] We, like monks and nuns, must find a way to silence so we can sharpen our ability to hear the Word of God. To do so is to sharpen our covenant relationship with God.

One of the best ways to break from legalism without compromising sin is to view God differently. I love the way Holt puts it in *Thirsty for God:* "We are told that a monk given thirty seconds to describe life in his monastery for a television interviewer replied, 'We fall down, then we get up. We fall down, then we get up. We fall down, then we get up...'"[129] This is how life really works. We fall down and then we get up. Legalism keeps us down. The getting up is what a covenant relationship is all about. So I, along with your loving heavenly Father, say to you in the name of a covenant relationship: "Get up; God loves you and is ready to go on a walk with you."

Morality seeks the best in humanity. Immorality seeks the beast in humanity. We strengthen relationships when we live in covenant. Relationships drown in the cesspool of selfishness and self-centeredness. Covenant relationships are centered in God. I like the way Donald Miller states it, "I need to know that God has things figured out, that if my math is wrong we are still going to be okay."[130] We may not have the theology right. The doctrine may be lacking, but these days I am far more concerned with my covenant relationship with God than I am with dotting the "i's" and crossing the "t's."

Larry Crabb is an incredible writer to the Christian community. In his book, *Connecting, A Radical New Vision*, he writes, "It's time for the people of God to enter the primary battle we're all fighting to connect with each

---

[127] Boa, *Conformed to His Image*, 336.

[128] Maas & O'Donnell, *Spiritual Traditions for the Contemporary Church*, 60.

[129] Holt, *Thirsty for God*, 10.

[130] Miller, *Blue Like Jazz*, 206.

other not about problems but about our desire to know God."[131] Indeed, to know God is the heartthrob of covenant. It changes every perspective in life when that becomes our desire.

Marriage is a process. It takes a lifetime to really know somebody. It took me 25 years to remember that Joanie does not like black olives. Every Thanksgiving and each time I ordered a pizza with olives, she reminded me she did not like black olives. Thank God for time. It took me 25 years to remember this fact, but now I have it in my memory banks. It takes a lifetime to really know God. Please do not stop short of really knowing Him. He is worth knowing. I am certain He likes black olives, too!

Crabb sums up this section best as he states, "A community that heals is a community that believes the gospel provides forgiveness of all sin, a guaranteed future of perfect community forever, and the freedom now to indulge the deepest desires of our hearts, because the law of God is written within us—we have an appetite for holiness."[132] The new norm for Christianity is freedom, not bondage. The law of God is written in our hearts, not our heads. As long as it is in our heads it is a chore. When it is in our hearts it becomes a blessing. It is time for Christians to start indulging, but not in sin. We have done that and that gets us nowhere. It is time for Christians to indulge in God!

The Ten Commandments

The Ten Commandments help give definition to a covenant relationship with God. I love the Ten Commandments. They would make perfect sense even if I were not a Christian. They provide a good code of conduct. If they had not come from the Bible, I am somewhat certain they would not be in question in the political arena today.

I am a covenant Christian. The Ten Commandments for me are not a chore nor a challenge, but a cherished way of demonstrating my obedience to God. Remember, a covenant relationship requires relationship and obedience. I desire to have a union with God, a covenant relationship with

---

[131] Crabb, *Connecting, A Radical New Vision* (Nashville: Word Publishing, 1997), 130.
[132] Ibid, 31.

God. Please put on the lens of the Covenant Renewal Model and look with me briefly at all ten from a covenant perspective.

Remember, whatever faults you see in the Ten Commandments come from faulty relationships. Some today in Christianity see the Ten Commandments as a failed policy; however, it's the relationship that is flawed, not the Ten Commandments.

Let me begin by saying the Ten Commandments are not the foundation for legalism. They are the foundation for covenant. Lodahl and Oord write in their book, *Relational Holiness:* "Legalism is lethal to holiness."[133] Again, the Ten Commandments are not a call to legalism. They are a call to covenant.

In *Posers, Fakers, & Wannabes*, we read, "Frederick Buechner, John Eagan, Anne Lamott, Thomas Merton, Mike Yaconelli, the whole chorus of voices in this chapter, call us to stop running and start resting in God's promise that we are totally loved."[134] A covenant relationship with God is about being totally loved by God. This would include the Ten Commandments. Once you and I can trust this, then we will run to Scripture; in running to Scripture we actually are running into a covenant with God!

Command #1: "You shall have no other gods before Me" (Exodus 20:3). In covenant relationships union is the key word, so why would you or I want to jeopardize an awesome relationship with God by inviting another god into the relationship? Yet people do it all the time. Each time this happens, covenant is damaged. Leech states, "But Christians can only address God as 'Abba' in so far as they are incorporated into Christ; their relationship is derived from His."[135] Command #1 is not about an impersonal bully telling us what to do; it is about a request from our "Abba."

Command #2: "You shall not make for yourself an idol, or any likeness of what is in heaven above or on the earth beneath or in the water under the earth. You shall not worship them or serve them; for I, the LORD your God, am a jealous God, visiting the iniquity of the fathers on the children, on the third and the fourth generations of those who hate Me, but showing

---

[133] Lodahl & Oord, *Relational Holiness* (Kansas City: Beacon Hill Press, 2005), 51.

[134] Manning & Hancock, *Posers, Fakers, & Wannabes (Unmasking the Real You)*, 66.

[135] Leech, *Experiencing God*, 85.

lovingkindness to thousands, to those who love Me and keep My commandments" (Exodus 20:4-6). Simply put, idolatry is forbidden. Idolatry is to God what a mistress is to a marriage!

Command #3: "You shall not take the name of the LORD your God in vain, for the LORD will not leave him unpunished who takes His name in vain" (Exodus 20:7). Covenant forbids misusing the Lord's name. Misusing His name is like calling your bride a "whore" during your wedding ceremony. Someone living in covenant will never misuse the name of the one with whom they are in union. It is theologically possible but covenantally impossible. That is why good covenant makes for good theology; good theology does not necessarily make good covenants.

Command #4: "Remember the sabbath day, to keep it holy" (Exodus 20:8). Covenant relationships demand sabbath rest. Covenant relationships require memory and wholeness. Covenant breaks down when we fail to invoke memory. Wholeness follows covenant.

A number of years ago, I performed a wedding on a Saturday. It was a small wedding, so I had no coordinator or others to assist me. While waiting for several more guests to arrive, I entertained those who were already seated in a small chapel just off what was then our main sanctuary.

I went to the back of the sanctuary to look out into the parking lot. Since I saw no one else coming, I turned to quickly run through the sanctuary to rejoin the wedding party.

Our old sanctuary is held up by six very large beams. I am thrifty and rarely turn lights on in order to save money. (While we're at it, I might as well confess that I am the one who unplugs the drinking fountains as well in order to save electricity. Wow! I feel much better getting that one off my chest!) As I ran through the sanctuary (something I had done a thousand times before), I lost track of where I was and hit one of those six large beams, knocking myself out and falling to the floor.

When I came to, everyone was still in the chapel waiting for me. I have no memory of that day. I got home and Joanie noticed the big lump on my head. I told her what I thought had happened and rested the remainder of that day. The following day, I preached two services in the morning but had no memory of preaching. Joanie took me to the hospital and the tests showed I had a serious concussion. To this day there are names and faces and even years of my life with my children that I cannot remember at all. A covenant relationship with God restores memory that is taken away by the cruelty of living in this world. Rest allows us to remember God.

Sabbath rest is God's gift to us to renew our covenant with God every week. On the subject of gathering on the sabbath, Leech writes, "For it is in community that God makes His presence known."[136] Unfortunately, for many, church services are not like that. They are more like what Ravenhill describes in his work, *Revival Praying:* "No longer do people go to the house of God to meet God; people go to the house of God just to hear a sermon about God."[137] Those in a covenant relationship with God go to church to meet God in community; first with God, then within, then with community. This is God's plan for His church. Anything short of this fails the test of covenant.

Command #5: "Honor your father and your mother, that your days may be prolonged in the land which the LORD your God gives you" (Exodus 20:12). Simply put, if we as parents do not live out covenant relationships before God, our children will abandon covenant relationships and live in rebellion to our authority over them, and worse, God's authority over them.

Command #6: "You shall not murder" (Exodus 20:13). Covenant does not even think in these terms, including abortion. This is not a tough commandment to obey for the covenant-minded individual.

Command #7: "You shall not commit adultery" (Exodus 20:14). This seems to be the greatest enemy in a covenant relationship with God. Once you give yourself fully to God, this commandment becomes much easier to keep. In fact, when in covenant with God, yourself, and your spouse, those in covenant do not even flirt!

Command #8: "You shall not steal" (Exodus 20:15). Covenant relationships fully satisfy. Therefore the need to steal is a moot subject. Covenant relationships never take from other relationships. By nature, those in covenant relationships are givers, not takers. That is not a tough commandment to obey when living in covenant.

I remember my first big crime as a child. As a four-year-old, I went everywhere my dad went in our truck. One day we stopped at the market

[136] Ibid, 65.
[137] Ravenhill, *Revival Praying,* 113.

near our home. "Where did you get that candy?" Dad asked as we got back in the truck. I told him I had taken it from the counter in the store. He told me I had stolen it. I began to cry. He made me go back in the store, pay the man double what it cost (one cent), and apologize. To this day that store is still standing. It is a memorial to what my life may have been without Christ.

Command #9: "You shall not bear false witness against your neighbor" (Exodus 20:16). False witnessing is a foreign concept to covenant relationships. There is never a need to deceive—ever.

Command #10: "You shall not covet your neighbor's house; you shall not covet your neighbor's wife or his male servant or his female servant or his ox or his donkey or anything that belongs to your neighbor" (Exodus 20:17). Covenant relationships are content relationships. Peter L. Steinke states, "The church is a gathering of dissimilar parts. It is not necessary that the parts be identical to one another. It is necessary that they be identified with one another. Those who have the same Lord are to have the same care for one another."[138] In covenant relationships, we are inventing ways to give, not take!

The Covenant Renewal Model takes a unique approach to the Ten Commandments. It seeks to embrace them in obedience. Covenant loves Commandments! Why? The Ten Commandments are tangible ways to demonstrate union. They are not a chore to keep. They are opportunities to cherish. Kotter states, "Often the most powerful way to communicate a new direction is through behavior."[139] Covenant relationships produce both good and godly behavior.

Guder writes, "Within North American culture the usual application of moral standards is impersonal, judgmental, and legalistic."[140] Those who view the Ten Commandments in this light have no concept of a covenant relationship with God. Those who do have a covenant relationship with God would disagree one hundred percent with Guder's statement.

Crabb writes, "Or we try to scold people into holier living."[141] Covenant never scolds. Covenant relationships go far beyond the Ten Commandments.

---

[138] Steinke, *How Your Church Family Works*, 57.

[139] Kotter, *Leading Change* (Boston: Harvard Business School Press, 1996), 95.

[140] Guder, *Missional Church*, 170.

[141]   Crabb, *Connecting, a Radical New Vision*, 21.

You could give the person living in a covenant relationship one hundred commandments and they would not even flinch. You could give them one thousand commandments and they would simply look at you and yawn, as if to say, "The more commands you give me, the more ways I have to demonstrate my love to God."

Chapter 11 Reflection and Discussion: Creating Covenant

1. Describe a culture without morality as defined in Scripture.

2. Describe a culture with biblical covenants.

3. Describe a culture without biblical boundaries.

4. Describe a culture without biblical laws.

5. Describe a culture in love with God.

6. Describe a culture in love with the world.

7. Identify a verse in the Bible that will help you see God's protection for you in His laws.

8. Find a story in the Bible where God's commands save people from harm.

VOCATION, COMMUNITY, WITNESS AND COVENANT

I f the Covenant Renewal Model is everything I am claiming it to be, it has to work in every area of life. The real test of covenant relationships comes with those relationships we have at church, in our social circles, our workplace and the places life takes us as a witness for Jesus Christ.

Roger E. Olson, in an article in *Christianity Today*, writes, "Like Luther, we must be open to the possibility that the Holy Spirit may break forth new light from Scripture that reforms even the ancient thinking of the church."[142] Perhaps what I am advocating is new light for the church. Perhaps it is old light made new. However one chooses to judge this work on covenant, it is light that is much needed in Christianity. I first will connect covenant with vocation. Second, I will connect the communities in which we function with covenant. Third, I will connect the witness of the Christian to covenant. This is a practical chapter showing the daily outworking of how covenant relationships transform within and with others.

Vocation and Covenant

Walter Brueggemann, author of *Hopeful Imagination,* makes this observation taken from an argument by Gilkey, a noted Protestant theologian: "Gilkey argues that the overriding spiritual and cultural fact in our generation is the end of the Enlightenment which is a model of life concerned for

---

[142] Olson, "The Tradition Temptation," *Christianity Today*, November 2003, 55.

control through knowledge, scientific, economic, political, psychological, that is now ending."[143] Brueggemann wrote this statement in 1986, three years prior to the "official" transition from modernism to postmodernism.

In every generation, God raises up men and women who are visionaries and prophets in times of spiritual confusion and darkness. D. Elton True-blood was, and I believe is, God's man for our time, who in the 20th century wrote with remarkable precision a path for us to travel in the 21st century. It is the path of the Covenant Renewal Model.

Trueblood came from a rich Quaker heritage going all the way back to 1682. Upon receiving his PhD, he worked as chaplain at Stanford University from 1936–1945. Sensing a call from God, Trueblood went to Earlham College in Indiana where he would serve out the remainder of his career. He is a noted author, theologian, philosopher, preacher, intellectual, and professor. His qualifications serve him well for the thrust of this chapter. As earlier stated, I have called him a prophet for our day, which will be evident in the pages that follow.

Keep in mind that the purpose of this section is to draw the connection between our vocation and covenant. On the subject of vocation as an evidence of being led by the Holy Spirit (or as Quakers would put it, "being guided by the light of Christ"), Trueblood writes, "The word 'vocation' has been debased in the modern world by being made synonymous with 'occupation,' but it is one of the gains of our time that the old word is beginning to regain its original meaning of 'calling.'"[144]

Related to this topic and lending weight as to its validity to covenant, Trueblood quotes another noted Quaker scholar, Dr. Arthur Roberts of George Fox University: "We can be grateful to Arthur Roberts for warning against the danger of fraudulence in our service theme. Though he makes the point by asking questions, it is clear that he believes the chief form of service for most Christians must be found in the normal vocations of life."[145] We begin to see the importance of covenant relationships to our vocations of life. A strong relationship with God enables us to be more effective in the

---

[143] Brueggemann, *Hopeful Imagination*, 17.

[144] Trueblood, *Your Other Vocation* (New York: Harper & Brothers, 1952) , 63.

[145] Trueblood, *The Incendiary Fellowship* (New York: Harper & Row, 1967), 93.

workplace. Our vocation, seen as a calling, challenges us to get it right with God so that we will get it right with others.

Trueblood defines further his meaning of vocation in the Christian context by stating, "The vocation of the Christian is threefold: he is called to pray, to serve, and to think, and he is called to do all three together."[146] He did not separate his Christianity from his vocation. For Trueblood they were synonymous.

My point to us is the same as that of Trueblood: There is a direct connection between my covenant relationship with God and what I do in my vocation. My vocation is not separate from my relationship with God; the two complement one another. For Trueblood, vocation is Christianity. It is the covenant relationship at work in the workplace. He would add, "Historically, Christianity has glorified work and has given to the modern world the marvelous idea of vocation."[147]

In my generation, there has been a disconnect between my work (vocation) and my relationship with God. What I do on Monday through Saturday is not connected with—or related to—going to church on Sunday. In fact, my relationship with God has been often defined by church. However, I am redefining it in light of the Covenant Renewal Model.

What we call "full-time Christian service," meaning ministry within the walls of the church, is not what Trueblood means. We have narrowed the definition to exclude anything outside the work of the church. But Trueblood is inclusive, not exclusive; to him vocation is the work of the church, not something that is done outside the scope of the church. According to Trueblood's definition, your vocation as a realtor or a carpenter or a beautician is just as much full-time Christian service as my being a pastor. This is an enormous paradigm shift for the 21st century church culture. If we can make this shift, a floodgate of new possibilities opens for the church.

In other words, just as the preacher needs to make really sure his relationship with God is current and "on fire" because of the work he does, so it is for all Christians—no matter what their vocation in life. They too, need

---

[146] Trueblood, *The New Man for Our Time* (New York: Harper and Row, 1970), 35.

[147] Trueblood, *The Company of the Committed* (New York: Harper & Brothers, 1961), 14.

to be current and "on fire" because the work they do is equally as important as the work done by the preacher. In this way, a covenant relationship with God is critically important because we no longer go to work to make a dollar; we go to work to represent God!

Trueblood was not the only voice of his day. There have been others who have agreed with his philosophy on the subject of vocation. H. Richard Niebuhr, in his book, *Christ and Culture,* writes, "No increase of scientific and technical knowledge can renew the spirit within us; but the right spirit will impel us to seek knowledge and skill in our special vocations in the world in order that we may render service."[148] Niebuhr speaks of the "right spirit." The right spirit is a covenant relationship with God. It will transform where we work because we are first transformed.

Trueblood would phrase it accordingly: "The pietist is one who stresses chiefly the roots; the activist is one who stresses chiefly the fruits. Service without devotion is rootless; devotion without service is fruitless."[149] He adds, "A Christian is asked to include in his life both piety and service."[150] Trueblood viewed vocation as an outflow of an inner life. In this, God's Spirit is always calling the Christian to His will within the daily routines of life, within vocation. I am advocating the connection between the need for a covenant relationship with God in order to be effective and realize the purpose for which we each have been created in light of our vocations.

Two people come to my mind when I think about vocation as ministry. Jeff, a friend of mine, has invited many people to church and has led some of them to the Lord. His business has nothing to do with inviting people to church or to the Lord. Yet, like other Christians, Jeff sees his vocation as the mission field where God has placed him.

Another person I think of is Conrad. He is a dear friend of mine who I have known since high school when the team won the state football title. I recall his choice to go to Western Oregon College to study business and play football. By the end of his college freshman year, he had invited and was responsible for bringing more than 20 people to our college Bible study

---

[148] Niebuhr, *Christ and Culture* (New York: Harper and Row, 1951), 176.

[149] Trueblood, *The New Man for Our Time,* 25.

[150] Ibid, 31.

from his school. Conrad saw his college days as a mission field. These two men understand the importance of ministry within vocation.

I have addressed the church and covenant in another chapter, but a brief word is important at this juncture for this chapter. Trueblood addresses the role of the church in vocation as well. He has sharp admonitions for the church and the message given to the laity on the subject of vocation. He states in no uncertain terms, "This is because the task of the church is the penetration of all of life."[151] Trueblood would insist, "There is still much to do if we are to make the ordinary carpenter believe that he has a holy calling."[152]

I must confess that this philosophy on vocation has changed the vocabulary I use in my ministry. As you read this, and you consider your vocation, know that you have a special, critical, vital role in the kingdom of God this side of Heaven. You must develop that covenant relationship with God within you in order to be prepared to do the work of ministry within the place where you work.

Trueblood said, "Invade the weekday."[153] The Covenant Renewal Model is about a total invasion of your world. There is no area of your life that is not touched by a covenant relationship with God. It will dramatically change your view toward your job. It will become driven by purpose because your life is driven by a covenant relationship with God. The covenant relationship is bigger than you and I. It is about God. We are the beneficiaries of such a relationship. We are transformed. Others are transformed. God is glorified!

Community and Covenant

I turn our attention now to an important aspect of covenant: community. It is critical to understand that any dimension of covenant relationships must be understood in the context of community. Each of us lives in community. In fact, we live in multiple communities. Each social group we're in—from home, to work, to country club, to civic organizations—is a community.

---

[151] Trueblood, *The Yoke of Christ*, 40.

[152] Trueblood, *Your Other Vocation*, 58.

[153] Ibid, 61.

Concerning the Israelites in Isaiah's day, "The central task of 2 Isaiah is to invite people home, to create a sense of that prospect of hope."[154] Mary Moehlman writes, "The sign of covenant is a people gathered by God into obedience to the Light."[155] The climax of our covenant relationship with God is being with Him in Heaven. Every move of God toward us this side of Heaven is Him preparing us for that day when we will be with Him forever in Heaven without interruption, without sin, and without the presence of Satan.

For Trueblood, community begins with Christ and then immediately, simultaneously spreads to other people. He writes, "We need a new sense of life's meaning to end our mood of futility, and this comes only by a saving faith. This faith, in turn, is nurtured by a special kind of fellowship in which Christ himself is the central member."[156] We must always remember that covenant is about God. The relationships that come from a relationship with God are marvelous and a gift from God, but the central theme, the central focus, of covenant relationships is God. I suggest that writers from the emerging church movement, in their language on being incarnational, are trying to imply what I am boldly stating: To live in covenant with God is to be incarnational.

Trueblood stands against modern thought, which is individualistic and self-serving. He always presses for the individual to be complete within community. This is another grand theme for the Postmodern. Trueblood writes, "Any man who has begun to understand the weakness of individualism knows that he needs something to buttress his feeble little life."[157] This was written at a time when the United States was at war with the world. The United States is at war with the world today as well! Worse, we are at war within our hearts and souls. A covenant relationship with God is a solution to both wars!

In Trueblood's book, *The Company of the Committed,* he writes about the role of the Holy Spirit within the context of community and covenant:

---

[154] Brueggemann, *Hopeful Imagination*, 111.

[155] Moehlman, "Children of the Covenant Children of the Light," *Quaker Religious Thought* 24, No. 2, no. 72 (1989–1990), 18.

156 Trueblood, *Alternative to Futility* (New York: Harper & Brothers, 1948), 124.

[157] Trueblood, *The Logic of Belief* (New York: Harper & Brothers Publishers, 1942), 71.

"Little is gained without the Spirit, and the Spirit cannot be maintained by separated individuals. Therefore the church or something like it must be cherished, criticized, nourished, and reformed."[158] Covenant relationships are not about me; they are about a web of relationships all spun from the center of the web—God. God catches us in His web of covenant love and we are joined with others who are likewise yoked with Christ. Trueblood indeed connects community and covenant by making Jesus Christ the focus of the community—any community, every community.

Likewise, Trueblood links community and vocation and covenant too. For him they are all one, not isolated and separated components of life. He writes, "There, then, is our clue. The Christian Faith must rediscover its own essential genius, which is the union of the secular and the sacred, of matter and spirit, the common and the divine."[159] The covenant relationship states that God wants to touch every area of His world this side of Heaven. He begins by touching you and I; we then touch one another, and then we touch our world. Covenant relationships are about bringing the world together, not isolating some people from other people as the church has done.

Trueblood also speaks directly to the church. He writes, "We know something important about the Christian Church when we know that it is clearly intended to be a company."[160] He likewise believed that church was not to be reduced to one hour a week with God. He writes, "If we wish to have a really important religion we must make a complete break with the one-hour-a-week concept"[161] The Covenant Renewal Model does not lead us to doing the minimum with God, but the maximum with and for Him.

Sick relationships seek to do as little as possible with one another. Healthy relationships seek to do as much as possible with one another. The Covenant Renewal Model is all about healthy relationships.

There are some who are moving away from God in an attempt to get closer to God. They view the "church" as the cause for spiritual emptiness.

---

[158] Trueblood, *The Company of the Committed*, 2.

[159] Trueblood, *The Common Ventures of Life*, 35.

[160] Trueblood, *The Company of the Committed*, 45.

[161] Trueblood, *The Common Ventures of Life*, 20.

Trueblood addresses this subject too: "Life is simpler if we are not required to participate."[162] However, covenant relationships are not about isolation; they are about participation. The Covenant Renewal Model does not remove burdens from life; it allows burdens to become lighter and more quickly removed from our life.

We cannot separate ourselves from the church because to do so is to separate ourselves from Christ. Moehlman writes, "Covenant is best understood as a relationship."[163] Relationships by definition do not live in isolation. God intends for our relationship with Him to be shared with others. My covenant relationship with God will spur on your covenant relationship with God. Your covenant relationship with God will spur on my covenant relationship with God.

Witness and Covenant

The final segment of this chapter is perhaps the most important of the three: witness. You and I are witnesses this side of Heaven—like it or not. We leave a spiritual footprint wherever we go. The question must be asked, "Why are not more Christians turned on to Christianity? Why is such a good thing so unattractive?" Perhaps, we need a different DNA. Perhaps what is needed is not a different God but a different approach to God. The Covenant Renewal Model is an attempt to approach relationships God's way. It is God's DNA that we are in need of when it comes to any and all relationships.

Another way of stating covenant is to talk about roots. We cannot offer people what we ourselves do not have. Christianity can be mimicked and faked—and even sustained for a short period of time. People do it all the time, especially when they are trying to impress people they want to marry!

Trueblood uses a phrase that I want you to remember. It touches on witness and covenant. Trueblood writes, "The terrible danger of our time consists in the fact that ours is a cut-flower civilization. Beautiful as cut flowers may be, and much as we may use our ingenuity to keep them looking fresh for a while, they will eventually die, and they die because they are

---

[162] Trueblood, *The Yoke of Christ*, 139.

[163] Moehlman, "Children of the Covenant Children of the Light," 9.

severed from their sustaining roots."[164] That's it! We have uncovered the key to a covenant relationship with God. This relationship with God has its foundation in the root system. We in the 21st century are all about appearance. The Covenant Renewal Model is all about authenticity. Authenticity comes when you nurture the roots of your relationship with God.

I used to do landscaping as a side job while in college and in my earlier years as a pastor. In Oregon, there is a tree—maybe it is a plant. At the very least it resembles a demon called bamboo. If you want it out of your yard, it takes an act of Congress to get it out. You can pull and cut and burn and plow and repeat that process over and over and bamboo will still come up the following year. It is the most relentless root I have ever seen. God wants our roots in Him to be relentless. He wants us to go deep with Him in His love. That way, there is no way Satan or the pull of this world can uproot us from a relationship with God.

A large part in understanding covenant is to understand the importance of nurturing our relationship with God. This requires time spent in the Bible. It requires prayer, meditation, fasting, singing, confession, contemplation, reading, and memorizing Scripture. It requires much alone time with God. It means having a devotional life, a prayer closet, a daily spiritual inspection. It means denying ourselves daily, taking up the cross and following Christ. It means crucifixion. It means service. It means sacrifice. It means surrender. It means suffering. It requires periods of silence before God. It requires accountability before God. It yields peace, joy, and contentment. A covenant relationship with God prepares us for the greatest assignment in life: witnessing!

Witnessing is personal. It is me communicating my story to another human being. Witnessing is not based on a set of formulas or propositions; it is personal. The items I listed in the previous paragraph are not meant to be a formula. They represent things we do with God in covenant relationship.

Witnessing is not a contractual obligation; it is a response out of a covenant relationship with God. The nature of covenant is to witness. And the nature of witness is the overflow of covenant. It is what people of covenant do.

---

[164] Trueblood, *The Predicament of Modern Man* (New York: Harper & Brothers, 1944), 59.

It is who they are. As Dan Greene so aptly states: "Witnessing is not a spare-time occupation or a once-a-week activity. It must be a quality of life. You don't go witnessing; you are a witness."

Witness must also include at its core the atoning work of Christ. In a series of four short articles, Dr. Arthur Roberts summarizes the importance of the atonement in relationship to witness and covenant. He states in a June 2002 article on atonement as a ransom, "Christ is our Savior in respect to sin, our Lord in respect to righteousness (justice)."[165]

Roberts develops this theme in another article where he writes about atonement as satisfying divine honor, "Sin is judged and righteousness raised up."[166] Note how he moves us from being debtors into people who are to be raised up in righteousness. He writes further on atonement as substitution: "Gethsemane is watered with real tears. Jesus is one of us."[167]

We see the progression of the atonement as it takes us *from* our sin *to* His righteousness in us, *to* a relationship, *to* the final point made in a concluding article on atonement as moral influence: "Love is energy, and suffering love the strongest."[168] Dr. Roberts concludes with the single greatest point of morality: love. What starts with sin ends with love. That is the core, the essence, of the covenant relationship with God. He takes us where we are in our sin and moves us through His showers of transformation into righteousness until we are fulfilled in His life-giving love that we are to share as a witness with the people of our world, His world!

Trueblood incorporates witness into all aspects of Christian living, but always seems to bring it around to the church. He makes a scathing—yet true—assertion: "Though the New Testament describes a hot fire, we prefer the damp wick."[169] The Covenant Renewal Model is not a damp wick.

---

[165] Roberts,"Atonement as Ransom" (Northwest Yearly Meeting of Friends, 2002), 1.

[166] Roberts, "Atonement as Satisfying Divine Honor" (Northwest Yearly Meeting of Friends, 2002), 1.

[167] Roberts, "Atonement as Substitution" (Northwest Yearly Meeting of Friends, 2002), 1.

[168] Roberts, "Atonement as Moral Influence" (Northwest Yearly Meeting of Friends,2002), 1.

[169] Trueblood, *The Incendiary Fellowship*, 26.

The Covenant Renewal Model is a hot fire that God intends to blaze bright within us this side of Heaven.

One November, on a hunting trip with some of my buddies from the church, we had an experience that was new to us. One of my buddies, Ken, who is now in Heaven, (not because of the story I am about to recall), loved munching on snacks all day long while out in the woods. That night around the campfire he was cleaning the crumbs out of his pocket and throwing them in the fire. The next thing I knew we were under attack—at least I thought we were being attacked. It turns out Ken had forgotten that mixed in with his crumbs were about 20 live rounds of .22 ammunition. If you are uncertain of what happens when you throw live ammunition into a fire, I can tell you it is not a pretty picture. We all went scrambling as we ducked for cover, hoping none of us had been hit. God's fire within us is intended to be explosive and safe!

There is a lot at stake in getting our relationship with God "right." We have much to gain and much to lose. Trueblood states, "An empty, meaningless faith, a faith not taken seriously, may thus be actually worse than none."[170] A covenant relationship with God is not meaningless faith. It is the most meaningful of all faiths. As God's witnesses, we need to be in covenant with Him so that our faith is attractive to others who are watching us.

Trueblood repeatedly takes us back to the foundation for living this life—whether in vocation, community or witness—with one central theme: "Modern man can be helped immeasurably by the realization that at the heart of all that is, stands not mere power, but a Person."[171] The Covenant Renewal Model is about the person of Jesus Christ. Nothing else matters. Get this one right, and you get it right for all of life, for all of eternity!

Trueblood concludes our chapter on vocation, community and witness by adding, "What we seek is the total penetration of our total culture by the total gospel."[172] Covenant is the total penetration in relationship building. Get the covenant piece right and our culture will be penetrated by the

---

[170] Trueblood, *Foundations for Reconstruction* (New York: Harper & Brothers, 1946), 34.

[171] Trueblood, *The New Man for Our Time*, 119.

[172] Trueblood, *Alternative to Futility*, 120.

gospel of covenant. Brueggemann writes concerning the prophet Jeremiah, "Jeremiah keeps listening."[173] Covenant requires listening to God. Here lies the secret to a covenant relationship with God! As we listen to God in covenant, He will direct us in our vocation, our communities, and our witness.

---

[173] Brueggemann, *Hopeful Imagination*, 14.

Chapter 12 Reflection and Discussion: Creating Covenant

1. How can covenant relationships make communities better?

2. How can covenant clarify our purpose for life where we work?

3. How can our witness to others be enhanced through covenant relationships?

4. What bridges can you build to your community through covenant relationships?

5. What bridges can you build in your workplace?

6. What bridges can you build with people living in broken relationships? (That is just about everybody!)

7. Identify a verse from the Bible on forgiveness. Do it!

8. Find a story in the Bible that addresses getting along with your neighbor. Do it!

CHURCH AND COVENANT

Church

I love the church, but not nearly as much as Jesus loves the church! I attend church. I pastor a church. Church is all I have ever known. Jesus died for the church. I get paid by my church. Jesus paid the price for the church. The church was not my idea. The church is God's idea. The church is within each of us and the church is outside of us. The church is at the heart of covenant. The church is not the enemy, nor is it the answer to the problems of life. Jesus is the answer! Satan is the enemy. The church will always have problems; it is filled with people! God has empowered the church. God has ordained the church. God has blessed His church.

In today's pop culture there is division over the church, within the church, and outside the church concerning the church. Covenant sees the church within the context of community as was written about in the previous chapter. The first church was the church of the Holy Trinity: Father, Son and Holy Spirit. They existed within community and were and are one.

God is our model for church unity. God loved community so much He added to the community by creating humans. I exclude animals, not because they are not part of God's kingdom, but because they do not have an eternal soul. Therefore, there is no comparison between animals and humankind, though animals and all of God's creation (including my dog Tammy, and your pet too) are important to Him. Everything was fine until human beings stepped out of the community. Covenant is God's redemptive plan to bring us back into His community.

It is impossible for covenant to exist outside of a community. By nature, covenant is community and community is covenant. Rather than judging the community, let's look at it the way God looks at His church: with great love. Perhaps you don't like the church; you are not alone. However, with a covenant mind-set, you could be the catalyst God uses to transform the organization He created and loves.

There are some things to look for when looking for a church. The denomination of the church used to be important. It is not so much so in the 21st century. There used to be high walls between Calvinists and Wesleyan-Arminians. There used to be walls between Pentecostals and those who thought Pentecostals were filled with demons. There used to be walls between Baptist and, well ... everybody else! My point is that each segment of the Christian community each thought they had a corner on God. They did not, and do not!

Then there was a move away from denominationalism altogether. It became popular to be a community church or an independent church. Then style became the issue: contemporary or traditional, emerging or non-emerging. Imagine what we look like to those who want nothing to do with church. We do not need an enemy; we are our own worst enemy!

The following are the core values I believe are important when considering a church where covenant relationships have a chance to thrive:

1. Consider a church that is Trinitarian.
2. Consider a church that always comes back to the cross.
3. Consider a church that preaches and teaches from the Bible every week.
4. Consider a church that carves out time for corporate prayer.
5. Consider a church that speaks much about the work of the Holy Spirit.
6. Consider a church that makes Jesus the centerpiece.
7. Consider a church that talks about the blood of Jesus, the forgiveness of sin and Jesus as the only way to salvation.
8. Consider a church that believes in a literal Heaven and a literal hell.
9. Consider a church that is missional both locally and globally.
10. Consider a church that reaches out to people who are not Christians.
11. Consider a church that believes the Bible to be authoritative and the inspired Word from God.

12. Consider a church that gives invitations where people can respond to the message of salvation.
13. Consider a church that teaches and practices generous giving.
14. Consider a church that loves and lives in community.

These are 14 important qualities I believe a church should be practicing in order to cultivate an atmosphere where covenant relationships can thrive. You will grow as a Christian in a church practicing these qualities.

There are many good churches of many different backgrounds that possess these qualities. I am neither an Arminian nor a Calvinist. I am neither a Pentecostal nor a Quaker. I am neither a contemporary Christian nor a traditional Christian. I am a covenant Christian.

Christian A. Schwarz, in his work, *Natural Church Development*, states, "Yet our research indicates that there is a highly significant relationship between the ability of a church to demonstrate love and its long-term growth potential."[174] Love is the greatest of the 14 qualities I have identified in finding a covenant relationship based church. If there is not love, there is not a covenant relationship.

Likewise, Schwarz states, "All living things in God's creation are characterized by their ability to bear fruit."[175] Covenant relationships lead to fruit-bearing. Fruit-bearing Christians make for churches that bear fruit. It is a neat deal God set up.

Christianity

I completed my Doctor of Ministry degree in 2007 and was not expecting to receive anything more than a degree. I also received a transformed heart and a transformed life. I now look at Christians and our world much differently than before. I realize my prior views were narrow, rigid, biased and unhealthy. I moved into a covenant relationship with God. Are you willing to do the same?

Your journey is not my journey—nor should it be—but we both have the same God who wants the very best for all of us. My heart now sees

---

[174] Schwarz, *Natural Church Development* (St. Charles, Ill.: ChurchSmart Resources, 2000), 36.
[175] Ibid, 76.

through the lens of covenant. Covenant changes how I read my Bible. It changes how I treat and interact with people. The Covenant Renewal Model has affected every area of my life for the better. I have never been happier as a Christian. I would love for you to experience covenant in your life, too.

The cross is a magnification of covenant. Jesus died on the cross not only to save me from my sins (penal view), He also died on the cross to restore my relationship with Him (covenant view). I now call the cross "the cross of covenant."

Pentecost is a magnification of covenant. The Holy Spirit was given to the church and to Christians for many reasons. Primarily, the Holy Spirit came to make Jesus Christ known that we might be redeemed by God, as well as reconciled to Him. That is the essence of the Covenant Renewal Model.

The rapture of the church and the second coming of Jesus Christ is the ultimate in covenant. All relationships in Christ will be reclaimed (I am not advocating universalism; I am speaking about Christians—not the sum of humanity), then our covenant in Christ will be complete because it will not be on this side of Heaven; it will be in Heaven! All relationships in Christ will be made whole, to the glory of God the Father, the author of covenant relationships.

The new covenant of Jesus Christ spoken about in the New Testament is the redemption of all previous covenants. Covenant no longer becomes a chapter in the book. It is the book! Jesus Christ will bring together all in covenant into one covenant with Him at His appearing.

We discover the cross in the New Testament, which is the equivalent of Gilgal in the Old Testament. It is the place where God and His people meet to renew the covenant.

Spiritual poverty is not so much a life of depravity as it is a failure to embrace a covenant relationship with God.

I remember one night while attending seminary. Joanie and I took a break from my studies and we went to the mall. Like most seminary students, we had little money. In fact, we were broke. My grandmother gave us groceries each week just so we could eat. It was a dark, stormy night with rain pounding down sideways in the parking lot. I was looking down on the ground for money, something I have done my entire life. Once in a while you get lucky. That night in the shopping mall parking lot I looked down and in a darkened puddle of water I saw a $20 bill. Manna from Heaven! You would have thought we had just won the lottery.

A covenant relationship with God is like finding a $20 bill, only better!

To embrace God's covenant offer is to embrace God. To embrace God's covenant offer is to then embrace ourselves. And to embrace God's covenant offer is to then embrace all others on planet earth. To embrace others is to embrace God. For when we do it to the least of these, we do it unto God. A failure to embrace covenant is a failure to embrace God.

Perhaps you're beginning to long for covenant relationships in your life. First, have a heart-to-heart talk with God. He has been waiting a long time to have this conversation with you. Remember, every good conversation requires listening. God is a gentleman. He will wait until you are finished speaking. He is a very good listener! Emil Brunner, in his work, *The Silence of God*, teaches us that God's strongest messages come to our hearts without a word being spoken, so wait in God's presence. Remember, every healthy relationship requires time.

Second, read your Bible as much as you can in light of the Covenant Renewal Model. You will see Scripture in a totally different light.

Third, receive the cross as a cross of covenant. Personalize the cross and call it your cross of covenant. Though Jesus died on it, we are each one to pick up our own cross and follow Him.

Fourth, receive Pentecost without discriminating against the Holy Spirit. Allow Him to lead you into a covenant relationship with God. Remember, covenant is not only about you giving yourself to God; it also includes you receiving all of God!

One final word in this section comes from the Old Testament, from Exodus 20. (By the way, I despise using the phrases Old Testament and New Testament. It is one book, one story, one narrative. We break it up and compartmentalize it way too much.) It is a single story of a single God offering a covenant relationship to humankind.

As a seal on covenant in Exodus 20, God gave His people the Ten Commandments. The Ten Commandments were a tool from God for us to live in a covenant relationship with God. It is an error to say that one breaks the Ten Commandments. What is broken is covenant. The Ten Commandments can be disobeyed, but not broken. The only thing broken in this world is the relationship we have with God and with ourselves and with one another.

Traditional Christianity says "tell me." Covenant Christianity says "show me." One is propositional. The other is relational. One comes from the head, the other from the heart. Let's join the ranks of covenant relationships within Christianity and stop talking about it and start showing others what it means to be friends with God. Join me in covenant relationships.

The Covenant Renewal Model has made me an optimist. I see hope for Christianity. However, if hope is to be realized, we are in need of a heart surgeon, not another spiritual pill. The work of covenant relationships requires transformation, nothing less. Covenant relationships are revolutionary. Covenant relationships can change the world. I invite you as a fellow Christian to join me in this journey.

Hell

There is never a really good time to talk about hell. I began writing a book on it years ago and decided to scrap that project. Who wants to read about what they are living? I thought, however, that by making some statements on hell, I can show you what covenant is not. By showing you what covenant is not, you will be able to better understand what covenant is. I classify this portion under the chapter of church and covenant because it is within the life of the church that this subject needs to be addressed.

Hell is a subject being avoided by the church. When was the last time you heard a sermon on hell? Besides, the opposite of covenant is hell, both literally and figuratively.

Covenant is everything hell is not. Hell is everything covenant is not. My favorite images in describing hell are found in that familiar passage in Luke 16:19–31 where we are given at least 11 features of hell. We see that hell is the ultimate rejection of a relationship with God.

Hell includes missed opportunities, the opposite of covenant relationships. Hell includes painful memories, just the opposite of covenant relationships, which are built on cherished memories. Hell includes literal pain while covenant relationships are a release from pain. Hell includes regret while covenant relationships include tremendous reward, with no regrets. Hell is ultimate rejection while covenant relationships are the ultimate in acceptance. Hell is an absence of relationships, living in total isolation forever.

Covenant relationships are the epitome of relationships. Hell is the absence of God, while covenant relationships are all about God. Hell is forever as is a covenant relationship with God. That is the only thing hell and covenant relationships have in common.

Figuratively speaking, hell on earth is isolation from God. Hell is selfish and self-centered and self-serving. Covenant relationships thrive on others, not self anything.

Ultimately, hell is a failure to embrace God. A failure to embrace God is a failed relationship. Hell is simply an absence of relationships, and starting with God, it excludes me and all others. Covenant is the presence of all relationships gifted to us by God, beginning with Him. We love who we are and we love who others are. That is the outflow of covenant.

As I conclude this chapter on the church and covenant, I am keenly aware there must be a starting point for covenant relationship in your life. A preexisting bad relationship must be approached differently than a healthy relationship. How you view yourself must be handled differently than how you view others. I have already elaborated in this chapter on four suggestions for getting started with God.

Schwarz attempts to answer the question of how churches can start from where they are in order to improve themselves. I like his response. He states, "The believers first must be gripped by a new devotion to Jesus."[176] Our starting point is a new devotion to Jesus Christ. This is the direction every church needs to move toward—a deeper, greater devotion to Jesus Christ!

---

[176] Schwarz, *Natural Church Development*, 107.

Chapter 13 Reflection and Discussion: Creating Covenant

1. Why do people dislike going to church?

2. Why do people like going to church?

3. Define church.

4. How are you making your church better?

5. If you were the only person attending church in the world, is your example good enough that others can follow it, making it all the way to Heaven? Why? Why not?

6. Take time and pray for your church!

7. Identify a verse in the Bible that speaks positively about the church.

8. Find a story in the Bible that would be a great model for the church in the 21st century.

MONEY AND COVENANT

Unfortunately, the subject of money needs to be discussed in light of the Covenant Renewal Model. It needs to be discussed because it has been observed by people far smarter than me that there are over 2,000 verses on money in the Bible. Usually how we handle money is our big downfall. We seem to have either not enough money, or in some instances, too much money. Money is not the problem, generally speaking. Covenant helps put money in its proper place. If money is an issue in your life, then this chapter should prove very helpful to you.

Materialism

The Bible says, "But godliness actually is a means of great gain when accompanied by contentment" (1 Timothy 6:6). Contentment is gained through covenant. Only when we have a covenant relationship with God will we fully realize the full blessing of being content. We can only be satisfied when we have gained the ultimate. The ultimate is God. A covenant relationship with God is the ultimate relationship in the universe. If one has a covenant relationship with God, contentment follows.

The Bible says, "For we have brought nothing into the world, so we cannot take anything out of it either" (1 Timothy 6:7). This is referencing materialism. Of course there is something we can take out of this world, a covenant relationship with God. This relationship makes materialism totally unnecessary. There is no need for materialism when referencing covenant because a covenant relationship with God leads to riches untold on the other side of earth, Heaven.

God's covenant with us this side of Heaven is the winning ticket to wealth in Heaven. Materialism is an earthly term for earthly people. We are Heaven-bound citizens. We will have no need of material goods once in Heaven.

Therefore, God is telling us to let go of those things we hang on to so tightly. He is teaching us to stop our fist-clenching. He is inviting us to let go of the things of this world and cling to Him. That is another way of stating covenant. It is a letting go of the security that materialism falsely provides on earth and clinging to a relationship with God that will carry us all the way to the winner's circle. (I am not a horse fan, but my wife is; that line was for her).

The Bible says, "If we have food and covering, with these we shall be content" (1 Timothy 6:8). The reason we are not content with food and covering is that we lack a covenant relationship with God. I challenge you to go 90 days without buying anything but food. Many will struggle at this challenge because we derive our contentment from materialism.

Should you accept my challenge, then give away all the money you saved during those 90 days. That makes people cringe even more. It is a simple test to show our dependence on the things of this world over a relationship with God. We have a relationship with God and the things of this world. A covenant relationship with God moves us further and further away from the things of this world.

The Bible says, "But those who want to get rich fall into temptation and a snare and many foolish and harmful desires which plunge men into ruin and destruction" (1 Timothy 6:9). Being rich in this passage is not a good thing. Rich toward God is always a good thing. The Bible discourages us from pursuing money and encourages us instead to pursue God ... *and then* God will give us other things (Matthew 6:33).

In the United States, we have a lot of stuff, yet, few would describe themselves as rich. Rich is a matter of perspective and opinion. I travel to Haiti from time to time. Please believe me when I tell you that we are rich. It is an issue of priorities. God is helping us see that our priority ought to be a relationship with Him more than a relationship with money. Many Christians have an affair with money and are keeping it a secret in their closet. Christians need to come out of the closet on this issue.

The Bible says, "For the love of money is a root of all sorts of evil, and some by longing for it have wandered away from the faith and pierced themselves with many griefs" (1 Timothy 6:10). This is a zinger verse for us. The issue with money is about misplaced love and devotion.

A covenant relationship with God is an insurance policy against wandering away from the faith. It is an insurance policy against undue pain in our lives brought on by the love of money. It is an insurance policy against being involved in anything evil. We all know what it is to make money and what it takes to make more of it. A covenant relationship with God asks that we put the same energy and devotion into loving God as we do into loving money and the things it provides.

The Bible says, "But flee from these things, you man of God, and pursue righteousness, godliness, faith, love, perseverance and gentleness" (1 Timothy 6:11). How? Covenant! The sum parts of this verse equal a covenant relationship with God. It is the only thing that does add up in this passage that focuses on money. In an era when tolerance is the theology of the day, we don't flee from much of anything today, yet in regard to money, the Bible tells us to flee from the love of it. I have discovered a way to obey this passage of Scripture. I obey it by living in a covenant relationship with God. My energy is given to being rich in my relationship with God rather than the love of money.

I have a safe in my home. I certainly am not going to tell you where it is. In it I have some things that are valuable to me. They are items I don't want anyone to steal. There is a safe in each of our hearts. In that safe there ought to be more of God than anything else. Guard it with your life!

The Bible says, "Fight the good fight of faith; take hold of the eternal life to which you were called, and you made the good confession in the presence of many witnesses" (1 Timothy 6:12). This verse gets us to the reason for living in a covenant relationship with God: eternal life. The question I ask you is this: "When does eternal life begin?" I always thought it began when I died and went to Heaven. Today, I believe it begins when I enter into a relationship with Jesus Christ in which I receive Him into my heart as my Savior. I am enlightened to this truth when I make Jesus Lord of my life by fully engaging in a covenant relationship with Him.

A covenant relationship with God is an eternal relationship with God. It begins this side of Heaven and continues in Heaven. In light of this eternal truth, why in the world would I cling to materialism when God is offering me something of far greater value? I urge you to make a paradigm shift both in your thinking about money and your closet materialism.

Consumerism

I remember a quote in a sermon by my pastor during my high school years. This would be one of those rare moments when I was actually listening. The quote states, "How much does it take to please man? The answer is, 'Just a little more.'" This sums up consumerism: just a little more. In some instances, a lot more!

Our country is in a financial crisis. Worse, we are in a spiritual crisis! Finances are not our real problem in the United States. We have a relationship problem. We are the nation of 100 golden calves. (To their credit, the Hebrews only had one golden calf.) We have been making one golden calf a day all throughout the 20th century and into the 21st. As long as the gold is flowing, we are happy.

Why is it that so many people who call themselves Christians are so unhappy? I believe it is because we are in a relationship crisis. Really, we are in an identity crisis. We do not know *who* we are because we do not recognize *whose* we are. A covenant relationship with God reestablishes *whose* we are. Our values shift, our priorities shift, our interests shift, our goals shift, our wants shift, everything shifts from consuming the earth to consuming Heaven. *Heaven's covenant with earth* is about consuming God. A covenant relationship with God is to consume Heaven.

Consumerism gets in the way of our life with God. When we spend time and energy consuming the temporary, we leave little room to consume that which is eternal. Our souls are eternal. Heaven and hell are eternal. God is eternal. I am asking you and I to move from the temporary to the eternal. Covenant is eternal. Covenant is not temporary. Covenant is permanent.

The United States is sucking fumes financially right now because we base our civilization on consuming. As long as we consume, we feel alive. The problem with this philosophy is it cannot sustain itself over time. We are at that point in our history where we must find an alternate solution. I am offering a covenant relationship with God as that alternative to consumerism.

Green

A covenant relationship with God is Green! You want to be Green, living in covenant with God. You'll be so Green you'll blend in at a golf course. You'll be so Green you won't need camouflage when you go hunting. You'll be so Green you'll only need to buy red decorations for Christmas next year. It is currently in vogue to be Green—to care about environmental quality.

Heaven's covenant with earth is a Green covenant. Covenant is Green in that it focuses on God instead of on consuming. Covenant is Green in that it focuses on a relationship with God, not on materialism. Covenant is Green in that it focuses on helping others get over selfish living. Covenant is Green in that it thrives in giving, not getting. Covenant is Green in that it moves us away from craving the things of earth to craving the things of Heaven. Covenant is Green.

A covenant relationship with God enjoys all of God's creation. Covenant is not plastic! Covenant is authentic! Covenant is not generic! Covenant is genuine! Covenant is not selfish! Covenant is selfless! Covenant is not about me! Covenant is about God in me! Covenant is Green!

Like the relationship with God I articulate in this book, I did not know I was Green until it became more newsworthy in recent years. I keep the heat low in the house. I rarely turn the heat above 62° F. At night I turn the heat off no matter how freezing it is outside. We have no air-conditioning. I recycle just about everything. I drive a scooter to work during the nicer days of the year. My carbon footprint is quite small. I was Green before Al Gore invented the internet! My wife has another name for it: cheap!

Giving

A tangible way to move toward a covenant relationship with God is to practice generous giving. A covenant relationship with God demands generous giving. God pours Himself into us that we might pour our lives into others on His behalf. Randy Alcorn, in *The Treasure Principle,* gives six treasure principle keys. He also states a very simple treasure principle from which the keys flow. He states, "You can't take it with you—but you can send it on ahead."[177]

---

[177] Alcorn, *The Treasure Principle*, 93.

From this treasure principle he lists six keys in relationship to giving. They are:

- "God owns everything. I'm His money manager."[178]
- "My heart always goes where I put God's money."[179]
- "Heaven, not earth, is my home."[180]
- "I should live not for the dot but for the line."[181]
- "Giving is the only antidote to materialism."[182]
- "God prospers me not to raise my standard of living, but to raise my standard of giving."[183]

Of these six treasure principle keys, there is one that is very covenant in nature. When Alcorn references living for the line not the dot (#4), picture a line across a paper in front of you. Place a dot the size of your pencil tip on the left end of the line. That dot represents your life on earth. The line, which has no end, is your life in eternity. A covenant relationship with God has no end. It has a beginning, but it has no end.

In light of covenant, the dot represents the things of earth that are so very temporal. We cling to them as though they were eternal. The Covenant Renewal Model is a model that moves us toward generous giving and generous living. It is a model that places the highest value on my time with God. A covenant relationship with God, like all good relationships, requires time. The more time you spend with God, the more generous your giving will be. It just works out that way every single time.

My son understood covenant. The month before the Lord gave him the keys to his home in Heaven, Kevin had spent a lot of time in his bedroom during Christmas break. Because he loved golf, he made a putting course in his bedroom, with tape marking different distances.

He also had on his table three tennis ball cans (which are still in the same place as when he left them). In one can he had the word "savings." In

---

[178] Ibid.

[179] Ibid..

[180] Ibid.

[181] Ibid..

[182] Ibid.

[183] Ibid.

another can he had the word "tips." This was because he worked at the local golf course and would get tips. The third can said "tithe." I noticed he had written 20% on that can. I asked him why he did that. I told him a tithe is only 10%. "I know," he answered, "but I want God to know that I really love Him and plan to give Him at least 20% my whole life."

Just days later, my son moved from earth to Heaven. Several weeks after the memorial service, I was given the envelope that Kevin had put in the offering plate the day before he went to Heaven. He had given 20%. Indeed, he kept his promise of giving God at least 20% his whole life!

We cannot know how much more time we have on this planet. I urge you to love God as Kevin loved God. Most 16-year-old boys save for a car. Most 16-year-old boys have big plans with money. Kevin had big plans too. Those plans included God! I am so glad I did not talk Kevin into reducing that tennis can from 20% to 10%. My first lesson in covenant relationships came from my son that day.

Need/Want

We each have many needs in this life. God knows our needs. Our problem is we draw a fuzzy line between needs and wants. A covenant relationship with God makes that fuzzy line more clear. In fact, the greater the covenant relationship, the less you will want.

Wants come from a lack of contentment. Contentment comes from covenant. Covenant is the antidote for wants. Covenant will likewise redefine your wants. Covenant will also redefine what you need. In other words, covenant redefines all of life. It puts life in harmony with God. It places us in union with God.

A covenant relationship with God gives us a perspective on the whole of life, including our needs and our wants. Alcorn writes, "Jesus actually gives the man five commands: *go, sell, give, come,* and *follow.* Knowing the state of the man's heart, Christ issues the specific commands he knew were best."[184]

---

[184] Alcorn, *Money, Possessions, and Eternity* (Wheaton, Ill.: Tyndale House Publishers, Inc., 2003), 287.

It really is a matter of trusting God. We trust God in every area but money. Alcorn writes, "Why is this truth so hard for us to accept? If we believe that God can create us, redeem us, and bring us through earth to spend eternity with him, why can't we take him at his word when he says he'll provide for our material needs?"[185] The answer is that we do not really trust God. We hate admitting to such a raw truth; but it is the truth. God has the means to get us from earth to Heaven, yet we distrust him this side of Heaven. I believe that as you enter into a covenant relationship God, you will find yourself trusting God, especially in the area of money.

I read *Money Possessions and Eternity* in May of 2003, just months after my tragedy with Kevin. I wrote this at the bottom of page 422 and dated it May 26, 2003: "On this memorial day I will not dwell on the death of my son, for he is alive. But I will dwell on the death to myself and the things of this world."

I was moving toward a covenant relationship with God. I was beginning to view this world differently. Randy Alcorn wrote his book with eternity in mind. My lenses have taken his theme of Heaven and eternity and I have added another set of lenses called covenant relationships. I see everything now through the lenses of covenant. I have written about some of those subjects in this book. Covenant applies to all areas of life this side of Heaven, and it better prepares us for what is on the other side of earth: Heaven.

Concluding Thoughts on Money and Covenant

The best book I have ever read on money and eternity is *Money, Possessions, and Eternity* by Randy Alcorn. An eternal perspective is critical when interpreting money in our culture. Equally important is a covenant perspective to interpreting money in our culture. The problem with an eternal perspective (not that there is one) is that it seems like eternity is a long ways away. The value in a covenant perspective is that it *connects* Heaven with earth. This is a critical missing link in Christianity. I believe that if you embrace a covenant perspective on life, you can cross the bridge to an eternal perspective. Your life will be transformed and your life will be renewed.

---

[185] Ibid, 350.

If the relationships with covenant are applied, money will be put in its proper place in our lives. Covenant trumps money. Under covenant, the focus in life shifts from "me" to "we." This paradigm shift will have a dramatic effect on our handling of money.

Ultimately, in the Covenant Renewal Model, the focus in life shifts from an earthly perspective to a heavenly perspective. Covenant relationships move us from the temporal to the eternal. We move from fleshly perspectives to a spiritual perspective. A covenant relationship with God has a higher value than money. In this, we gain authenticity.

Money is not bad; it is a tool, a necessary tool. The covenant mind-set leaves us wanting "a little more covenant" instead of "a little more money." How can I free myself from the love of and the worry about money? I free myself by entering into a covenant with God. It is a covenant whose roots are not in a contract, but a relationship. When we focus on covenant, we stop focusing on money. Money will take care of itself. God will take care of you!

Chapter 14 Reflection and Discussion: Creating Covenant

1. What is the connection between money and materialism?

2. What is the connection between money and poverty?

3. Define rich!

4. Do you live within your means?

5. Define generous giving, as well as generous living.

6. Do you need divine intervention regarding your money?

7. Identify a verse from the Bible that will give you peace and direction concerning your money or the lack of it.

8. Find a story from the Bible that addresses the proper use of money. Then find a story where money was used improperly.

CHAPTER 15

SPIRIT, SOUL, BODY AND COVENANT

The Bible says, "Now may the God of peace Himself sanctify you entirely; and may your spirit and soul and body be preserved complete, without blame at the coming of our Lord Jesus Christ." (1 Thessalonians 5:23). This verse is the final verse I give you on covenant, though there are many others. This chapter is the final chapter of this book. The God of peace, interpreted, the *God of covenant,* will sanctify us entirely. Part of this deal maker is the inclusion of the whole person: spirit, soul and body.

Platonic thought says the soul is good and the body is bad. Plato was wrong. Whatever is wrong with us, God redeems through His covenant with us. God would not preserve something that is evil and sinful. God, in covenant, sanctifies us entirely. In that process God transforms our life, which includes spirit, soul, and body. A covenant relationship with God is His full meal deal for us. We lose nothing and we gain everything in the Covenant Renewal Model. God loses nothing and gains everything in the Covenant Renewal Model too. He gets us! I do not mean this in an arrogant way. It was God's idea, not ours, to live in covenant. It was God's idea to have us share in His inheritance in Heaven for all of eternity. We mean something to God. You mean something to God! Don't you get it? God loves you! That is what a covenant relationship is all about. It is our opportunity to experience His love! To experience God is to experience love. To experience love is to experience God. God is love. His covenant is a love covenant.

Life can take its toll on us human beings. Live long enough and you, too, will be affected by life. I love getting Christmas letters from people. Generally, they are a summary of the highlights of the year of the family sending the letter. They should be called brag letters. What they actually are is a series of events in their life that make my life look pathetic! The section you are about to read is about real life. I have little to brag about except what God has done for me. I credit Him with all that is good in my life.

There are three areas I want to relate to covenant in this closing chapter. Actually, covenant relates to them more than the other way around. Our self-esteem is impacted by covenant as is our emotions. I also want to say a word about something we each have: addictions. Most addictions are good; some are not so good. This may be the most practical of all the chapters you read in this book. Certainly, it is the most transparent chapter. I believe my self-esteem is connected with my spirit. I believe my emotions are connected to my soul. I believe addictions are connected to my body. All three are affected by a covenant relationship with God.

Self-Esteem and Spirit

Whatever self-esteem I had as a child, school took care of that. School did not make me feel smarter; it made me feel dumber! Grading on a curve was torture for me, elation for others. I now realize I made lots of scholarship money for my friends in high school with my grades. My crummy testing abilities enabled them to score above me on a curve, giving them the grades needed to get scholarships to college. You are welcome! There are some straight "A" students who owe their success in part to me!

It was popular in the 1960s to begin school on the younger side of life rather than the later side of life. Having a September birthday meant I was always on the small side of things, and that is the understatement of the century. I will write more on that as you hear my story of low or no self-esteem.

In the first grade they discovered I struggled with hearing the sounds of certain letter combination. I was separated from my classmates and was taught "phonics." I still cannot make certain sounds. My self-esteem, though I did not know what it was at that time, had been affected.

In the third grade I was standing in line with my classmates, one in front of the other with hands to our sides, not touching or moving (yeah right, a third grade boy not touching or moving—the military doesn't even require that) and the girl behind me barfed. That's right, she barfed. In the 1960s the most sought after winter coat was a fake fur one with a big hood. My hood was not on my head and served as a perfect barf bag for the girl behind me. I was known as barf bag for many days following that dreadful event. School can be a real treat! My self-esteem took another hit.

In the sixth grade (I must move this along as I could write volumes on the horrors of my life), I vividly remember a game of flag football. Girls and boys were combined back in the dark ages when I was in grade school. The teacher chose two captains and each captain picked the people to be on their team. The picking of teams took longer than the game. I now see this as a tremendous teaching technique when you have nothing to teach. Of course, I was chosen last because I was the shortest, the chubbiest and the smallest boy on the field. The one time I did get the ball, it was only because the teacher made the quarterback give it to me and I proceeded to drop the ball. What self-esteem?

In junior high gym class, I had to "dress down" and "shower" for the first time in my life with total strangers. I remember going shopping with my mom for my "required" P.E. clothes before the school year began. What a treat to buy those "special" items with my mother. This was another low point in my life.

I remember that dreaded first day of gym class. Mr. Finn walked in and barked, "Everybody strip down and put on your gym clothes." I was terrified. I was afraid to look at the other boys, and the one boy I did look at accidentally looked like a gorilla. For a seventh grader this is a major crisis. We talk about a financial crisis. We have all read about the Cuban missile crisis. I was in a crisis.

I quickly stripped only to realize my next great crisis: Which way does an athletic supporter (a.k.a. jockstrap) go on? It looked more like a hat than anything else. I used all previous learning from my past and thought the label went in the back. Crisis solved. WRONG! I heard loud laughter break out in a split second. It was laughter directed at me and the fact I had put my jockstrap on backwards. I suppose I would have laughed too had it not been me. My self-esteem was knocked down yet another notch at the ripe old age of 11.

Move over junior high, here comes four years of living hell, otherwise known as high school. Of course, it did not help being 4 foot 9 inches tall and weighing in at 74 pounds! We were required to have a red pen in my ninth grade creative writing class. During the 55-minute class, I began to daydream, using the pen as a mechanism for hiding the terror on my face. I thought the cap was on the ink end of the pen. It was not.

For nearly 55 minutes I covered my face with red ink. I did not know I had done this. The bell rang and the girl sitting in front of me turned around and began laughing out of control as did the other students. It was the same kind of laughter I had heard in the locker room in junior high. I thought they were laughing at me as a person, so I ran into the bathroom in tears and then saw what I had done to my face. I wanted to die! I spent 30 minutes trying to rub that hellish red ink off my face. You can't wash off pain. My self-esteem took another hit.

During my junior year, I took the S.A.T. (I still have no idea what that stands for.). I scored in the bottom 5%. This was another highlight of my high school career. My self-esteem took another hit.

This will be the shortest paragraph in this book. It is the paragraph about my love life. Had it not been for one kind girl at church camp I would have had a perfect "0" during high school. This was another blow to my self-esteem.

My freshman year in college I was told that based on my S.A.T. scores, I probably would not do well in school. My self-esteem was ravaged again.

In seminary the president called me in to his office to tell me I might want to consider a profession other than pastoral ministry. After graduation, I pastored a church and lasted only 11 months. It seemed the president of the school was right after all. My self-esteem was whacked again.

Just when you're thinking, *how much more punishment can a person endure*, my "self-esteem," which became "no esteem" began to turn around in January of 1980. A girl by the name of Joanie looked at me through covenant eyes and saw something nobody else saw, including me. I thank God for that girl, who has now been my wife for almost 30 years.

Next to my covenant with God, my covenant relationship with Joanie is Heaven on earth (most of the time). I know I would not be where I am today without her.

It has been said, "All roads lead to Rome." Perhaps, all roads in Christianity lead to covenant. At least for me they do. I have shared with you some of the humorous stories of my life that at the time were very painful. I want you to see that self-esteem and spirit are interrelated. Had I not known God throughout my life, the painful experiences may have been reason enough to end my life. Covenant keeps you close to God, especially when life is brutal. God watched over my fragile spirit in my early years. It was His commitment to His covenant with me that sustained me. Years later, I would see His commitment, His covenant to me. I trust you're beginning to see it for your life. Covenant kept my spirit close to God. Covenant will keep your spirit close to God too, especially when life is brutal and unfair. Covenant says, "I will never leave you or forsake you."

Emotions and Soul

We all have emotions. God has emotions. Emotions and the soul are closely linked together. Covenant can affect our emotions. Further, a covenant relationship with God can affect our emotions in a very positive way. Archibald Hart writes on depression in his book, *"Coping with Depression in the Ministry and other Helping Professions*: "Simply stated it is this: All reactive depression is, in some way, a response to loss."[186] That is at the heart of life on earth. We are continually dealing with loss.

Some cultures deal with loss better than other cultures. It appears Americans do a poor job of dealing with loss, certainly death. Perhaps it is because we have so much that we are not used to loss. Perhaps we are not used to losing anything. Yet life is about gaining and losing. This I know about God and Satan: Satan is always taking things away from Christians, and God is always giving things to us. The Bible says, "The thief comes only to steal and kill and destroy; I came that they may have life, and have it abundantly." (John 10:10). Abundant life in Christ is the covenant relationship. A premise of covenant is

---

[186] Hart, *Coping with Depression in the Ministry and Other Helping Professions* (Dallas, London, Sydney, Singapore: Word Publishing, 1984), 42.

that even in death nothing is lost. God is forever redeeming that which is temporarily lost. Depression results when there is a loss in our life. A covenant relationship with God can paralyze depression. I have personally experienced this power of God in the years since Kevin went to Heaven.

Every person has damaged emotions. I have damaged emotions. You have damaged emotions. Welcome to planet earth. There have been some great books written on the subject of damaged emotions. David Seamands writes about the healing and recovery of damaged emotions. Another good author is Edwin H. Friedman, who wrote *Generation to Generation*. He talks much about our family of origin. He teaches on how to use differentiation to become balanced in life emotionally. He writes, "From a family systems point of view, stress is less the result of some quantitative notion such as 'overwork' and more the effect of our position in the triangle of our families." [187] For Friedman, families, which are supposed to be a blessing, can sometimes be an emotional drain. Covenanting with God can ease the emotional stress this creates.

I believe damaged emotions can be healed with covenant relationships. I have given evidence and definition in this book to support this claim. A covenant relationship with God will touch our damaged emotions every single time because God in covenant first touches our soul. When our soul is touched by God, our damaged emotions are healed by God.

As a child I experienced divorce. As an adult I have experienced the death of a child. These are the two big life-changing events in my life. Events like this will either take you away from God or draw you to God. You either become bitter, or you become better. I became better; most do not! I am speaking to any who have walked away from God during a hard place in life. He wants to enter into a covenant relationship with you. He wants to heal your damaged emotions. I qualify for one who has damaged emotions. You probably do too. The healing of my damaged emotions is in direct proportion to the extent I have availed myself of God's invitation to a covenant relationship with Him.

I urge you to open up your soul to God. To open up your soul is to open up your emotions to God. Open up your soul, your spirit, your body to covenant. Covenant is the bed upon which these areas of life can find rest.

---

[187] Friedman, *Generation to Generation*, 1.

Contemplate how long you have carried a damaged emotion, an event, a circumstance, a person, or a situation in which the pain has not gone away. I urge you to enter into a covenant relationship with God so He can heal your damaged emotions, your soul.

Your emotional health is dependent on a covenant relationship with God. Your mental health may be dependent on a covenant relationship with God. Your physical health may be dependent on a covenant relationship with God. Certainly, your spiritual well-being is completely dependent on a covenant relationship with God. The longer I walk in covenant with God, the healthier I become. The longer you walk in a covenant with God, the healthier you will become.

Addictions and Body

My experience with addictions may not be your experience. Nobody is free from addictions. The myth in Christianity is that when we are in Christ, we are freed from addictions. While I believe God sets us free from harmful addictions, we nonetheless possess addictions in some form or another throughout our life. I do not make excuses for unhealthy addictions. I also do not pretend addictions are not a part of life.

This book is not about addictions. It is about a covenant relationship with God and how this unique relationship can impact addictions. Our body is the stage upon which addictions act out the play. We must always make room for covenant to be on the stage at all times. The theme of covenant is simple: The more I am in union with God, the less control addictions will have over my body. Putting it another way, the closer I move to God, the further I move away from addictions. Dr. Hart writes in *Adrenaline and Stress:* "Whenever we are threatened physically or psychologically, a chain of responses is set in motion to prepare us for what has been described as the 'fight or flight' response. More accurately, it should be called the 'fight, fright, or flight response.'" [188] A covenant relationship with God equips us to fight, keeps us from fright, and never gives us a need to run from our problems.

---

[188] Hart, *Adrenaline and Stress* (Dallas, London, Vancouver, Melbourne: Word Publishing, 1995), 7.

Addictions can affect every area of our lives. Hart writes, "So before you golf, jog, cycle, ski on your Nordic Track, do your pushups, or even eat your fish, do one important thing: make sure you are at peace with yourself and the world."[189] As I have stated repeatedly throughout this book, the only way I know to gain genuine lasting peace is to have a covenant relationship with God. Then all of life falls into place. Life becomes a symphony. Your life becomes the strings upon which God makes the music.

I am not minimizing addictions. I am maximizing covenant. My addictions become subdued, corralled by a covenant relationship with God. I do not believe they totally all go away this side of Heaven. A recovering alcoholic will tell you this. So will a recovering pornography addict. But there can be total and complete victory. That is the point of a covenant relationship with God. You and I can have total and complete victory when we live in covenant with God.

Assuming God wants me addicted only to Him, addiction will remain a part of life this side of Heaven. It is a journey of the soul. Referencing the late Dag Hammarskjöld, who once stated, "The longest journey of any person is the journey inward." In *The Emotionally Healthy Church*, Scazzero says: "Most of us feel much more equipped to manipulate objects, control situations, and 'do' things than take that very long journey inward."[190] The path of the Covenant Renewal Model is the path that leads to the long journey inward. Once inside, we find God. Once we find God, we are able to better deal with issues of the spirit, soul and body.

Scazzero, in the work I just mentioned, has some excellent advice for leaders and leaders of churches. The advice is so good that it can be applied to addictions, emotions, and self-esteem. He gives six principles that lead to emotional health. I suggest they also lead to a covenant relationship with God. They are:

"1. Look beneath the iceberg.

2. Break the power of the past.

3. Live in brokenness and vulnerability.

---

[189] Ibid, 100.

[190] Scazzero & Bird, *The Emotionally Healthy Church* (Grand Rapids, Mich.: Zondervan, 2003), 72.

4. Receive the gift of limits.

5. Embrace grieving and loss.

6. Make incarnation your model for loving well."[191]

Look past yourself. Give God your past. Live in brokenness of spirit. Receive the gift of humanity with its need for God. Embrace grief and loss as temporary. Make a covenant relationship with God the model so others can see Christ in you as you live in love.

God cares about the whole person: spirit, soul, and body. When I first heard about the Covenant Renewal Model over four years ago, a light came on inside my heart, my mind, my soul. I discovered that a covenant relationship with God strips away everything that has gummed onto my life. Covenant leaves just God and me. Covenant leaves just God and you. He leaves us with a simple invitation, not a scolding. His invitation is similar to the invitation in the Garden of Eden, when He said to Adam, "Where are you?" (Genesis 3:9).

Don't hide from the invitation. Come out from behind the bushes and receive a covenant relationship with God. It is the solution to life this side of Heaven. I call this incredible relationship *Heaven's covenant with earth*. By the way, earth has a name. It has many names. For me "earth" translates to "Randy Robert Butler." Your translation will be your name. Heaven has only one translation: God!

---

[191] Ibid, 193.

Chapter 15 Reflection and Discussion: Creating Covenant

1. What is the connection between your spirit and the Holy Spirit?

2. Is your soul in intimate communion with God? What steps will you take to make it a better covenant relationship?

3. Is Jesus Christ being glorified through your body and life? How so?

4. What do you need God to do in your heart at this very moment?

5. Describe, define the Covenant Renewal Model.

6. How can you share the Covenant Renewal Model through your life?

7. Identify a verse from the Bible that empowers you to live closer to God.

8. Find a story in the Bible of a person who really walked with God.

THE REST OF MY STORY AND COVENANT

A covenant relationship with God is my solution for Christianity in the 21st century. I have fleshed it out with Moderns, Postmoderns, Scripture, the Holy Spirit, spiritual formation, Heaven, marriage, children, church history, spiritual warfare, morality, the Ten Commandments, community, vocation, witness, church, money, spirit, soul, and body.

I have articulated what it looks like and how it works. I have taken Christianity beyond reason and science back to its roots of faith and experience and miracles. It is a miracle each time God touches the human heart, much less transforms it. Faith is seeing the unseen. A covenant relationship with God requires faith. It is a relationship that is spiritual. It touches the mental, the emotional, the physical, but is birthed within the spiritual realm.

I have shared with you through my stories the experiences of covenant. They are real. They warrant being told and considered by all people. If real for others, this testimony of a covenant relationship with God will spread quickly. If this testimony is just another theory, then it will die just as quickly as it began. This is not a new paradigm. It is as old as the Garden of Eden. I have simply dusted it off so that you can see it for yourself.

Greer says in his book, *Mapping Postmodernism*: "Because of its complicity with modernism, systematic theology—in both its liberal and conservative traditions—reduced our ability to hear the voice of God."[192]

---

[192] Greer, *Mapping Postmodernism, a Survey of Christian Options* (Downers Grove, Ill.: InterVarsity Press, 2003), 20.

Hearing God's voice is central to the Covenant Renewal Model. Discerning His voice is equally important. Covenant expands the capacity to hear God's voice, whereas previous theology has limited such an experience.

The authors of *The Language of the Emerging Church* state, "Modernity was preoccupied with correct beliefs and believing, but only in a narrowly defined sense. For moderns, so enthralled with rational, conceptual correctness, 'believe' was normally married to the conjunction 'that,' rather than the preposition 'in.'"[193]

I have defined a covenant relationship with God not so much in a rational way as much I have defined it experientially. I have defined covenant in a descriptive way rather than a prescriptive way. Moderns love prescriptions. I have not described a pill for humanity. I have described an interpersonal relationship with God.

Correct beliefs have never been enough, yet correct beliefs are what most Christians over the past two hundred years have settled for. Donald Miller says, "I think the most important thing that happens within Christianity is when a person falls in love with Jesus."[194] I make this statement quite often: "I love Jesus with all my heart." In fact, it's a statement we have people repeat when they join our church.That says it all, for me.

I sometimes close my prayers in church by saying, "And Lord, please keep us clean and close to You." Another way of saying that is in the words of the missionary Bill Borden whose life was abruptly halted by a fatal illness during his first days in Africa. When his father learned of his death and received his son's Bible, the wealthy father who owned Borden's Dairy thereafter gave millions to missions.

Thousands of missionaries felt called to the mission field after being inspired by the life of Bill Borden. Written in his Bible are the following words, which I now have in my Bibles and it is my theme for life: "No Reserve! No Retreat! No Regret! For outside a faith in Christ, there is no explanation for such a life."

That is a covenant relationship with God. It is not a religion. It is a relationship. Sometimes, relationships do not make sense. This relationship

---

[193] Sweet et al, *The Language of the Emerging Church* (Grand Rapids, Ill: Zondervan, 2003), 42.

[194] Miller, *Blue Like Jazz*, 86.

with God makes perfect sense to me, because I am *experiencing* it. You must take the words of this book and make them your own in an experience with God.

The Covenant Renewal Model is not about legislating morality. Larry Crabb writes, "It's about time to go beneath the moralism that assumes that the church's job is done when it instructs people in biblical principles and then exhorts them to do right."[195] The intent of covenant is to have an encounter with God, a good encounter that lasts a lifetime.

Larry Shelton writes, "However, the faithful are no longer motivated by duty or obligation, but by obedience to their inward knowledge of a God—knowledge which transforms the Law from an external standard that legislates moral action into an internal spiritual attitude of God's Law written upon their hearts."[196]

When a relationship is governed by duty, it flows from the head. When a relationship is governed by obedience, it flows from the heart. The Covenant Renewal Model flows from the heart. My center of gravity is no longer my mind, but my heart. When my heart is transformed, my mind follows. This is a paradigm shift away from modernity and its claims of propositional thinking.

It is amazing to me how far from Scripture the church can find itself. With so many great theologians in ages past, I am puzzled about how we ended up where we are. An example of this would be the subject of Heaven.

I am amazed that Randy Alcorn is one of a handful of authors to write with such clarity and revelation on the subject. Praise God for Randy Alcorn.

Likewise, I am amazed that so little has been written on a covenant relationship with God. Plenty has been written on the dissection of the standard eight covenants in Scripture. But little has been said about covenant in the terms described by Larry Shelton. Praise God for Larry Shelton. I am adding to his foundation giving covenant skin. Larry Shelton laid the theological foundation for covenant. I am building the walls. I am excited for the one who will come in after me and do all the interior decorating.

---

[195] Crabb, *Connecting, a Radical New Vision*, xvi.

[196] Shelton, *Cross & Covenant, Interpreting the Atonement for 21st Century Mission*, 76.

I love the way Leonard Sweet has framed the issue in *Summoned to Lead:* "A professor at a ripe old age was still studying, reading, and learning as if he were a first-year student. In a response to someone's 'Why?' he responded, 'I would rather my students drink from a running stream than a stagnant pool.'"[197]

Christianity has been offering water from a cesspool for far too long. It may be fine for the pets to drink out of the toilet bowl, but not the children of God. God is the headstream of a river that is flowing by your heart. He has invited you and I to drink from the water He offers. It is fresh, living water. The name of the river is Covenant. God desires for the Covenant River to flow through the regions of your heart and life. This river water is pure, fresh, and transforming.

The Rest of My Story

The rest of my story is not about the half of me that died in January 2003; rather my story is about the half that is alive. My covenant relationship with God has given me new life. I am going to make it to the finish line. When I cross the finish line, I will have people waiting to see me.

First and foremost I will see Jesus. I will spend the first 1,000 years thanking Him for eternal life and for all the other things He has done for me.

Then at some point I anticipate Him saying to me, "You have waited long enough." At that moment, He will have a 16-year-old boy by his side whose name is Kevin. Kevin and I will pick up right where we left off on earth. The reunion in Heaven is real. The Bible says, "Brethren, I do not regard myself as having laid hold of it yet; but one thing I do: forgetting what lies behind and reaching forward to what lies ahead, I press on toward the goal for the prize of the upward call of God in Christ Jesus." (Philippians 3:13–14). I am looking forward. I am looking to Heaven. I am looking forward to renewed, restored, redeemed, reconciled relationships.

Has covenant made my pain all go away? No! Has covenant made life on earth the same as life in Heaven? No! Has covenant taken away the loss of my son? No!

---

[197] Sweet, *Summoned to Lead* (Grand Rapids, Mich.: Zondervan, 2004), 129.

Has covenant lessened my pain? Yes! Has covenant made life more like Heaven on earth? Yes! Has covenant lessened the loss of my son? Yes! Covenant this side of Heaven is just that: covenant this side of Heaven. I am not there yet, but until then, I have something that has made life on earth worth living in the midst of personal loss and tragedy.

Kevin's Friends

You represent many people just like you who have lost a friend and are reading this book. I trust this book will help all of you experience God and live life to its fullest, even if the one you love is temporarily gone. As my wife states it, "we now live with a new normal." Nothing will ever be the same. It is simply a new normal. Love God, love one another, and find someone new to love in the name of Jesus. That is what Kevin would tell you from Heaven. He would also tell you to have fun; he finally got what he wanted most in life: to be in Heaven. You will be rejoined with your friend again one day. I look forward to seeing that reunion when each of you sees Kevin for the first time in Heaven.

Kevin's best friend was Dusty Bowers. I spoke with Dusty today on the phone. He was grieving the loss of his best friend. Best friends become best friends because they understand covenant relationships. To all the Dustys who have lost a best friend, we serve a God who will restore all things, especially best friends!

Joanie

One day, some weeks after that eternal week in January of 2003, Joanie and I were having an intense, emotion filled, tear-flowing discussion. She trotted over to the other side of the bedroom, drew her foot across the carpet and said, "There is the line, either you believe God is who He says He is or not. I cannot decide for you. You have to decide for yourself." That was the turning point in my life. It was that event that moved me from what I believed to what I was about to experience. I knew what I was supposed to believe. What I needed was an experience. God met the need of my heart and life and flooded my soul with His presence and has never left. God is real in my life. He can be real in your life, too!

Kristi

My daughter Kristi, who is a stronger Christian than I will ever be, wrote me a note on March 9, 2003 on an offering envelope. I carry it with me in my Bible wherever I go. Kristi captured the heart of the Covenant Renewal Model. She found it before I did. Her note to me says, "I love you with all my heart. I know our family is way different now, but our love is still the same. Just think—Kevin is in Heaven—imagine the firework show from above Disneyland! Life is short—but while it seems like forever we must patiently endure! Don't give up—Kevin hit a home run, but our ball game isn't up yet. Play hard for me. All my love, Kristi."

Our ball game isn't up yet. You need to play hard for someone in your life. I am playing hard for the people in my life. My journey led me to a covenant relationship with God. It is the closest thing to Heaven we can have this side of Heaven. Play hard!

Invitation to a Covenant Relationship with Jesus Christ

The following speech was given by Kristi at the Mayor's Prayer Breakfast on May 1, 2003. If you do not know Jesus as your Savior, or if you have fallen away from God, my daughter said it best at that prayer breakfast.

"Good morning. When I sat down and thought what the word prayer meant to me, a couple of things come to my mind. I thought about my life and the times I've needed to pray. Just so you know a little bit about me: My dad is the pastor at Salem Evangelical Church and all I've ever known is church. I accepted Jesus as my Savior as a little girl and I have never strayed from my faith.

Prayer has always been a huge part of my church; therefore making it a huge part of my life. Prayer was always important to me as an individual because it meant I had a friend I could talk to anytime and he would listen, no matter how ridiculous I sounded. This last January my brother Kevin went to Heaven. When he was in the hospital, prayer was about the only thing I could lean on. Life had never been anything but perfect for my family until this point in my life. I found myself praying with a faith I had never known before.

Never really seeing the answer to my prayer the way I wanted to see it, I became very frustrated. I began to question if God was going to do what I asked Him.

I was doing everything right in my mind. I had a strong solid relationship with the Lord and I prayed with faith that would move mountains, yet Kevin wasn't improving. The night he went to Heaven, I realized God's wisdom is far greater and much higher than my prayers. It says in the Bible that God's thoughts are not our thoughts, neither are His ways our ways, and I clearly understood that.

So why did I pray for something I wasn't going to get? Well, because faith is the foundation of my relationship with God, and I need that faith to believe that my God is all-knowing, all-powerful and in control of my life. Prayer forces me to daily have a conversation with my Savior and my friend.

I stand before you today as someone who doesn't understand God, but someone who trusts God. I cannot tell you I love my life right now because honestly I don't. However, I can tell you that myself, along with my mom and dad, are going to make it. I love the Lord more than ever.

I promise you a relationship with the Lord is worth it. We live in a world full of sin, and it takes a fully committed heart to survive and not let the devil win.

I constantly tell myself that life is short, and Heaven is just a breath away. But at the same time, I had better do something for God's kingdom because my short life could mean eternity for someone else.

Sure, I have reason to sit at home and cry my life away, but I choose not to let the devil win this one. I find my strength in the Lord and I will forever serve Him.

Today as you pray, have more faith than you have ever known, but trust God even more. I don't know what the future holds, but I know who holds the future. Thank you."

Conclusion Reflection and Discussion: Creating Covenant

1. The next chapter is yours to write. How can the Covenant Renewal Model shape the remainder of your life?

2. Will you allow tragedy to become God's victory in your life?

3. How does the covenant model prepare you for the future mountains you will undoubtedly climb?

4. Do you find the word "quit" in covenant? (The correct answer is No!)

5. In what ways do you see love in the Covenant Renewal Model?

6. Start living in a covenant relationship with God, within your own soul, and with others.

7. Identify a verse from the Bible with the word "covenant" in it.

8. Find a story from the Bible that reflects the Covenant Renewal Model. (Hint: There is a story on every single page of the Bible!)

APPENDIX

The purpose of this appendix is to give you a concise picture of Jesus. There are many ways it can be used in a Bible study. I have used this appendix in my own church on numerous occasions. I have used it in the classroom as well.

You may look for themes within the texts as one means for observation.

You may look for keywords within the text as another means for finding the puzzle pieces of covenant.

You may look for reoccurring phrases that define Jesus and our relationship to Him.

You may simply read it in its entirety in one sitting and do so for a week. You will discover Jesus in ways you have never known Him before.

Likewise, you may read it one line at a time and let each line speak truth into your heart! This is my favorite approach to this appendix.

The intent of this appendix is to lead you to a covenant relationship with God through His Son Jesus Christ. I pray the Holy Spirit will guide you as you use the life of Jesus in Scripture as your foundation for covenant relationships.

WHAT JESUS SHOWED US AND TOLD US

Compiled by Randy R. Butler

*denotes a quote of Jesus from The New American Standard Bible

MATTHEW

1. 3:15* "Fulfill all righteousness."

2. 3:15 Jesus was baptized.

3.   3:16 The Spirit of God descended on Jesus.

4.   3:17 This is my Son with whom I am pleased.

5.   4:1 Jesus was led by the Spirit into the wilderness to be tempted by the devil.

6.   4:2 He fasted 40 days and 40 nights and became hungry.

7.   4:4* "It is written, 'Man shall not live on bread alone, but on every word that proceeds out of the mouth of God.'"

8.   4:7* "It is written, 'You shall not put the Lord your God to the test.'"

9.   4:10* "Go Satan! For it is written, 'You shall worship the Lord your God, and serve Him only.'"

10.   4:17* Jesus began to preach and say, "Repent, for the kingdom of heaven is at hand."

11.   4:19* "Follow Me, and I will make you fishers of men."

12.   4:23 Jesus taught in the synagogues, proclaiming the gospel of the kingdom and healing disease and sickness.

13.   5:3* "Blessed are the poor in spirit."

14.   5:4* "Blessed are those who mourn."

15.   5:5* "Blessed are the gentle."

16.   5:6* "Blessed are those who hunger and thirst for righteousness."

17.   5:7* "Blessed are the merciful."

18.   5:8* "Blessed are the pure in heart."

19.   5:9* "Blessed are the peacemakers."

20.   5:10* "Blessed are those who have been persecuted for the sake of righteousness."

21.   5:11* "Blessed are you when people insult you and persecute you, and falsely say all kinds of evil against you."

22.   5:12* "Rejoice and be glad."

23.   5:13* "You are the salt of the earth."

24.   5:14* "You are the light of the world."

25. 5:16* "Let your light shine before men in such a way that they may see your good works."

26. 5:17* "Do not think that I came to abolish the Law or the Prophets; I did not come to abolish but to fulfill."

27. 5:19* "Whoever then annuls one of the least of these commandments, and teaches others to do the same, shall be called least in the kingdom of heaven; but whoever keeps and teaches them, he shall be called great in the kingdom of heaven."

28. 5:20* "Unless your righteousness surpasses that of the scribes and Pharisees, you will not enter the kingdom of heaven."

29. 5:22* "Everyone who is angry with his brother shall be guilty before the court; ... and whoever says 'You fool,' shall be guilty enough to go into the fiery hell."

30. 5:24* "First be reconciled to your brother, and then come and present your offering."

31. 5:25* "Make friends quickly with your opponent at law."

32. 5:28* "Everyone who looks at a woman with lust for her has already committed adultery with her in his heart."

33. 5:29* "If your right eye makes you stumble, tear it out."

34. 5:30* "If your right hand makes you stumble, cut it off."

35. 5:32* "Everyone who divorces his wife, except for the cause of unchastity, makes her commit adultery; and whoever marries a divorced woman commits adultery."

36. 5:34–36* "Make no oath at all."

37. 5:37* "Let your statement be, 'Yes, yes' or 'No, no'"

38. 5:39* "Do not resist an evil person; but whoever slaps you on your right cheek, turn the other to him also."

39. 5:40* "If anyone wants to sue you, and take your shirt, let him have your coat also."

40. 5:41* "Whoever forces you to go one mile, go with him two."

41. 5:42* "Give to him who asks of you, and do not turn away from him who wants to borrow from you."

42. 5:44* "Love your enemies and pray for those who persecute you."

43. 5:48* "Therefore, you are to be perfect, as your heavenly Father is perfect."

44. 6:1* "Beware of practicing your righteousness before men to be noticed by them."

45. 6:3* "When you give to the poor, do not let your left hand know what your right hand is doing."

46. 6:6* "When you pray, go into your inner room, close your door and pray to your Father who is in secret."

47. 6:7* "When you are praying, do not use meaningless repetition."

48. 6:9–13* "Pray, then, in this way: Our Father who is in heaven, hallowed be Your name. Your kingdom come. Your will be done, on earth as it is in heaven. Give us this day our daily bread. And forgive us our debts, as we also have forgiven our debtors. And do not lead us into temptation, but deliver us from evil."

49. 6:14* "If you forgive others … your heavenly Father will also forgive you."

50. 6:15* "If you do not forgive others, then your Father will not forgive your transgressions."

51. 6:17* "When you fast, anoint your head and wash your face."

52. 6:19* "Do not store up for yourselves treasures on earth."

53. 6:20* "Store up for yourselves treasures in heaven."

54. 6:24* "No one can serve two masters; …You cannot serve God and wealth."

55. 6:25* "Do not worry about your life … eat … drink … clothing."

56. 6:33* "Seek first His kingdom and His righteousness."

57. 6:34* "Do not worry about tomorrow."

58. 7:1* "Do not judge."

59. 7:5* "First take the log out of your own eye."

60. 7:6* "Do not give what is holy to dogs, and do not throw your pearls before swine."

61. 7:7* "Ask, and it will be given to you; seek, and you will find; knock, and it will be opened to you."

62. 7:12* "Treat people the same way you want them to treat you."

63. 7:13* "Enter through the narrow gate."

64. 7:15* "Beware of the false prophets."

65. 7:21* "Not everyone who says to Me, 'Lord, Lord,' will enter the kingdom of heaven, but he who does the will of My Father who is in heaven will enter."

66. 7:24* "Everyone who hears these words of Mine and acts on them, may be compared to a wise man."

67. 7:26* "Everyone who hears these words of Mine and does not act on them, will be like a foolish man."

68. 7:29 He taught them as one having authority.

69. 8:3 He stretched out His hand and touched the leper.

70. 8:13 He healed the paralyzed servant of the centurion.

71. 8:15 He healed Peter's mother-in-law.

72. 8:16 He cast out demons and healed all who were sick.

73. 8:18 He saw the crowd and gave orders to depart to the other side.

74. 8:22* "Follow Me, and allow the dead to bury their own dead."

75. 8:24 He was asleep in the boat in a storm.

76. 8:26 He rebuked the wind and it became perfectly calm.

77. 8:32 He cast out demons from two men into some pigs.

78. 8:34 Jesus is asked to leave.

79. 9:2 He forgave sin.

80. 9:6 He heals the paralytic.

81. 9:9 He said, "Follow Me," to Matthew.

82. 9:10 Jesus dined with many sinners.

83. 9:13* "Go and learn what this means."

84. 9:22 Jesus healed a woman who believed all she had to do was touch Him for healing.

85. 9:25 Jesus brought a dead girl back to life.

86. 9:29–30 Jesus healed two blind men.

87. 9:33 Jesus cast a demon out of a mute man.

88. 9:35 Jesus went to the cities and the villages teaching in their synagogues, proclaiming the gospel of the kingdom, and healing every kind of disease and sickness.

89. 9:36 Seeing the multitudes, He felt compassion.

90. 9:38* "Beseech the Lord of the harvest to send out workers into His harvest."

91. 10:1 He summoned His twelve disciples and gave them authority to cast out unclean spirits and to heal every kind of disease and every kind of sickness.

92. 10:5 Jesus sent out these twelve after instructing them.

93. 10:5–6* "Do not go to … the Gentiles … but rather go to the lost sheep of the house of Israel."

94. 10:7* "Preach saying, 'The kingdom of heaven is at hand.'"

95. 10:8* "Heal the sick, raise the dead, cleanse the lepers, cast out demons."

96. 10:9* "Do not acquire gold, or silver, or copper for your money belts."

97. 10:11 He told the twelve that when they arrived at a city, they were to inquire who is worthy in a city and stay there.

98. 10:12* "As you enter the house, give it your greeting."

99. 10:14* "Whoever does not receive you … shake the dust off your feet."

100. 10:16* "Be shrewd as serpents and innocent as doves."

101. 10:17* "But beware of men."

102. 10:19* "Do not worry about how or what you are to say."

103. 10:20* "It is not you who speak, but it is the Spirit of your Father who speaks in you."

104. 10:22* "It is the one who has endured to the end who will be saved."

105. 10:23* "Whenever they persecute you in one city, flee to the next."

106. 10:26* "Do not fear them."

107. 10:27* "What I tell you in the darkness, speak in the light; and what you hear whispered in your ear, proclaim upon the housetops."

108. 10:28* "Do not fear those who kill the body."

109. 10:31* "Do not fear."

110. 10:32* "Everyone who confesses Me before men, I will also confess him before My Father who is in heaven."

111. 10:33* "Whoever denies Me before men, I will also deny him before My Father who is in heaven."

112. 10:34* "I did not come to bring peace, but a sword."

113. 10:37* "He who loves father or mother ... and ... son or daughter more than Me is not worthy of Me."

114. 10:38* "And he who does not take his cross and follow after Me is not worthy of Me."

115. 10:39* "He who has found his life will lose it, and he who has lost his life for My sake will find it."

116. 11:1 He departed from there to teach and preach in their cities.

117. 11:5* "The blind receive sight and the lame walk, the lepers are cleansed and the deaf hear, the dead are raised up, and the poor have the gospel preached to them."

118. 11:20 He began to reproach the cities in which most of His miracles were done because they did not repent.

119. 11:25* "I praise You, Father."

120. 11:28–29* "Come to Me, all who are weary and heavy-laden, and I will give you rest. Take My yoke upon you and learn from Me, for I am gentle and humble in heart, and you will find rest for your souls."

121. 12:13 Jesus healed the man's hand on the Sabbath.

122. 12:15 He healed them all.

123. 12:22 Jesus healed and cast out a demon from a possessed man.

124. 12:30* "He who is not with Me is against Me; and he who does not gather with Me scatters."

125. 12:31* "Whoever speaks against [blasphemes] the Holy Spirit, it shall not be forgiven him."

126. 12:37* "By your words you will be justified, and by your words you will be condemned."

127. 12:50* "Whoever does the will of My Father who is in heaven, he is My brother and sister and mother."

128. 13:3 He spoke many things to them in parables.

129. 13:12* "For whoever has, to him more shall be given, and he will have an abundance; but whoever does not have, even what he has shall be taken away from him."

130. 13:16* "Blessed are your eyes, because they see; and your ears, because they hear."

131. 13:18–23 Parable of the four kinds of seed.

132. 13:24–30 Parable of the tares and wheat.

133. 13:31–32 Parable of the mustard seed.

134. 13:33 Parable of the leaven.

135. 13:36–50 Explanation of the four parables.

136. 13:54 He began teaching in the synagogue.

137. 13:57* "A prophet is not without honor except in he hometown and in his own household."

138. 13:58 He did not do many miracles there because of their unbelief.

139. 14:13 When He heard about John the Baptist's death, He withdrew to a lonely place by Himself.

140. 14:14 He felt compassion and healed the sick.

141. 14:19 He blessed the food and gave it away.

142. 14:22 He sent the multitudes away.

143. 14:23 He went up to the mountain by Himself to pray; He was there alone.

144. 14:25 He came to them walking on the sea.

145. 14:27* "Take courage, it is I; do not be afraid."

146. 14:28 Peter asked Jesus to command him to come to Him on the water.

147. 14:31 Immediately, Jesus stretched out His hand and took hold of him.

148. 14:36 As many as touched the fringe of His cloak were healed.

149. 15:11* "It is not what enters into the mouth that defiles the man, but what proceeds out of the mouth, this defiles the man."

150. 15:24* "I was sent only to the lost sheep of the house of Israel."

151. 15:28 He healed a demon-possessed daughter.

152. 15:30 He healed them.

153. 15:32* "I feel compassion for the people."

154. 15:36 He took the seven loaves and the fish, gave thanks for them, broke them and started giving them to the disciples to give to the people.

155. 15:39 He sent away the crowds.

156. 16:4 He left them and went away.

157. 16:6* "Watch out and beware of the leaven of the Pharisees and Sadducees."

158. 16:15* "But who do you say that I am?"

159. 16:21 He must suffer, be killed, and be raised up on the third day.

160. 16:24* "If anyone wishes to come after Me, he must deny himself, and take up his cross and follow Me."

161. 17:7* "Get up, and do not be afraid."

162. 17:18 Jesus rebukes a demon in a boy and he is healed.

163. 17:20* "If you have faith the size of a mustard seed, you will say to this mountain, 'Move from here to there,' and it will move; and nothing will be impossible to you."

164. 17:21* "This kind does not go out except by prayer and fasting."

165. 17:24–25 Tax collectors inquire about whether or not Jesus pays a particular tax. The answer is, yes.

166. 18:3* "Unless you are converted and become like children, you will not enter the kingdom of heaven."

167. 18:4* "Whoever then humbles himself as this child, he is the greatest in the kingdom of heaven."

168. 18:5* "Whoever receives one such child in My name receives Me."

169. 18:6* "Whoever causes one of these little ones who believe in Me to stumble, it would be better for him to have a heavy millstone hung around his neck, and to be drowned in the depth of the sea."

170. 18:10* "See that you do not despise one of these little ones."

171. 18:11* "For the Son of Man has come to save that which was lost."

172. 18:15* "If your brother sins, go show him his fault in private."

173. 18:16* "But if he does not listen to you, take one or two more with you, so that by the mouth of two or three witnesses every fact may be confirmed."

174. 18:18* "Whatever you will bind on earth shall be bound in heaven; and whatever you loose on earth shall be loosed in heaven."

175. 18:22 The rule for forgiveness is not seven times, but seventy times seven.

176. 18:35* "My heavenly Father will also do the same to you, if each of you does not forgive his brother from your heart."

177. 19:2 He healed great multitudes

178. 19:9* "Whoever divorces his wife, except for immorality, and marries another woman commits adultery."

179. 19:15 Jesus lays His hands on children and prays for them.

180. 19:21* "If you wish to be complete, go and sell your possessions and give to the poor, and you will have treasure in heaven; and come, follow Me."

181. 119:29* Everyone who has left houses or brothers or sisters or father or mother or children or farms for My name's sake will receive many times as much, and shall inherit eternal life."

182. 20:16* "The last shall be first, and the first last."

183. 20:26* "Whoever wishes to become great among you shall be your servant."

184. 20:27* "Whoever wishes to be first among you shall be your slave."

185. 20:28* "The Son of Man did not come to be served, but to serve, and to give His life a ransom for many."

186. 20:34 Moved with compassion, Jesus healed two blind men.

187. 21:12 Jesus cast out all who were buying and selling in the temple.

188. 21:13* "My house shall be called a house of prayer."

189. 21:14 The blind and the lame came to Him in the temple, and He healed them.

190. 21:18 He became hungry.

191. 21:22* "All things you ask in prayer, believing, you will receive."

192. 21:23 He was teaching in the temple.

193. 22:21* "Render to Caesar the things that are Caesar's; and to God the things that are God's.

194. 22:33 They were astonished at His teaching.

195. 22:37* "You shall love the Lord your God with all your heart, and with all your soul, and with all your mind."

196. 22:39* "You shall love your neighbor as yourself."

197. 23:1–39 Seven woes.

198. 24:4* "See to it that no one misleads you."

199. 24:6* "See that you are not frightened."

200. 24:13* "But the one who endures to the end, he will be saved."

201. 24:23* About the antichrist: "Do not believe him."

202. 24:26* About false messiahs and false prophets: "Do not believe them."

203. 24:32 The parable from the fig tree.

204. 24:33* "Recognize that He is near, right at the door."

205. 24:42* "Be on the alert, for you do not know which day your Lord is coming."

206. 24:44* "For this reason you also must be ready."

207. 25:13* "Be on the alert then, for you do not know the day nor the hour."

208. 25:35–36* "For I was hungry, and you gave Me something to eat; I was thirsty, and you gave Me something to drink; I was a stranger, and you invited Me in; naked, and you clothed Me; I was sick, and you visited Me; I was in prison, and you came to Me."

209. 26:26–29 Communion—breaking of bread with the disciples at the Last Supper.

210. 26:30 Jesus sang a hymn with His disciples.

211. 26:36* "Sit here while I go over there and pray."

212. 26:37 Jesus began to be grieved and distressed.

213. 26:38* "Keep watch with Me."

214. 26:39 He fell on His face and prayed.

215. 26:41* "Keep watching and praying that you may not enter into temptation; the spirit is willing, but the flesh is weak."

216. 26:42 He prayed a second time.

217. 26:44 He prayed a third time.

218. 26:52* "Put your sword back into its place; for all those who take up the sword shall perish by the sword."

219. 26:63 Jesus kept silent.

220. 26:67 They spit in His face and beat Him with their fists; and others slapped Him.

221. 27:11* "It is as you say," in answer to Pilate's question, "Are you the King of the Jews?"

222. 27:12 While He was being accused, He did not answer.

223. 27:14 He did not answer the governor in regard to even a single charge, much to the governor's amazement.

224. 27:46* "My God, My God, why have You forsaken Me?"

225. 27:50 Jesus cried out again with a loud voice, and yielded up His spirit.

226. 28:3 His appearance was like lightning and His garment as white as snow.

227. 28:9 Jesus met the women and greeted them. They took hold of His feet and worshipped Him.

228. 28:10* "Do not be afraid; go and take word to My brethren."

229. 28:19–20* "Go therefore and make disciples of all the nations, baptizing them in the name of the Father and the Son and the Holy Spirit, teaching them to observe all that I commanded you; and lo, I am with you always, even to the end of the age."

MARK

230. 1:12 Immediately the Spirit impelled Him to go out into the wilderness.

231. 1:14 He preached the gospel of God.

232. 1:15* "Repent and believe in the gospel."

233. 1:17* "Follow Me, and I will make you become fishers of men."

234. 1:20 Immediately He called them; they left their nets and followed Him.

235. 1:21 He entered the synagogue and began to teach.

236. 1:25 Jesus casts out an unclean spirit.

237. 1:31 Jesus heals Peter's mother-in-law of a fever.

238. 1:34 He healed many who were ill with various diseases and cast out many demons.

239. 1:35 Early in the morning while still dark, He went alone to pray.

240. 1:38* "Let us go … to the towns, so that I may preach there."

241. 1:39 He preached in the synagogues and cast out demons.

242. 1:41 He was moved with compassion.

243. 1:41 He cleansed a man with leprosy.

244. 1:44* "Show yourself to the priest and offer for your cleansing what Moses commanded."

245. 2:2 He was speaking the word to them.

246. 2:5 Seeing their faith, Jesus forgives sin.

247. 2:8 Immediately, Jesus was aware in His spirit.

248. 2:11 Authority to forgive sins—He physically heals a paralytic.

249. 2:13 He was teaching them.

250. 2:14* "Follow Me!"

251. 2:15 He ate with many sinners.

252. 2:17* "I did not come to call the righteous, but sinners."

253. 3:1 He entered again into a synagogue.

254. 3:5 He looked at them with anger, for He was grieved at their hardness of heart.

255. 3:5 He healed the man's hand.

256. 3:7 Jesus withdrew to the sea with His disciples.

257. 3:10 He healed many.

258. 3:13 He went up to the mountains and summoned those whom He Himself wanted.

259. 3:14–15 And He appointed twelve, that they might be with Him, and that He might send them out to preach, and to have authority to cast out demons.

260. 3:20 He came home.

261. 3:23 He began speaking to them in parables.

262. 3:29* "Whoever blasphemes against the Holy Spirit never has forgiveness, but is guilty of an eternal sin."

263. 3:35* "For whoever does the will of God, he is My brother and sister and mother."

264. 4:1 He began to teach again by the sea.

265. 4:2 He was teaching them many things in parables.

266. 4:9* "He who has ears to hear, let him hear."

267. 4:10 As soon as He was alone, His followers, along with the twelve, began asking questions about the parables.

268. 4:24* "Take care of what you listen to."

269. 4:33 With many such parables He spoke the word to them as they were able to hear it.

270. 4:34 He did not speak to them without a parable.

271. 4:34 He explained everything privately to His own disciples.

272. 4:36 And He left the multitude.

273. 4:38 He was in the stern, asleep on the cushion.

274. 4:39* He rebuked the wind and said to the sea, "Hush, be still."

275. 5:8* "Come out of the man, you unclean spirit."

276. 5:30 Jesus immediately perceived that the power proceeding from Him had gone forth.

277. 5:36* "Do not be afraid any longer, only believe."

278. 5:41–42 Jesus brings a 12-year-old dead girl back to life.

279. 6:2 He began to teach in the synagogue.

280. 6:4* "A prophet is not without honor except in his hometown and among his own relatives and in his own household."

281. 6:5 He could do no miracle there except that He laid His hands on a few sick people and healed them.

282. 6:6 He went around the villages teaching.

283. 6:7–9 He summoned the twelve and began to send them out in pairs. He gave them authority over the unclean spirits and instructed them to take nothing for their journey, except a staff—no bread, no bag, no money in their belt.

284. 6:10–11* "Wherever you enter a house, stay there until you leave town. Any place that does not receive you or listen to you, as you go out from there, shake the dust off the soles of your feet for a testimony against them."

285. 6:31* "Come away by yourselves to a secluded place and rest a while."

286. 6:34 He felt compassion for them.

287. 6:34 He began to teach them many things.

288. 6:37* "You give them something to eat."

289. 6:41 Looking up toward Heaven, He blessed the food and broke the loaves and He kept giving them to the disciples.

290. 6:46 He departed to the mountain to pray.

291. 6:48 He came to them walking on the sea.

292. 6:50* "Take courage; it is I, do not be afraid."

293. 7:14* "Listen to Me, all of you, and understand."

294. 7:17 After leaving the multitude, He entered the house.

295. 7:20* "That which proceeds out of the man, that is what defiles the man."

296. 7:29 He cast a demon out of a daughter.

297. 7:33 He took him aside from the multitude by himself.

298. 7:34 He looked up to Heaven.

299. 8:2* "I feel compassion for the people because they have remained with Me now three days and have nothing to eat."

300. 8:6 He gave thanks and broke the loaves and started giving them to His disciples to serve the multitude.

301. 7 After He blessed the fish, He had them served as well.

302. 8:12 He sighed deeply in His spirit.

303. 8:13 He left them.

304. 8:15* "Watch out! Beware of the leaven of the Pharisees and the leaven of Herod."

305. 8:23 He spit on the blind man's eyes and laid His hands on him.

306. 8:25 Again, He laid His hands on the man's eyes.

307. 8:27 He questioned His disciples.

308. 8:29 He continued to question them.

309. 8:30 He warned them to tell no one about Him.

310. 8:31 He began to teach them.

311. 8:34–35* "If anyone wishes to come after Me, he must deny himself, and take up his cross and follow Me. For whoever wishes to save his life will lose it, but whoever loses his life for My sake and the gospel's will save it."

312. 8:38* "For whoever is ashamed of Me and My words in this adulterous and sinful generation, the Son of Man will also be ashamed of him when He comes in the glory of His Father with the holy angels."

313. 9:2 He took Peter, James, and John up to a high mountain by themselves.

314. 9:23* "'If you can?' All things are possible to him who believes."

315. 9:25 He rebuked the unclean spirit.

316. 9:27 Jesus took him by the hand and raised him, and he got up.

317. 9:29* "This kind cannot come out by anything but prayer."

318. 9:31 He was teaching His disciples.

319. 9:35* "If anyone wants to be first, he shall be last of all and servant of all.

320. 9:36 He took a child in His arms.

321. 9:37* "Whoever receives one child like this in My name receives Me; and whoever receives Me does not receive Me, but Him Who sent Me."

322. 9:50* "Have salt in yourselves, and be at peace with one another."

323. 10:1 He once more began to teach them.

324. 10:9* "What therefore God had joined together, let no man separate."

325. 10:11–12* "Whoever divorces his wife and marries another woman commits adultery against her; and if she herself divorces her husband and marries another man, she is committing adultery."

326. 10:13–14 Jesus was indignant when the disciples tried to turn the children away.

327. 10:15* "Whoever does not receive the kingdom of God like a child will not enter it at all."

328. 10:16 He took the children in His arms and began blessing them, laying His hands on them.

329. 10:21 Jesus felt a love for the rich young man.

330. 10:21* "One thing you lack: go and sell all you possess and give to the poor, and you will have treasure in heaven; and come, follow Me."

331. 10:23* "How hard it will be for those who are wealthy to enter the kingdom of God!"

332. 10:31* "Many who are first will be last, and the last, first."

333. 10:32 Again He took the twelve aside.

334. 10:45* "For even the Son of Man did not come to be served, but to serve, and to give His life a ransom for many."

335. 10:52 Jesus heals blind Bartimaeus.

336. 11:12 He became hungry.

337. 11:15–16 He entered the temple and began to cast out those who were buying and selling there. He overturned the tables of the moneychangers and the seats of those who were selling doves. He would not permit anyone to carry goods through the temple.

338. 11:17* "My house shall be called a house of prayer for all the nations. But you have made it a robbers' den."

339. 11:22* "Have faith in God."

340. 11:24* "All things for which you pray and ask, believe that you have received them, and they will be granted you."

341. 11:25* "Whenever you stand praying, forgive, if you have anything against anyone, so that your Father also who is in heaven will also forgive you your transgressions."

342. 11:26* "But if you do not forgive, neither will your Father who is in heaven forgive your transgressions."

343. 11:27 He was walking in the temple.

344. 12:1 He began to speak to them in parables.

345. 12:14 You are truthful, and defer to no one; for You are not partial to any, but teach the way of God in truth.

346. 12:17 * "Render to Caesar the things that are Caesar's, and to God the things that are God's."

347. 12:30–31* "'You shall love the Lord your God with all your heart, and with all your soul, and with all your mind, and with all your strength.' The second is this, 'You shall love your neighbor as yourself.' There is no other commandment greater than these."

348. 12:35 He taught in the temple.

349. 12:37 The crowds enjoyed listening to Him.

350. 12:38* "Beware of the scribes."

351. 12:41 He sat down opposite the treasury and began observing how the people were putting money into the treasury.

352. 13:5* "See to it that no one misleads you."

353. 13:7* "When you hear of wars and rumors of wars, do not be frightened."

354. 13:9* "Be on your guard."

355. 13:11* "Do not worry beforehand about what you are to say, but say whatever is given you in that hour; for it is not you who speak, but it is the Holy Spirit."

356. 13:13* "The one who endures to the end, he will be saved."

357. 13:21* "If anyone says to you, 'Behold here is Christ'; ... do not believe him."

358. 13:23* "Take heed."

359. 13:28* "Now learn the parable from the fig tree."

360. 13:29* "When you see these things happening, recognize that He is near."

361. 13:33* "Take heed, keep on the alert."

362. 13:35* "Therefore, be on the alert."

363. 13:37* "Be on the alert!"

364. 14:17 When it was evening He came with the twelve.

365. 14:22 He took some bread, and after a blessing He broke it; and gave it to them.

366. 14:22* "Take it; this is My body."

367. 14:23 When He had taken a cup, and given thanks, He gave it to them; and they all drank from it.

368. 14:32* "Sit here until I have prayed."

369. 14:33 He began to be very distressed and troubled.

370. 14:34* "My soul is deeply grieved to the point of death; remain here and keep watch."

371. 14:35 He fell to the ground and began to pray.

372. 14:36* "Yet not what I will, but what You will."

373. 14:38* "Keep watching and praying that you may not come into temptation; the spirit is willing, but the flesh is weak."

374. 14:39 Again He went away and prayed the same words.

375. 14:61 He kept silent and gave no answer.

376. 15:5 Jesus made no further answer; Pilate was amazed.

377. 15:37 Jesus uttered a loud cry, and breathed His last.

378. 16:9 He first appeared to Mary Magdalene, from whom He had cast out seven demons.

379. 16:14 He reproached them for their unbelief and hardness of heart.

380. 16:15* "Go into all the world and preach the gospel to all creation."

LUKE

381. 2:46 When He was about 12 years old, His parents found Him in the temple, sitting in the midst of the teachers, both listening to them, and asking them questions.

382. 2:49* "Did you not know that I had to be in My Father's house?"

383. 2:51 He continued in subjection to His parents.

384. 2:52 Jesus kept increasing in wisdom and stature, and in favor with God and men.

385. 3:21–23* Jesus was also baptized, and while He was praying, Heaven was opened, and the Holy Spirit descended upon Him in bodily form like a dove, and a voice came out of Heaven, "You are My beloved Son, in You I am well-pleased."

386. 3:23 Jesus was about thirty years of age when He began His ministry.

387. 4:1–2 Jesus, full of the Holy Spirit, returned from the Jordan and was led about by the Spirit in the wilderness for forty days; and when those days had ended, He became hungry.

388. 4:4* "It is written, 'Man shall not live on bread alone.'"

389. 4:8* "It is written, 'You shall worship the Lord your God and serve Him only.' "

390. 4:12* "It is said, 'You shall not put the Lord you God to the test.'"

391. 4:14 Jesus returned to Galilee in the power of the Spirit.

392. 4:15 He began teaching in their synagogues and was praised by all.

393. 4:16 As was His custom, He entered the synagogue on the Sabbath, and stood up to read.

394. 4:18–19* "The Spirit of the Lord is upon Me, because He anointed Me to preach the gospel to the poor. He has sent Me to proclaim release to the captives, and recovery of sight to the blind, to set free those who are oppressed, to proclaim the favorable year of the Lord."

395. 4:20 He closed the book, gave it back to the attendant, and sat down.

396. 4:24* "No prophet is welcome in his hometown."

397. 4:30 But passing through their midst, He went His way.

398. 4:31 He was taught them on the Sabbath.

399. 4:35* Jesus rebuked him, saying, "Be quiet and come out of him!"

400. 4:39 Standing over Simon's mother-in-law, He rebuked the fever, and it left her.

401. 4:40–41 Laying His hands on every one of them, He healed them. And demons also came out of many.

402. 4:42 When day came, He departed and went to a lonely place.

403. 4:43* "I must preach the kingdom of God to the other cities also, for I was sent for this purpose."

404. 4:44 He kept on preaching in the synagogues of Judea.

405. 5:3 He sat down and began teaching the people from the boat.

406. 5:10* "Do not fear, from now on you will be catching men."

407. 5:13* He stretched out His hand and touched him, saying, "I am willing; be cleansed." And immediately the leprosy left him.

408. 5:15 Great crowds gathered to hear Him and to be healed of their sicknesses.

409. 5:16 But He Himself would often slip away to the wilderness and pray.

410. 5:17 And it came about one day that He was teaching.

411. 5:20 And seeing their faith.

412. 5:24* "'But so that you may know that the Son of Man has authority on earth to forgive sins,'—He said to the paralytic—'I say to you get up, and pick up your stretcher and go home.'"

413. 5:27* To Levi the tax collector: "Follow Me."

414. 5:32* "I have not come to call the righteous but sinners to repentance."

415. 5:36 He told them a parable.

416. 6:6 On another Sabbath, He entered the synagogue and taught.

417. 6:10 Jesus heals a withered hand on the Sabbath.

418. 6:12 He went off to the mountain to pray, and He spent the whole night in prayer to God.

419. 6:13 He called His disciples to Him and chose twelve of them.

420. 6:19 All the people were trying to touch Him, for power was coming from Him and healing them all.

421. 6:27–31* "But I say to you who hear, love your enemies, do good to those who hate you, bless those who curse you, pray for those who mistreat you. Whoever hits you on the cheek, offer him the other also; and whoever takes away your coat, do not withhold your shirt from him either. Give to everyone who asks of you, and whoever takes away what is yours, do not demand it back. Treat others the same way you want them to treat you."

422. 6:35* "But love your enemies, and do good, and lend, expecting nothing in return."

423. 6:36* "Be merciful, just as your Father is merciful."

424. 6:37* "And do not judge, and you will not be judged; and do not condemn, and you will not be condemned; pardon, and you will be pardoned."

425. 6:38* "Give, and it will be given to you. They will pour into your lap good measure—pressed down, shaken together, and running over. For by your standard of measure, it will be measured to you in return."

426. 6:39 He also spoke a parable to them.

427. 6:41* "Why do you look at the speck that is in your brother's eye, but do not notice the log that is in your own eye?"

428. 6:47–49* "Everyone who comes to Me, and hears My words and acts on them, I will show you whom he is like: he is like a man building a house, who dug deep and laid a foundation on the rock; and when a flood occurred, the torrent burst against that house and could not shake it, because it had been well built. But the one who has heard, and has not acted accordingly, is like a man who built a house upon the ground without any foundation; and the torrent burst against it and immediately it collapsed, and the ruin of that house was great."

429. 7:1 He completed all His discourse in the hearing of the people.

430. 7:9* "I say to you, not even in Israel have I found such great faith" (healing of the centurion's servant).

431. 7:13 He felt compassion for her.

432. 7:15 The dead man sat up and began to speak.

433. 7:21 He cured many people of diseases and afflictions and evil spirits, and He gave sight to many who were blind.

434. 7:23* "Blessed is he who does not take offense at Me."

435. 7:36 He entered the Pharisee's house and reclined at the table to eat.

436. 7:47* "For this reason I say to you, her sins, which are many, have been forgiven, for she loved much; but he who is forgiven little, loves little."

437. 8:1 He began going around from one city and village to another, proclaiming and preaching the kingdom of God; and the twelve were with Him.

438. 8:4 He spoke by way of a parable.

439. 8:18* "So take care how you listen; for whoever has, to him more shall be given; and whoever does not have, even what he thinks he has shall be taken away from him."

440. 8:21* "My mother and My brothers are these who hear the word of God and do it."

441. 8:23 But as they were sailing along, He fell asleep.

442. 8:24 When the disciples woke Jesus, He rebuked the wind and the surging waves, and they stopped, and it became calm.

443. 8:33 The demons came out from the man (Legion) and entered the swine.

444. 8:39* "Return to your house and describe what great things God has done for you" (to the man from whom the demons came out).

445. 8:48* "Daughter, your faith has made you well; go in peace" (to the woman who had touched Jesus in a crowd).

446. 8:50* "Do not be afraid any longer; only believe, and she will be made well."

447. 8:55 Jesus brings Jairus' 12-year-old daughter back to life. (Jairus was an official of the synagogue.). When her spirit returned, she got up immediately and Jesus gave orders for something to be given her to eat.

448. 9:1-2 He called the twelve together and gave them power and authority over all the demons, and to heal all diseases. He sent them out to proclaim the kingdom of God, and to heal diseases.

449. 9:10 Taking the disciples with Him, He went to a city called Bethsaida.

450. 9:11 Welcoming the crowds, He spoke to them about the kingdom of God and cured those who had need of healing.

451. 9:16 He took the five loaves and two fish, and looking up to heaven, He blessed them, and broke them, and kept giving them to the disciples to set before the people.

452. 9:18 He was praying alone.

453. 9:23* "If anyone wishes to come after Me, he must deny himself, and take up his cross daily and follow Me."

454. 9:24* "For whoever wishes to save his life will lose it, but whoever loses his life for My sake, he is the one who will save it."

455. 9:26* "For whoever is ashamed of Me and My words, the Son of Man will be ashamed of him when He comes in His glory, and the glory of the Father and of the holy angels."

456. 9:28 He took Peter, John, and James up to the mountain to pray.

457. 9:42 Jesus healed a boy with convulsions.

458. 9:47 Jesus knew what they were thinking in their hearts.

459. 9:48* "Whoever receives this child in My name receives Me, and whoever receives Me receives Him who sent Me; for the one who is least among you, this is the one who is great."

460. 9:56* "For the Son of Man did not come to destroy men's lives, but to save them."

461. 9:59* "Follow Me."

462. 9:60* "Allow the dead to bury their own dead; but as for you, go and proclaim everywhere the kingdom of God."

463. 10:1 The Lord appointed seventy others and sent them in pairs ahead of Him to every city and place where He Himself was going to come.

464. 10:2* "Therefore beseech the Lord of the harvest to send out laborers into His harvest."

465. 10:19–20* "Behold, I have given you authority to tread on serpents and scorpions, and over all the power of the enemy, and nothing will injure you. Nevertheless do not rejoice in this, that the spirits are subject to you, but rejoice that your names are recorded in heaven."

466. 10:21 At that very time, He rejoiced greatly in the Holy Spirit.

467. 10:37* To conclude the parable of the good Samaritan: "Go and do the same."

468. 11:1 While He was praying, His disciples asked Him to teach them to pray.

469. 11:2–4* "When you pray, say: 'Father, hallowed be Your name. Your kingdom come. Give us each day our daily bread. And forgive us our sins, for we ourselves also forgive everyone who is indebted to us. And lead us not into temptation.'"

470. 11:9* "Ask, and it will be given to you; seek, and you will find; knock, and it will be opened to you."

471. 11:14 He cast out a demon who had made a man mute.

472. 11:17 He knew their thoughts.

473. 11:23* "He who is not with Me is against Me; and he who does not gather with Me, scatters."

474. 11:28* "On the contrary, blessed are those who hear the word of God and observe it" (speaking against blessing Mary His mother).

475. 11:35* "Then watch out that the light in you is not darkness."

476. 11:41* "But give that which is within as charity, and then all things are clean for you."

477. 11:39–52 Woes upon the Pharisees.

478. 12:1* "Beware of the leaven of the Pharisees, which is hypocrisy."

479. 12:4* "My friends, do not be afraid of those who kill the body and after that have no more that they can do."

480. 12:5* "But I will warn you whom to fear: fear the One who, after He has killed, has authority to cast into hell; yes, I tell you, fear Him!"

481. 12:7* "Do not fear."

482. 12:8–10* "Everyone who confesses Me before men, the Son of Man will confess him also before the angels of God; but he who denies Me before men will be denied before the angels of God. And everyone who speaks a word against the Son of Man, it will be forgiven him; but he who blasphemes against the Holy Spirit, it will not be forgiven him."

483. 12:11–12* "Do not worry about how or what you are to speak in your defense, or what you are to say; for the Holy Spirit will teach you in that very hour what you ought to say."

484. 12:15* "Beware, and be on your guard against every form of greed."

485. 12:16 He told them a parable.

486. 12:21* "So is the man who lays up treasure for himself, and is not rich toward God."

487. 12:22* "Do not be worry about your life, as to what you will eat; nor for your body, as to what you will put on."

488. 12:24* "Consider the ravens."

489. 12:27* "Consider the lilies."

490. 12:29* "Do not seek what you will eat and what you will drink, and do not keep worrying."

491. 12:31* "But seek His kingdom."

492. 12:32* "Do not be afraid."

493. 12:33* "Sell your possessions and give to charity."

494. 12:35* "Be dressed in readiness, and keep your lamps lit."

495. 12:40* "You too, be ready," regarding the return of Jesus.

496. 13:3* "Unless you repent, you will all likewise perish."

497. 13:5* "Unless you repent, you will all likewise perish."

498. 13:6 He began telling a parable.

499. 13:10 He taught in one of the synagogues on the Sabbath.

500. 13:11–12 Jesus healed a woman who had been sick for 18 years with a spirit.

501. 13:13 He laid His hands on her.

502. 13:22 He passed through from one city and village to another, teaching and proceeding on His way to Jerusalem.

503. 13:24* "Strive to enter through the narrow door; for many, I tell you, will seek to enter and will not be able."

504. 14:1 He went into one of the Pharisee's house on the Sabbath to eat.

505. 14:4 Jesus healed a man with dropsy.

506. 14:7 He began to speak a parable to the invited guests.

507. 14:11* "For everyone who exalts himself will be humbled, and he who humbles himself will be exalted."

508. 14:13* "When you give a reception, invite the poor, the crippled, the lame, the blind."

509. 14:26–27* "If anyone comes to Me, and does not hate his own father and mother and wife and children and brothers and sisters, yes, and even his own life, he cannot be My disciple. Whoever does not carry his own cross and come after Me cannot be My disciple."

510. 14:33* "So then, none of you can be My disciple who does not give up all his own possessions."

511. 15:3 He told them a parable.

512. 15:7* "I tell you that in the same way, there will be more joy in heaven over one sinner who repents than over ninety-nine righteous persons who need no repentance."

513. 15:10* "In the same way, I tell you, there is joy in the presence of the angels of God over one sinner who repents."

514. 16:9* "Make friends for yourselves by means of the wealth of unrighteousness, so that when it fails, they will receive you into the eternal dwellings."

515. 16:10* "He who is faithful in a very little thing is faithful also in much; and he who is unrighteous in a very little thing is unrighteous also in much."

516. 16:13* "No servant can serve two masters … You cannot serve God and wealth."

517. 16:18* "Everyone who divorces his wife and marries another commits adultery, and he who marries one who is divorced from a husband commits adultery."

518. 17:3–4* "Be on your guard! If your brother sins, rebuke him; and if he repents, forgive him. And if he sins against you seven times a day, and returns to you seven times, saying 'I repent,' forgive him."

519. 17:6* "If you had faith like a mustard seed, you would say to this mulberry tree, 'Be uprooted and be planted in the sea'; and it would obey you."

520. 17:14* "Go and show yourselves to the priest" (the healing of the ten lepers).

521. 17:17–8* "Were there not ten cleansed? But the nine—where are they? Was no one found who returned to give glory to God, except this foreigner?"

522. 17:19* "Stand up and go; your faith has made you well."

523. 17:32* "Remember Lot's wife."

524. 17:33* "Whoever seeks to keep his life will lose it, and whoever loses his life will preserve it."

525. 18:1 He told them a parable to show that at all times they ought to pray and not to lose heart.

526. 18:9 He also told this parable to certain ones who trusted in themselves that they were righteous and viewed others with contempt.

527. 18:16–17* "Permit the children to come to Me, and do not hinder them, for the kingdom of God belongs to such as these. Truly I say to you, whoever does not receive the kingdom of God like a child will not enter it at all."

528. 18:22* "One thing you still lack; sell all that you possess and distribute it to the poor, and you shall have treasure in heaven; and come, follow Me."

529. 18:24* "How hard it is for those who are wealthy to enter the kingdom of God!"

530. 18:27* "The things that are impossible with people are possible with God."

531. 18:31 He took the twelve aside and spoke to them.

532. 18:42* "Receive your sight; your faith has made you well."

533. 19:5* "Zaccheus, hurry and come down, for today I must stay at your house."

534. 19:10* "For the Son of Man has come to seek and to save that which was lost."

535. 19:11 He went on to tell them a parable.

536. 19:26* "I tell you that to everyone who has, more shall be given, but from the one who does not have, even what he does have shall be taken away."

537. 19:41 When He approached, He saw the city and wept over it.

538. 19:45 He entered the temple and began to cast out those who were selling.

539. 19:46* "My house shall be a house of prayer, but you have made it a robbers' den."

540. 19:47 He taught daily in the temple.

541. 20:1 While He was teaching the people in the temple area and preaching the gospel, the religious leaders confronted Him.

542. 20:9 He began to tell the people a parable.

543. 20:23 He detected their trickery.

544. 20:25 * "Then render to Caesar the things that are Caesar's, and to God the things that are God's."

545. 20:46–47* "Beware of the scribes, who like to walk around in long robes, and love respectful greetings in the market places, and chief seats in the synagogues and places of honor at banquets, who devour widows' houses, and for appearance's sake offer long prayers. These will receive greater condemnation."

546. 21:1 He looked up and saw the rich putting their gifts into the treasury.

547. 21:2 He saw a poor widow putting in two small copper coins.

548. 21:8* "See to it that you are not misled."

549. 21:9* "When you hear of wars and disturbances, do not be terrified."

550. 21:14* "So make up your minds not to prepare beforehand to defend yourselves."

551. 21:19* "By your endurance you will gain your lives."

552. 21:28* "But when these things begin to take place, straighten up and lift up your heads, because your redemption is drawing near."

553. 21:29 He told them a parable.

554. 21:31* "So you also, when you see these things happening, recognize that the kingdom of God is near."

555. 21:34* "Be on guard, that your hearts may not be weighted down with dissipation and drunkenness and the worries of life."

556. 21:36* "But keep on the alert at all times, praying that you may have strength to escape all these things that are about to take place, and to stand before the Son of Man."

557. 21:37 During the day He taught in the temple, but at evening He went out and spent the night on the mount that is called Olivet.

558. 22:17 He took the cup and gave thanks.

559. 22:19* When He had taken some bread and given thanks, He broke it and gave it to them, saying, "This is My body which is given for you; do this in remembrance of Me."

560. 22:26* "The one who is the greatest among you must become like the youngest, and the leader like the servant."

561. 22:32* "But I have prayed for you, that your faith may not fail; and you, when once you have turned again, strengthen your brothers."

562. 22:39 He came out and proceeded as was His custom to the Mount of Olives.

563. 22:40* "Pray that you may not enter into temptation."

564. 22:41 He withdrew from them about a stone's throw, and He knelt down and began to pray.

565. 22:42* "Father, if You are willing, remove this cup from Me; yet not My will, but Yours be done."

566. 22:44 In agony, He prayed very fervently, and His sweat became like drops of blood.

567. 22:46* "Get up and pray that you may not enter into temptation."

568. 22:51* "Stop! No more of this" (as He healed the ear of the guard).

569. 23:9 Pilate questioned Jesus at some length, but He answered him nothing.

570. 23:34* "Father, forgive them; for they do not know what they are doing."

571. 23:43* "Truly I say to you, today you shall be with Me in Paradise."

572. 23:46 Jesus cried out with a loud voice.

573. 24:25* "O foolish men and slow of heart to believe in all that the prophets have spoken!"

574. 24:27 He explained to them the things concerning Himself in all the Scriptures.

575. 24:30 He took the bread and blessed it, and breaking it, He began giving it to them.

576. 24:38* "Why are you troubled, and why do doubts arise in your hearts?"

577. 24:40 He showed them His hands and His feet.

578. 24:42–43 He took a piece of broiled fish and ate it before them.

579. 24:45 Then He opened their minds to understand the Scriptures.

580. 24:47* "And that repentance for forgiveness of sins would be proclaimed in His name to all the nations, beginning from Jerusalem."

581. 24:49* "But you are to stay in the city until you are clothed with power from on high."

582. 24:50 He led them out as far as Bethany, and He lifted up His hands and blessed them.

JOHN

583. 1:12 But as many as received Him, to them He gave the right to become children of God, even to those who believe in His name.

584. 1:14 And the Word became flesh, and dwelt among us, and we saw His glory, glory as of the only begotten from the Father, full of grace and truth.

585. 1:43* "Follow Me" (to Philip).

586. 2:1–11 Turning water to wine was the beginning of the signs Jesus did in Cana of Galilee to manifest His glory; and His disciples believed in Him.

587. 2:15 He made a scourge of cords, and drove the money changers out of the temple, with the sheep and the oxen that were being sold; and He poured out the coins of the money changers and overturned their table.

588. 2:16* "Take these things away; stop making My Father's house a place of business."

589. 2:23 Many believed as they observed the signs Jesus was doing.

590. 2:24 For His part, Jesus did not entrust Himself to them, for He knew all men.

591. 3:3* "Unless one is born again he cannot see the kingdom of God."

592. 3:5* "Unless one is born of water and the Spirit, he cannot enter into the kingdom of God."

593. 3:7* "Do not be amazed that I said to you, 'You must be born again.'"

594. 3:15* "Whoever believes will in Him have eternal life."

595. 3:16* "Whoever believes in Him shall not perish, but have eternal life."

596. 3:18* "He who believes in Him is not judged; he who does not believe has been judged already."

597. 3:21* "But he who practices the truth comes to the Light, so that his deeds may be manifested as having been wrought in God."

598. 3:22. He spent time with the disciples and baptizing.

599. 4:2 Although Jesus Himself was not baptizing, His disciples were.

600. 4:6 Jesus, weary from His journey, sat down by the well.

601. 4:7* "Give Me a drink."

602. 4:13* "Everyone who drinks of this water will thirst again."

603. 4:14* "Whoever drinks of the water that I will give him shall never thirst."

604. 4:24* "God is spirit, and those who worship Him must worship in spirit and truth."

605. 4:32* "I have food to eat that you do not know about."

606. 4:41 Many more believed because of what Jesus said.

607. 4:48* "Unless you people see signs and wonders, you simply will not believe."

608. 4:50 Jesus heals a father's son.

609. 4:54 Jesus performed a second sign after He came out of Judea into Galilee.

610. 5:5–6 When Jesus saw the man lying by the pool of Bethesda, He knew that he had been in that condition for a long time.

611. 5:8 Jesus healed a man who had been sick for 38 years.

612. 5:13 Jesus slipped away in the crowd.

613. 5:14* "Do not sin anymore, so that nothing worse happens to you."

614. 5:24* "He who hears My word, and believes Him who sent Me, has eternal life, and does not come into judgment, but has passed out of death into life."

615. 5:38* "You do not have His word abiding in you, for you do not believe Him whom He sent."

616. 5:39* "You search the Scriptures because you think that in them you have eternal life."

617. 5:40* "And you are unwilling to come to Me so that you may have life."

618. 5:46–47* "For if you believed Moses, you would believe Me, for he wrote about Me. But if you do not believe his writings, how will you believe My words?"

619. 6:3 Jesus went up on the mountain and sat there with His disciples.

620. 6:5 Jesus saw a large crowd coming to Him.

621. 6:6 He tested Philip; He knew what He intended to do.

622. 6:11 After giving thanks for the bread, Jesus distributed it to those who were seated and did likewise with the fish, giving the people as much as they wanted.

623. 6:12* "Gather up the leftover fragments that nothing will be lost."

624. 6:15 Jesus perceived their intention to come and take Him by force to make Him king; He withdrew again to be alone.

625. 6:19 The disciples saw Jesus walking on the sea.

626. 6:20* "It is I; do not be afraid."

627. 6:27* "Do not work for the food which perishes, but for the food which endures to eternal life."

628. 6:29* "This is the work of God, that you believe in Him whom He has sent."

629. 6:35* "He who believes in Me will never thirst."

630. 6:43* "Do not grumble among yourselves."

631. 6:47* "He who believes has eternal life."

632. 6:51* "I am the living bread that came down out of heaven; if anyone eats of this bread, he will live forever."

633. 6:53–54* "Unless you eat the flesh of the Son of Man and drink His blood, you have no life in yourselves. He who eats My flesh and drinks My blood has eternal life, and I will raise him up on the last day."

634. 6:56* "He who eats My flesh and drinks My blood abides in Me, and I in him."

635. 6:58* "He who eats this bread will live forever."

636. 6:59 He taught in the synagogue in Capernaum.

637. 6:61 Jesus knew that His disciples grumbled at what He said.

638. 6:63* "It is the Spirit who gives life; the flesh profits nothing; the words that I have spoken to you are spirit and are life."

639. 6:64 Jesus knew from the beginning who they were who did not believe, as well as who it was that would betray Him.

640. 6:65* "No one can come to Me unless it has been granted him from the Father."

641. 7:1 After these things, Jesus walked in Galilee (and not in Judea) because the Jews were seeking to kill Him.

642. 7:10 He went up to the feast, but not publicly.

643. 7:14 In the midst of the feast, Jesus went up into the temple and began to teach.

644. 7:24* "Do not judge according to appearance, but judge with righteous judgment."

645. 7:37–38* "If anyone is thirsty, let him come to Me and drink. He who believes in Me, as the Scripture said, 'From his innermost being will flow rivers of living water.'"

646. 8:2 Early in the morning, He came again into the temple, and all the people came to Him; He sat down and taught them.

647. 8:6 Jesus stooped down, and wrote on the ground with his finger.

648. 8:7* "He who is without sin among you, let him be the first to throw a stone at her."

649. 8:8 Again He stooped down and wrote on the ground.

650. 8:11* "I do not condemn you either. Go. From now on sin no more."

651. 8:12* "He who follows Me will not walk in the darkness, but will have the Light of life."

652. 8:19* "If you knew Me, you would know My Father also."

653. 8:20 He taught in the temple.

654. 8:24* "Unless you believe that I am He, you will die in your sins."

655. 8:30 As He spoke, many came to believe in Him.

656. 8:31–32* "If you continue in My word, then you are truly disciples of Mine; and you will know the truth, and the truth will make you free."

657. 8:47* "He who is of God hears the words of God; for this reason you do not hear them, because you are not of God."

658. 8:51* "If anyone keeps My word he will never see death."

659. 8:59 They picked up stones to throw at Him, but Jesus hid Himself and went out of the temple.

660. 9:1 As He passed by him, Jesus saw a man who had been blind from birth.

661. 9:6 He spit on the ground and made clay of the spittle, then applied the clay to the blind man's eyes.

662. 10:9* "I am the door; if anyone enters through Me, he will be saved, and will go in and out and find pasture."

663. 10:27* "My sheep hear My voice, and I know them, and they follow Me."

664. 11:3 He whom You love is sick (speaking of Lazarus).

665. 11:5 Jesus loved Martha and her sister Mary and their brother Lazarus.

666. 11:25* "He who believes in Me will live even if he dies."

667. 11:33 Mary wept; Jesus was deeply moved in spirit and was troubled.

668. 11:35 Jesus wept.

669. 11:38 Jesus was deeply moved within.

670. 11:43–44 Jesus raises Lazarus from the dead.

671. 11:54 Jesus therefore no longer continued to walk publicly among the Jews, but He went away from there to the country near the wilderness into a city called Ephraim and stayed there with the disciples.

672. 12:8* "You always have the poor with you, but do not always have Me."

673. 12:24–26* "Unless a grain of wheat falls into the earth and dies, it remains alone; but if it dies, it bears much fruit. He who loves his life loses it, and he who hates his life in this world will keep it to life eternal. If anyone serves Me, he must follow Me; and where I am, there My servant will be also; if anyone serves Me, the Father will honor him."

674. 12:35–36* "Walk while you have the Light, so that darkness will not overtake you; he who walks in the darkness does not know where he goes. While you have the Light, believe in the Light, so that you may become sons of Light."

675. 12:36 Jesus departed and hid Himself from them.

676. 12:44* "He who believes in Me, does not believe in Me but in Him who sent Me."

677. 12:46* "That everyone who believes in Me will not remain in darkness."

678. 12:48* "He who rejects Me and does not receive My sayings, has one who judges him; the word I spoke is what will judge him at the last day."

679. 13:1 Having loved His own who were in the world, He loved them to the end.

680. 13:5 Jesus washed the disciples' feet.

681. 13:8* "If I do not wash you, you have no part with Me."

682. 13:11 He knew the one who was betraying Him.

683. 13:15* "For I gave you an example that you also should do as I did to you."

684. 13:34–35* "A new commandment I give to you, that you love one another, even as I have loved you, that you also love one another. By this all men will know that you are My disciples, if you have love for one another."

685. 14:1 * "Do not let your heart be troubled; believe in God, believe also in Me."

686. 14:12* "He who believes in Me, the works that I do, he will do also; and greater works than these he will do; because I go the Father."

687. 14:13–15* "And whatever you ask in My name, that will I do, so that the Father may be glorified in the Son. If you ask Me anything in My name, I will do it. If you love Me, you will keep My commandments."

688. 14:21* "He who has My commandments and keeps them is the one who loves Me; and he who loves Me will be loved by My Father, and I will love him and will disclose Myself to him."

689. 14:23* "If anyone loves Me, he will keep My word."

690. 14:27* "Do not let your heart be troubled, nor let it be fearful."

691. 15:2* "Every branch in Me that does not bear fruit, He takes away; and every branch that bears fruit, He prunes it so that it may bear more fruit."

692. 15:4–5* "Abide in Me, and I in you … apart from Me you can do nothing."

693. 15:6* "If anyone does not abide in Me, he is thrown away as a branch and dries up."

694. 15:7* "If you abide in Me, and My words abide in you, ask whatever you wish, and it will be done for you."

695. 15:9* "Abide in My love."

696. 15:10* "If you keep My commandments, you will abide in My love."

697. 15:12* "This is My commandment, that you love one another, just as I have loved you."

698. 15:14* "You are My friends if you do what I command you."

699. 15:16* "I chose you, and appointed you that you would go and bear fruit."

700. 15:17* "This I command you, that you love one another."

701. 15:23* "He who hates Me hates My Father also."

702. 15:27* "You will testify also, because you have been with Me from the beginning."

703. 16:20* "You will weep and lament, but the world will rejoice; you will grieve, but your grief will be turned into joy."

704. 16:24* "Ask and you will receive, so that your joy may be made full."

705. 16:33* "In the world you have tribulation, but take courage; I have overcome the world."

706. 17:1 * Jesus spoke, lifted his eyes to heaven, and said, "Father, the hour has come; glorify Your Son, that the Son may glorify You."

707. 17:2–26 Jesus prayed many specific prayers for His disciples.

708. 18:4 Jesus knew all the things that were coming on Him.

709. 18:11* Peter cuts off Malchus' ear. "Put the sword into the sheath."

710. 19:1 Pilate took Jesus and scourged Him.

711. 19:28* "I am thirsty."

712. 19:30 He bowed His head and gave up His spirit.

713. 19:34 One of the soldiers pierced His side with a spear, and immediately blood and water came out.

714. 20:17* "Stop clinging to Me, for I have not yet ascended to the Father; but go to My brethren, and say to them, 'I ascend to My Father and your Father, and My God and your God.'"

715. 20:19 Jesus came and stood in their midst.

716. 20:19* "Peace be with you."

717. 20:21* "Peace be with you; as the Father has sent Me, I also send you."

718. 20:22* "Receive the Holy Spirit."

719. 20:23* "If you forgive the sins of any, their sins have been forgiven them; if you retain the sins of any, they have been retained."

720. 20:26* "Peace be with you."

721. 20:29* "Blessed are they who did not see, and yet believed."

722. 20:30–31 In the presence of His disciples, Jesus performed many other signs, which are not written in this book; but these have been written so you may believe that Jesus is the Christ, the Son of God, and that believing you may have life in His name.

723. 21:1 After these things, Jesus manifested Himself again to the disciples.

724. 21:6* "Cast the net on the right-hand side of the boat and you will find a catch."

725. 21:10* "Bring some of the fish which you have now caught."

726. 21:12* "Come and have breakfast."

727. 21:15* "Tend My lambs."

728. 21:16* "Shepherd My sheep."

729. 21:17* "Tend My sheep."

730. 21:19* "Follow Me!"

731. 21:25 There are many other things that Jesus did, which if they were written in detail, even the world itself could not contain the books that would be written.

BIBLIOGRAPHY

Alcorn, Randy. *50 Days of Heaven*. Carol Stream, Ill.: Tyndale, 2006.

—*Heaven*. Wheaton, Ill.: Tyndale House Publishers, Inc., 2004.

—"Heaven: Our Certain Hope." Review of Reviewed Item. *Eternal Perspective Ministries*, 2007.

—*In Light of Eternity*. Colorado Springs: WaterBrook Press, 1999.

—*Money, Possessions, and Eternity*. Wheaton, Ill.: Tyndale House Publishers, Inc., 2003.

—"Overcoming the Myths About Heaven." Review of Reviewed Item. *Eternal Perspective Ministries*, 1999.

—"Rethinking Our Beliefs About Heaven." Review of Reviewed Item. *Eternal Perspective Ministries*, 2006).

—*The Treasure Principle*. Sisters, Ore.: Multnomah Publishers, 2001.

Ammerman, Nancy T., Jackson W. Carroll, Carl S. Dudley, and William McKinney. *Studying Congregations, a New Handbook*. Nashville: Abingdon Press, 1998.

Anderson, Ray S. *The Shape of Practical Theology*. Downers Grove, Ill.: Inter Varsity Press, 2001.

Baron, Renee. *What Type Am I? Discover Who You Really Are*. Harmondsworth, Middlesex, England: Penguin Group, 1998.

Bellah, Robert N. *Habits of the Heart*. New York: Harper & Row, 1986.

Boa, Kenneth. *Conformed to His Image*. Grand Rapids, Mich.: Zondervan, 2001.

Bonhoeffer, Dietrich. *Life Together.* New York: Harper & Row, 1954.

Brown, Raymond E. *The Church the Apostles Left Behind.* New York: Paulist Press, 1984.

Brueggemann, Walter. *Hopeful Imagination.* Philadelphia: Fortress Press, 1986.

Buckingham, Marcus and Donald O. Clifton. *Now, Discover Your Strengths.* New York: The Free Press, 2001.

Chittister, Joan. *Wisdom Distilled from the Daily.* San Francisco: HarperCollins, 1991.

Crabb, Larry. *Connecting, A Radical New Vision.* Nashville: Word Publishing, 1997.

Cymbala, Jim. *Fresh Wind, Fresh Fire.* Edited by Dean Merrill. Grand Rapids, Mich.: Zondervan, 1997.

de Mello, Anthony. *Awareness.* New York: Doubleday, 1990.

Evangelical Church of North America. *The Discipline 2002.* Minneapolis: Commission on the Discipline, 2002.

Farson, Richard. *Management of the Absurd.* New York: Touchstone, 1997.

Foster, Richard J. *Celebration of Discipline.* San Francisco: HarperSanFrancisco, 1998.

Friedman, Edwin H. *Generation to Generation.* New York, London: The Guilford Press, 1985.

Goleman, Daniel, Richard Boyatzis, and Annie McKee. *Primal Leadership, Learning to Lead with Emotional Intelligence.* Boston: Harvard Business School Press, 2004.

Greer, Robert C. *Mapping Postmodernism, a Survey of Christian Options.* Downers Grove, Ill.: InterVarsity Press, 2003.

Guder, Darrell L. *Missional Church.* Grand Rapids, Mich.: William B. Eerdmans Publishing Company, 1998.

Guroian, Vigen. *The Fragrance of God.* Grand Rapids, Mich: William B. Eerdman, 2006.

Hart, Archibald D. *Coping with Depression in the Ministry and Other Helping Professions.* Dallas, London, Sydney, Singapore: Word Publishing, 1984.
—*Adrenaline and Stress.* Dallas, London, Vancouver, Melbourne: Word Publishing, 1995.

Hauerwas, Stanley. *Character and the Christian Life.* San Antonio: Trinity University Press, 1985.

Holt, Bradley P. *Thirsty for God.* Minneapolis: Augsburg Fortress, 2005.

Howard, Evan. "Three Temptations of Spiritual Formation." *Christianity Today,* December 9, 2002, 46–49.

Johnston, Graham MacPherson. *Preaching to a Postmodern World: A Guide to Reaching Twenty-First Century Listeners.* Grand Rapids, Mich.: Baker Books, 2001.

Kotter, John P. *Leading Change.* Boston: Harvard Business School Press, 1996.

Leech, Kenneth. *Experiencing God.* San Francisco: Harper & Row, 1985.
—*True Prayer.* San Francisco: Harper & Row, 1980.

Lodahl, Michael and Thomas Jay Oord. *Relational Holiness.* Kansas City: Beacon Hill Press, 2005.

Maas, Robin and Gabriel O'Donnell. *Spiritual Traditions for the Contemporary Church*. Nashville: Abingdon Press, 1990.

Manning, Brennan and James H. Hancock. *Posers, Fakers, & Wannabes (Unmasking the Real You)*. Colorado Springs: NavPress, 2003.

May, Gerald G. *Addiction and Grace*. San Francisco: HarperCollins, 1988.

McIntosh, Gary L. and Samuel D. Rima. *Overcoming the Dark Side of Leadership*. Grand Rapids, Mich.: Baker Books, 2005.

McLaren, Brian D. *A Generous Orthodoxy: why I am a missional, evangelical, post/Protestant, liberal/conservative, mystical/poetic, biblical, charismatic/contemplative, Fundamentalist/Calvinist, Anabaptist/Anglican, Methodist, Catholic, Green, incarnational, depressed-yet-hopeful, emergent, unfinished Christian*. El Cajon, Calif.: Youth Specialties Books, published by Zondervan, Grand Rapids, Mich., 2004.

Merton, Thomas. *New Seeds of Contemplation*. New York: Abbey of Gethsemani, Inc., 1961.

Miller, Donald. *Blue Like Jazz*. Nashville: Thomas Nelson Publishers, 2003.

Moehlman, Mary. "Children of the Covenant Children of the Light." *Quaker Religious Thought* 24, No. 2, no. 72 (1989–1990), 6–21.

Mulholland, M. Robert, Jr. *Invitation to a Journey*. Downers Grove, Ill.: InterVarsity Press, 1993.

Niebuhr, H. Richard. *Christ and Culture*. New York: Harper and Row, 1951.

Noll, Mark A. *The Scandal of the Evangelical Mind*. Grand Rapids, Mich.: Wm. B. Eerdmans Publishing Co., 1994.

Nouwen, Henri J.M. *In the Name of Jesus*. New York: The Crossroad Publishing Company, 1996.

Nuttall, Geoffrey F. *The Holy Spirit in Puritan Faith and Experience*. Oxford: Basil Blackwell, 1947.

Olson, Roger E. "The Tradition Temptation." *Christianity Today*, November 2003, 52–55.

Post, Ron. *Created for Purpose*. Eagle Creek, Ore.: Coffee House Publishers, 1999.

Quinn, Robert E. *Deep Change*. San Francisco: Jossey-Bass Publishers, 1996.

Ravenhill, Leonard. *Revival Praying*. Minneapolis: Bethany House Publishers, 1984.

Rima, Samuel D. *Rethinking the Successful Church*. Grand Rapids, Mich.: Baker Books, 2002.

Rinehart, Stacy T. *Upside Down, the Paradox of Servant Leadership*. Colorado Springs: NavPress Publishing Group, 1998.

Roberts, Arthur O. *Exploring Heaven*. New York: Harper Collins, 2003.
—2002, "Atonement as Moral Influence." In Northwest Yearly Meeting of Friends. (accessed September, 2002).
—2002. "Atonement as Ransom." In Northwest Yearly Meeting of Friends. (accessed June, 2002).
—2002. "Atonement as Satisfying Divine Honor." In Northwest Yearly Meeting of Friends. (accessed July, 2002).
—2002. "Atonement as Substitution." In Northwest Yearly Meeting of Friends. (accessed August, 2002).

Scazzero, Peter L. and Warren Bird. *The Emotionally Healthy Church*. Grand Rapids, Mich.: Zondervan, 2003.

Schaeffer, Francis A. *The Church before the Watching World*. Downers Grove, Ill.: InterVarsity Press, 1976.
—*The Mark of the Christian*. Downers Grove, Ill.: InterVarsity Press, 1970.

Schwarz, Christian A. *Natural Church Development*. St. Charles, Ill.: ChurchSmart Resources, 2000.

Shelton, R. Larry. *Cross & Covenant, Interpreting the Atonement for 21st Century Mission*. Tyrone, Ga.: Paternoster, 2006.

Smith, Timothy L. *Revivalism and Social Reform*. New York: Harper and Row, 1957.

Steinke, Peter L. *How Your Church Family Works*. Herndon, Va.: The Albin Institute, 2002.

Sweet, Leonard I., Brian D. McLaren, and Jerry Haselmayer. *The Language of the Emerging Church*. Grand Rapids, Mich.: Zondervan, 2003.

Sweet, Leonard I. *Summoned to Lead*. Grand Rapids, Mich.: Zondervan, 2004.

Thurman, Howard. *Jesus and the Disinherited*. Boston: Beacon Press, 1996.

Trueblood, D. Elton. *The Logic of Belief*. New York: Harper & Brothers Publishers, 1942.
—*Alternative to Futility*. New York: Harper & Brothers, 1948.
—*The Common Ventures of Life*. New York: Harper & Brothers, 1949.
—*The Company of the Committed*. New York: Harper & Brothers, 1961.
—*Foundations for Reconstruction*. New York: Harper & Brothers, 1946.
—*The Incendiary Fellowship*. New York: Harper & Row, 1967.
—*The New Man for Our Time*. New York: Harper & Row, 1970.
—*The Predicament of Modern Man*. New York: Harper & Brothers, 1944.
—*The Yoke of Christ*. New York: Harper & Brothers, 1958.
—*Your Other Vocation*. New York: Harper & Brothers, 1952.

Tyson, John R. *Invitation to Christian Spirituality*. New York: Oxford University Press, 1999.

Wilkes, C. Gene. *Jesus on Leadership*. Wheaton, Ill.: Tyndale House Publishers, 1998.

Willard, Dallas and Randy Frazee. *Renovation of the Heart*. Colorado Springs: NavPress, 2005.

ABOUT THE AUTHOR

Randy Butler grew up in the church and always wanted to be a preacher. His family nicknamed him "Hallelujah Harry" for all the times he played "preacher," with them as his audience. While he was on the high school golf team, his coach nicknamed him "Preacher." His plans of being the first Protestant monk changed in college when he met and married Joan Hatfield. They live in Keizer, Oregon, near their daughter Kristi and son-in-law Charles. Their son Kevin died suddenly at 16 years of age in 2003.

While still loving to preach weekly at Salem Evangelical Church, at age 46 Randy became a volunteer police chaplain and received his Doctor of Ministry degree at age 48. At age 50, Randy now loves riding motorcycles, archery, politics, and writing.

If you have any questions or need spiritual help, please contact
Randy at randy@salemec.com
Salem Evangelical Church
455 Locust Street NE
Salem OR 97301
randybutlerbooks.com
randy@randybutlerbooks.com

Coming soon...

FORECASTING TEMPTATION

By Randy R. Butler

Introduction

I love storms! As a native Oregonian, I know we don't get a lot of severe weather. My family has enjoyed living in the Salem/Keizer area, in the heart of the Willamette Valley, since 1986. We get a fair amount of rain. The summers are pleasant and the winters are mild compared to the Midwest and the East. I live 60 miles from the ocean with a mountain range between me and it. The summit in the Coast range on my way to the ocean is about 700 feet. I live 60 miles from Mt. Hood as the crow flies. The summit of Blue Box pass on Mt. Hood is 4,024 feet. The Willamette Valley is nestled between the coastal range and the Cascade mountain range, making agriculture a very rich resource in the Willamette Valley.

I love winter because winter in the Willamette Valley means we might get one or two snow events a year. Usually, the forecast is more exciting than the storm itself. Whenever the first hint of a possible, maybe, sort of (but probably not going to happen) snow forecast appears my dad gives me a call just to get my hopes up. We have been doing this since I was a little boy.

I am now a 51-year-old man and we just did it again this week as the forecast is for the possibility, maybe, sort of (but probably not going to happen) for snow in the Willamette Valley. Actually, the forecast is for the lower elevations. When we hear the weatherman say there could be snow to the valley floor, then we have a chance of snow! To make snow a greater reality in my life, I sit on top of my roof trying to get closer to the snow!

Where I live, school gets cancelled whenever snow is even forecasted since we're such pansies in the Willamette Valley. My greatest year of snow was when I lived in Spokane, Washington 1984–1985. We had weeks of snow and weeks of freezing weather. It was awful. Actually being in the storm was awful. The romance of the idea of the storm seems much more appealing than the storm itself. And that's the way it is with temptation.

There are many temptations that look really good, but in reality they are very dangerous. In fact, if the temptation you're considering doesn't look really good, there are others out there that will look better if you look a little harder! That is the nature of temptation. It's like a drug and we go for more, bigger, better each and every time. We are rarely satisfied. It has been said that when asked what it would take to please man, then answer always comes back, "Just a little bit more." It begins as something very exciting and ends with a disaster. Not every time. Disaster comes when we think we are in control.

I invite you to join me in a very honest conversation on the subject of forecasting temptation. In the United States of America, there is an actual hurricane season. I have been in several hurricanes both in Florida on my way to Haiti and in Haiti itself. On that same trip, we flew over New Orleans right over the top of a hurricane. From that perspective, the hurricane was awesome to see, knowing we were not in any danger. But when our plane landed in Ft. Lauderdale, little did we know that would be one of three hurricanes that would affect our 18-day trip to Haiti.

If there were no damage and if nobody got hurt, hurricanes would be very exciting events worth experiencing. The reality is that hurricanes are very damaging and cause a great deal of harm. So does temptation. It is potentially damaging and hurtful. Temptation is a storm we must learn to stay far away from. With a hurricane, there is sometimes a siren that goes off to warn people to take cover. I wish there was a siren to go off every time you and I enter into the eye of temptation. It may seem calm; the reality is that all hell is about to break loose!

My goal for you is to discover your weaknesses, forecast the storms of your life, and discover ways to avoid the destruction temptation often leaves behind. I have had many close calls with temptation. I have had victory over temptation, and too many times I have been damaged and hurt by temptation. So have you.

I will carefully define temptation. We will then consider what happens when something is tried just once. Then I want to take those temptations in life and try to better forecast temptation, personalizing it for your life. I will ask some bold questions about temptation and then introduce ways to divert temptation. I will share pertinent information about temptation from all eras and then use three examples of people in the Bible who got it right with temptation so we can discover ways to do better with the beast of temptation.

Finally I want to close this discussion with ways you and I can taze temptation. I will share with you my experience with being tazed and its direct application to your ability to better forecast your personalized temptation. In other words, you and I will never be perfect Christians, but we do not have to be caught in the middle of the storm as often as seems to be the case.

The first chapter is my attempt to be both honest with you about my humanity and help you to embrace your humanity as well. I will do my best to help you see there are no perfect Christians. I think the idea of "perfect Christians" was perfected with the annual Christmas letter, more commonly called the brag letter. If your life is messed up like mine is, then you know who I am talking about. If your life is a bed of roses, this book will help you see that right beneath your beautiful buds are some really nasty thorns!

Christmas brag letters are both humorous and disgusting. Some people paint their year as though they spent most of it in heaven. Sure, we can all talk about the good things, but that isn't how the whole year fleshes out. Bragging about how good you have it is a real turnoff. If you have it good, then quietly go about your life, but do not make others feel like garbage at your expense. If we are honest about temptation—and this book calls for an honest evaluation and conversation—then next year's brag letter needs to be laced with some humble pie!

To capture the essence of what I am attempting to do in this book, I reflect on a Paul Harvey story from many years ago. I credit him with this story, though I have no idea if he was the author. It captures the essence of how beastly temptation really is and what it has done to all of us, including those whose brag letter leads us to believe otherwise. The following was read by Paul Harvey on his daily radio broadcast. It is entitled, "If I Were the Devil" and it reads:

"With the wisdom of a serpent I would whisper to people as I whispered to Eve: 'Do as you please.' To the young I would whisper that the Bible is a myth. I would convince them that man created God and not the other way around. I would confide that what's bad is good and what's good is square. And to the old I would teach them to pray after me: 'Our father which are in Washington.'

"I'd educate authors how to make lurid literature exciting so that anything else would appear dull and uninteresting. I'd threaten TV with dirtier movies and vice versa. I'd peddle narcotics to whom I could. I'd sell alcohol to ladies and gentlemen of distinction and tranquilize the rest with pills.

"If I were the devil, I'd soon have families at war with themselves, churches at war with themselves, and nations at war with themselves—until each in its turn was consumed. And with promises of higher ratings, I'd have media fanning the flame.

"If I were the devil, I'd encourage schools to refine young intellects but neglect to discipline emotions. Just let those run wild until before you knew it, you'd have to have drug-sniffing dogs and metal detectors at every schoolhouse door. Within a decade, I'd have prisons overflowing, judges promoting pornography.

"Soon I could have God evicted from the courthouse and then from the schoolhouse and then from the house of Congress. In his own churches, I would substitute psychology for religion. I would lure priests and pastors into misusing boys and girls and church money. If I were the devil, I would make the symbol of Easter an egg and the symbol of Christmas a bottle.

"If I were the devil, I would take from those who have and give to those who want it until I had killed the incentive of the ambitious. And what do you bet I could get whole states to promote gambling as the way to get rich.

"I would caution against extremes and hard work and patriotism and moral conduct, convince the young that marriage is old-fashioned, that swinging is more fun, and that what you see on TV is the way to be. Thus I could undress you in public and I could lure you into bed with diseases for which there is no cure.

"In other words, if I were the devil, I'd just keep right on doing what he's doing."

I might add that this was written before the age of the internet as we know it today. Indeed, Satan continues to use everything imaginable in this world for our destruction.

In Chapter 1, I share with you my reality check in life that made me realize becoming a perfect Christian is not possible after all. This was a real blow to my ego and my theology. I share how we are all the same at the foot of the cross and how nobody elevates above that level in this life. In fact, this phrase, "we are all the same at the foot of the cross," was spoken to me just after Joanie and I were married. I married into the Hatfield family and then-Senator Mark Hatfield mentioned this phrase when I visited with him briefly after our wedding. He reminded me that regardless of how high the position we hold in this world, "we are all the same at the foot of the cross." I have used that statement many times in my ministry.

In Chapter 2, I talk about the general descriptions of temptation—both what it is and what it is not. This is a helpful chapter that sets the stage for the remainder of the book.

In Chapters 3 through 7, I list and we have a conversation about 103 specific points that undress temptation. I offer solutions to temptations though the majority of those solutions are totally up to you.

In Chapter 8, I share a survey I conducted in my church one Sunday morning as well as the results. It is a survey for you to use personally and with others if you so choose. You have my permission to make copies of the survey if you don't want to buy a bunch of books—though that would be my preference! I also share the analysis of the surveys that my congregation turned in to me. It is an interesting chapter that was a surprise to me and I trust will be meaningful for you.

In Chapter 9, I do a verse-by-verse Bible study from three different passages using three different people from the Bible: Joseph, Job, and Jesus. This is my favorite chapter because it is a road map for me to follow to better combat temptation in my life. I wrote this book for you and for me! I need it as much or more than you because all of us are messed up as you will see in Chapter 1.

I finish things up with Chapter 10, which talks about tazing temptation. I am a chaplain for the local police department in my spare time. One of the events I had the opportunity to be a part of was getting tazed. Wow! What an experience. I will use that experience as a part of the imagery helpful in forecasting temptation in my final chapter of this book.

There are five passages of Scripture I use in eight lessons at the end of each chapter except the survey chapter. I develop Genesis 3:1–13, Genesis 39:1–23, Job 1:1–22, Matthew 4:1–11, and 1 John 2:1–6 throughout this book to help us see how to better forecast temptation from the vantage point of Scripture.

In addition, I give you ten passages of Scriptures in eight different chapters that are topical and each relate to temptation. I invite you the reader to have a conversation with other people about this subject so we can all do a better job in forecasting temptation. The context of these verses is very important. I include topical verses at the end of chapters 1 through 7 and 9. These 80 passages should be of great help to this conversation. I include them at the end of each chapter rather than inserting them within the chapter so they could be more easily recognized and discussed with friends and family.

Likewise, in chapters 3 through 7, I articulate 103 points in an attempt to dissect temptation. Each of these points is numbered in each chapter to serve as a means to easily discuss each of them or the ones that matter the most to you. So in actuality, this entire book is a discussion guide on the subject of temptation. It was written in a style meant to bring about a conversation. Use it in small groups, in Sunday school, for family devotions, in youth group, in church settings or wherever you so choose. It is meant to lead people to a lot of meaningful and helpful conversations so we can get a better handle on temptation.

I use the word temptation throughout the book in such a way as to almost give it an identity, a life of its own. I did this because I believe it does take on a life of its own. I know there are times I use the word temptation when you might think Satan or one of his other names would be more appropriate. I did this so we would not underestimate the beast I call temptation.

Lastly, I did not write this book as an authority. I wrote this book because I am a victim. Like you, I/we have been victimized by temptation. I am tired of seeing what it has done to my life and to many others I love. Our world is a mess because temptation is winning the battle. It is imperative that we win the war. To this end, I hope this book helps you to better forecast temptation.

Summer 2012, Deep River Books